When Loving Hurts and You Don't Know Why

- "I always felt pretty good about the way I looked until Ed started cutting ads out of magazines. He'd tell me he wanted me to look more like this one or that one.... I began to feel really unattractive."

- "He'd say, 'I've got a big meeting to handle this morning, so I need to have sex.' It had nothing to do with me."

- "I didn't dare run out of his cheese and special crackers and special wine because there'd be hell to pay."

- "He humiliated me so often that it just became too painful to have friends over. I was ashamed for them to see me taking it."

- "It was incredible how different I felt at work than I did at home. At work, people respected me, but the minute I walked in the front door I fell to pieces."

- "When Jim is in a bad mood, I feel heat starting in my stomach and then spreading all over me. It's the worst thing I've ever felt. It's sheer terror."

These women took back their lives from the men who were undermining their happiness. You can, too. Let this frank and compassionate guide show you how.

MEN WHO HATE WOMEN & THE WOMEN WHO LOVE THEM

WHEN LOVING HURTS AND YOU DON'T KNOW WHY

SUSAN FORWARD, PH.D.
AND JOAN TORRES

BANTAM BOOKS
NEW YORK TORONTO LONDON SYDNEY AUCKLAND

This edition contains the complete text
of the original hardcover edition
NOT ONE WORD HAS BEEN OMITTED.

MEN WHO HATE WOMEN & THE WOMEN WHO LOVE THEM

A Bantam Book
Bantam hardcover edition / September 1986
Bantam mass market edition / June 1987
Bantam trade paperback edition / January 2002

ISBN 978-0-553-38141-2

Published simultaneously in the United States and Canada

Bantam Books are published by Bantam Books, a division of Random House, Inc. Its trademark, consisting of the words "Bantam Books" and the portrayal of a rooster, is Registered in U.S. Patent and Trademark Office and in other countries. Marca Registrada. Bantam Books, New York, New York.

PRINTED IN THE UNITED STATES OF AMERICA

BVG   22 21 20 19 18 17

For Wendy and Matt

Contents

Acknowledgments

There are several people whose efforts and support are an important part of this book.

My collaborator, Joan Torres, took my ideas and my passion to tell this story and skillfully gave them form and shape.

Dorris Gathrid, Don Weisberg, and Larry Goldman helped it all happen.

Two treasured friends and colleagues gave unsparingly of their time and expertise. They are Nina Miller, M.F.C.C., and Arlene Drake, M.F.C.C. I can never thank them enough.

My editor, Toni Burbank, was relentless in her pursuit of excellence and a great source of comfort and encouragement when I needed it—which was often.

The friends and clients who gave me their stories must remain anonymous, but I bless them for their courage and their willingness to share their experiences.

Finally, my deepest gratitude to the thousands of women who have written me or called me over the radio and have touched my heart.

This book belongs to all of you.

A Personal Introduction

Nobody in his right mind would stay with someone in my condition. The only reason Jeff stays is because he loves me.

When Nancy first came to see me she was sixty pounds over-weight and had an ulcer. She wore old, baggy jeans and a shapeless smock; her hair was stringy, her fingernails were bitten down to the quick, and her hands shook. When she had married Jeff, four years before, she had been a fashion coordinator for a major Los Angeles department store. In her work she had traveled through Europe and the Orient selecting designer clothes for the store. She had always dressed in the latest fashions and dated fascinating men; she had been written about in a number of articles on successful women in the Los Angeles area—and she had accomplished this before she was 30. Yet, when I first saw her, at age 34, she was so ashamed of how she looked and felt about herself that she seldom left home.

The decline of Nancy's self-esteem seemed to have begun when she married Jeff. Yet, when I questioned her about her husband, she began with a long list of superlatives.

> He's a wonderful man. He's charming and witty and dynamic. He's always doing little things for me—he sent me flowers to commemorate the anniversary of the first night we'd made love. Last year he bought two surprise tickets to Italy for my birthday.

She told me that Jeff, a busy and successful entertainment lawyer, always found time to spend with her, and that despite her current appearance he still wanted her along for all his business dinners and outings.

> I used to love going out with him with his clients because we'd still hold hands like high-school lovers. I'm the envy of all my friends because of him. One friend said, "You've got the special one, Nancy." And I know he is. But look at me! I don't understand what's happened. I feel so low all the time. I've got to get myself back together or I'm going to lose him. A man like Jeff doesn't have to lug around a wife like me. He can have anyone he wants, including movie stars. I'm lucky he's hung in as long as he has.

As I listened to Nancy and observed her appearance, I asked myself, "What's wrong with this picture?" There was a basic contradiction here. Why would a competent and effective woman, in a loving relationship, get so ground down? What had happened to her in the four years of her marriage to make such a marked change in both her appearance and her sense of self-worth?

I pressed her to tell me more about her relationship with Jeff, and bit by bit a fuller picture emerged.

> I guess the only thing that really bothers me about him is how much he flies off the handle.

"What do you mean by 'fly off the handle'?" I asked. She laughed
a little.

> He does what I call his King Kong imitation, yelling and
> making lots of noise. He also puts me down a lot, like he did
> the other night when we were having dinner with friends. He
> was talking about a play and I interjected something and he
> just snapped at me, "Why don't you shut up?" Then he said
> to our friends, "Don't pay any attention to her. She's always
> got some stupid thing to say." I was so humiliated I felt like
> sinking into the upholstery. I could hardly swallow my food
> afterwards.

Nancy began to cry as she recalled several other humiliating
scenes in which Jeff had called her stupid, selfish, or thoughtless.
When enraged, he would often yell at her, slam doors, and throw
things.

The more I questioned her, the clearer the picture became. Here
was a woman trying desperately to figure out how to please a husband who was often angry and intimidating as well as charming.
Nancy said she often fell asleep long after he did with his cruel
words stinging in her ears. During the day, she had fits of crying for
no apparent reason.

It was at Jeff's insistence that Nancy had quit her job when they
married. Now she felt incapable of returning to her career. As she
described it:

> Now I wouldn't even have the nerve to go on an interview,
> much less a buying trip. I don't feel like I could make the de-
> cisions anymore because I've lost confidence in myself.

Jeff made all the decisions in their marriage. He insisted on total
control of every aspect of their life together. He oversaw all spending, selected the people with whom they socialized, and even made
decisions about what Nancy should do while he was at work. He

derided her for any opinion she had that differed from his, and he yelled at her, even in public, whenever he was displeased. Any deviation on her part from the course he had set for them resulted in a hideous scene.

I told Nancy we had a lot of work to do, but I assured her she would begin to feel less overwhelmed. I told her we would take a hard look at her relationship with Jeff and that the self-confidence she thought she'd lost was not really gone, only misplaced. Together, we would get it back again. When she left that first session, she felt a little steadier and less lost. But I began to feel shaky.

Nancy's story had hit me very hard. I knew that as a therapist, my reactions to a client were important tools. I make emotional connections with the people I work with, which helps me understand more quickly how they are feeling. But this was something else. After Nancy left my office, I felt very uncomfortable. This was not the first time a woman had come to see me with this type of problem, nor was it the first time I had reacted so strongly. I could no longer deny that what was affecting me was the fact that Nancy's situation was too close to my own.

On the outside, I appeared confident, fulfilled—a woman who truly had it all. All day long, at my office, at the hospital and the clinic where I practised, I worked with people to help them find confidence and a renewed sense of their own strength. But at home, it was another story. My husband, like Nancy's, was charming, sexy, and romantic, and I had fallen madly in love with him almost immediately after we met. But I soon discovered that he had a great deal of anger inside him and that he had the power to make me feel small, inadequate, and off-balance. He insisted on being in control of everything I did, believed, and felt.

The Susan who was a therapist could say to Nancy, "Your husband's behavior doesn't sound loving. In fact, it sounds as if there's a lot of psychological abuse going on." But what was I saying to myself? The Susan who went home at night twisted herself into a pretzel trying to keep her husband from yelling at her. That Susan kept telling herself that he was a wonderful man, that he was exciting to be with, and that, therefore, if something went wrong, it must be her fault.

Over the next few months, I looked more closely at what was going on both in my own marriage and in the relationships of my clients who appeared to be in similar situations. What was really happening here? What were the patterns? Although it was the women who usually sought my help, it was the behavior of the men that claimed my attention. As their partners described them, they were often charming and even loving, but they were able to switch to cruel, critical, and insulting behavior on a moment's notice. Their behavior covered a wide spectrum, from obvious intimidation and threats to more subtle, covert attacks which took the form of constant put-downs or erosive criticism. Whatever the style, the results were the same. The man gained control by grinding the woman down. These men also refused to take any responsibility for how their attacks made their partners feel. Instead, they blamed their wives or lovers for any and every unpleasant event.

I knew from my experience in working with couples that every marriage has two sides. However, it's easy for therapists to over-identify with the client when we only hear one side of the story. Certainly each partner contributes to whatever turmoil and conflict exists in a relationship. But once I began seeing some of my clients' male partners in counseling, I realized that they did not suffer nearly as much as they caused their partners to suffer. It was the women who were in pain. All of them had dramatic losses of self-esteem, and many had additional symptoms and reactions. Nancy had ulcers, was overweight, and had let her appearance go; others had severe problems with drug and/or alcohol abuse, migraines, gastro-intestinal complaints, eating disorders, and sleeping disorders. Their job performance had often suffered. Their once-promising careers had declined. Previously successful and competent women found themselves doubting their skills and their judgment. They experienced depressions, crying spells, and anxiety with alarming frequency. In every case, these problems had begun to appear during the partnership or marriage.

As I realized that I was seeing a distinct pattern in these relationships, I began to discuss it with my colleagues. They were all familiar with the type of man I described; each had treated women who either had been married to, had been in love with, or were the daughters of men who fit my description. What was so surprising to me was that while the type of behavior was so familiar to all of us, no one had yet described it in a cohesive way.

At this point I started reviewing the psychological literature. Because of the man's lack of sensitivity to the pain he was causing his partner, I first reexamined character disorders. People with character disorders have little capacity for guilt, remorse, or anxiety. These emotions are uncomfortable but necessary monitors of our ethical and moral interactions with other people.

I knew that there were two major types of recognized character disorders. First, there are the narcissists. These are people who are totally self-obsessed. They tend to make relationships primarily in order to be reassured of their own specialness in the world. Men who fall into this category often flit from one relationship to another in search of love and admiration. Some familiar names for this type of man are Peter Pans and Don Juans. They have been called "the people who cannot love."

The men in the relationships I was looking at were different. They appeared to love intensely, and in many cases they had been in a long-term relationship with one partner. Also, their primary need differed from that of the narcissist in that they seemed to need to *control* more than they needed to be *admired*.

At the other end of the character-disorder spectrum were the more extreme and dangerous sociopaths. These are people who create a whirlwind of chaos in their lives. They use and exploit anyone who comes into their orbit. Lies and deception are second nature to them. They can range from common criminals to prominent and successful professionals who are chronically involved in white-collar crime. The most striking feature about sociopaths is their total lack of conscience.

But the man I was attempting to define was often genuinely responsible and competent in his dealings with society. His destructive behavior was not generalized, as was that of the sociopath. In fact, it was very focused. Unfortunately, it was focused almost exclusively on his partner.

He used for weapons his words and his moods. While he tended not to physically abuse the woman in his life, he systematically wore her down through psychological battering, which in the end is every bit as emotionally devastating as physical violence.

I wondered whether these men got some sort of perverse pleasure out of the pain and suffering they were causing their partners. Were they, in fact, sadists?

After all, many of the people I discussed my discoveries with assured me that the women involved with these men were classic textbook masochists. This made me angry. I knew that the labelling of women in unhealthy relationships as masochistic—that is, seeking and enjoying suffering—has long been standard practice in my profession and in our culture. This is a convenient but highly dangerous way of attempting to explain why so many women fall into self-denying, submissive behavior with men. In reality, women learn these behaviors early, and are consistently rewarded and praised for them. The paradox here is that the behaviors that make a woman vulnerable to mistreatment are the very ones she has been taught are feminine and lovable. The concept of masochism is particularly dangerous because it serves to justify aggression against women—it confirms that "that's what women really want."

As I talked more extensively with the couples I was counseling, I found that neither of these terms applied. Rather than getting emotional or sexual pleasure from his partner's pain, as the sadist does, the man I was attempting to define felt both *threatened* and *enraged* by his partner's suffering. The woman was no more a masochist than the man was a sadist. She did not get any hidden sexual or emotional pleasure from her partner's abusive treatment of her. Instead, it severely demoralized her. Once again I found that the psychological categories and terminology were not adequate to describe what I was seeing in these relationships. The man I was attempting to define did not appear in the literature.

He was not a clear-cut sociopath, narcissist, or sadist, although some of these elements were often present in his character. The most dramatic difference between this man and those described in the psychological literature was that he was capable of engaging in a long-term relationship with one woman. In fact, his love seemed particularly hot and intense. The tragic part was that he did everything he could to destroy the woman he professed to love so deeply.

I know as a therapist that the words "I love you" don't necessarily indicate what is going on in a relationship. I know that it is behavior, not words, that defines reality. As I listened to my clients, I asked myself: Is this the way you treat someone you really love? Isn't this in fact the way you treat someone you hate?

I remembered the Greek word for "woman hater": *misogynist*, from *miso*, meaning "to hate," and *gyne*, meaning "woman." Although the word had been in the language for several hundred years, it was usually used to describe mass murderers, rapists, and others who acted out violently against women. Certainly these criminals were misogynists in the most lethal sense of the word. But I was convinced that the men I was trying to define were also misogynists. Only their choice of weapons was different.

The more I learned about misogynists and misogynistic relationships, the more I learned not only about my patients, but about my husband, myself, and our marriage. By this time, my situation at home had become extremely tense. I found myself inventing elaborate excuses at the end of each day to avoid leaving work. My children were under stress, and my self-esteem was at an all-time low. In fact, had there been any literature on misogynistic relationships, my husband and I would have been considered a classic case. As far as he was concerned, it was my fault if anything went wrong. He blamed me for everything from his business problems to the fact that his shoes weren't shined properly. Although my work was our major source of income at that time, he often ridiculed the psychotherapeutic profession in general and me in particular.

The more he labeled me selfish and uncaring, the more I tried to appease him by apologizing, by capitulating, and by purposely sabotaging much of my career progress. I had begun my marriage as a cheerful, energetic person; now, fourteen years later, I was anxious and frequently on the verge of tears. I found myself behaving in ways that I couldn't stand, nagging and interrogating him constantly, or retreating into sullen, angry silences instead of dealing directly with my feelings about our relationship.

Then came an incident which tipped the scales for me. I had begun to specialize in work with adults who had been sexually abused as children, and my persistence in bringing this issue to public awareness had begun to attract attention. I received a contract for my first book, *Betrayal of Innocence: Incest and Its Devastation*. That day I rushed home to my husband to share my excitement and delight. But the moment I walked in the door, I could tell that he'd had one of his bad days. I knew that my good news would only intensify his frustrations, so I went into the kitchen without saying a word about the book, poured myself a glass of wine, and had a solitary toast to celebrate. Instead of being able to share a joyous moment with the man who meant so much to me, I had to hide it for fear of upsetting him.

I knew then that something was terribly wrong. I realized that my husband and I—like the misogynist couples I was counseling—needed outside help with our problems. However, my husband was not willing to work on either his behavior or our relationship. Finally, painfully, I came to the conclusion that I could no longer stay in our marriage without totally giving up myself.

The grieving over this tremendous loss went on for a long time, but something else was happening to me as well. I discovered enormous amounts of creativity and energy in myself that hadn't been available to me before. Soon my professional life took a dramatic upward swing. My book was published, my practice was growing, and I had my own national radio call-in program. I found myself dealing more and more, both on the air and in my practice, with the same kind of psychological abuse as I had experienced in my marriage. Women called me on the radio who had been in these types of relationships anywhere from a few months to a half a century. Often, after they described only a few telling incidents to me, I would ask them the following questions about their relationships:

- Does he assume the right to control how you live and behave?
- Have you given up important activities or people in your life in order to keep him happy?
- Does he devalue your opinions, your feelings, and your accomplishments?
- Does he yell, threaten, or withdraw into angry silence when you displease him?
- Do you "walk on eggs," rehearsing what you will say so as not to set him off?
- Does he bewilder you by switching from charm to rage without warning?
- Do you often feel confused, off-balance, or inadequate with him?
- Is he extremely jealous and possessive?
- Does he blame you for everything that goes wrong in the relationship?

If they answered "yes" to most of my questions, I knew they were involved with misogynists. Once I had clarified for them what was going on in their lives, I could hear the relief in their voices, even over the air.

Convinced that I had discovered a major psychological disorder, I decided to test the waters further by discussing the topic on *A.M. Los Angeles*, a TV talk show. In my segment I described the tactics and behaviors of a typical misogynist.

The moment I went off the air, several of the women crew members on the show rushed over to me. They all seemed to have had some close personal experience with this type of man. The next day, the network reported that my segment had received one of the most overwhelming phone-call responses that they'd ever had.

Not long afterward, I appeared on another talk show, in Boston. This time I spent an entire hour on the subject, and there was an even greater response. When letters began pouring in from all over the country, I knew that I'd hit a nerve. The sense of urgency in the letters was tremendous. Women wanted to know where they could find a book on the subject of misogyny. They wanted to know more.

The women who wrote to me and offered me their stories touched me deeply. They needed to be reassured that what they'd been feeling in their relationships wasn't "crazy." They needed to know that it wasn't just "them"—that there were other people out there who understood and who would not define them in the negative terms used by their male partners.

Their reactions further reinforced for me that recognizing, clarifying, and understanding what is going on within such relationships can offer tremendous relief from the crushing burden of self-blame. I knew then that I had to write this book—not only to help women understand what was happening to them, but also what they could do about it.

Before any of us can change a relationship, we have to understand what is occurring in it. But understanding is not enough. By itself, understanding is just an intellectual exercise. In order for your life and your relationship to change, you have to *do* something differently, not just *think* about it differently.

To help you accomplish this, I have divided the book into two parts. In the first part, I describe how these relationships work and why they work. I will explore every aspect of the interaction, from the romantic and exciting beginnings to the confusion and pain eventually experienced by every woman who is in love with a misogynist. I describe the men themselves and how they came to behave the way they do, and I look also at how and why women learn to accept poor treatment from men.

Along the way, I will introduce to you a number of couples drawn from my practice, and we will follow some of them throughout the book. All names and identifying characteristics have of course been changed to preserve their privacy. But the situations they experienced and the words they used to describe them are as accurate as I can make them.

In the second part of the book I offer a group of effective behavioral techniques that I have honed over the last few years. These can be very instrumental in bringing about important changes in your relationship with your partner and with yourself. These techniques will help you become more self-protective, more assertive, more effective, and less vulnerable to the manipulation, confusion, and loss of self-confidence that always occur in misogynistic partnerships.

I know that some of the material in this book may stir up strong feelings for you, whether you are in a misogynistic relationship now, are recovering from one in the past, or have concerns about being vulnerable in the future. Although I can't be with you in person as you begin this journey, I want you to know that you will have my respect, my caring, and my encouragement every step of the way.

PART I

Men Who Hate Women

1 | *The Most Romantic Man in the World*

It's the Rodgers and Hammerstein way to fall in love. You see him across a crowded room, your eyes meet, and that certain thrill surges through you. Your palms grow damp when he stands near you; your heart beats faster; everything in your body seems to be more alive. This is the dream of happiness, sexual fulfillment, and completion. This man will appreciate and be responsive to you. Just being near him is exciting and wonderful. When it happens it's overpowering. We've come to call it *romantic love*.

Rosalind was 45 when she met Jim. She is a striking woman, tall, with auburn hair and a trim figure, which she works hard to keep in shape. She has a distinctive style of dressing that shows off her height and her artistic flair. She owns an antique shop and is a successful dealer, collector, and appraiser of advertising art, which is her specialty. Rosalind was married twice before and has a grown son. She was excited about meeting Jim because she'd heard so much about him from her friends. They took her to hear him play with a local jazz group. Afterward, when the four of them went out for a drink, Rosalind felt very drawn to Jim, who was tall, dark, and extremely good-looking.

> Jim and I were very attracted to each other. We talked about kids and music. He told me he'd been married before and that his two kids lived with him. I was impressed with that. He was interested in hearing about my antique shop because he was doing some furniture refinishing and was interested in the market in general. He asked me if he could see me again the next night. When the check came, I could see he didn't have much money, so I volunteered to make us dinner at my place for our next date. He took my hand and squeezed it and just caught my eyes with his for a moment. I could tell he was grateful that I'd understood his position.
>
> The next day I thought about him constantly, and when he came over that night it was wonderful. After dinner I put on the music to *A Star Is Born*, being the romantic nut that I am, and so there we were, dancing to this music in my living room; he's holding me so close and the world is just spinning around me. Here's this man who really likes me, who's strong, who's willing to work on a relationship. All this stuff is flashing through my mind while I'm floating away with him, feeling so terrific. It was the most romantic thing that ever happened to me.

Jim was 36 when he met Rosalind. He was as carried away as she was by their romance; she was the woman he'd been looking for all his life. As he later told me:

> She was beautiful and had a figure that wouldn't quit. She had her own business and was making a go of it by herself. She'd raised her son and seemed to have done a good job of that. I'd never met anyone like her. She was outgoing and bubbly and enthusiastic about everything I was doing with my life, even about my kids. She was perfect. I started calling all my friends to tell them about her. I even called my

mother. I tell you, I never felt like that before. I never thought about anyone so much or dreamed about them all the time like I dreamed about her. I mean, this was really different.

After their third date, Rosalind started writing her name with his last name to see how it looked. She canceled social engagements for fear of missing his calls; and Jim didn't disappoint her. Instead of behaving like a "typical man," he became as involved with her as she was with him. He always phoned when he said he would—no more waiting for weeks for a man to call—and he never put his work ahead of his need to see her. Together, they were on an exciting emotional roller-coaster.

My client Laura's whirlwind courtship started out literally "across a crowded room." At the time, she was a successful account executive for a major cosmetics firm, a very pretty woman with light brown hair, dark almond-shaped eyes, and a slender figure. She was 34 when she and Bob first met. She was out one evening with a woman friend at a restaurant:

> I had gone to make a phone call and when I returned to our table there was this very handsome man sitting there talking to my friend. He had noticed me and was waiting for my return. There was electricity between us from that first moment. I don't think I was ever so attracted to anyone before in my life. He had those flashing eyes that I just can't resist. I was so turned on by him that I couldn't wait to go to bed with him.
>
> We got together the next night for our first date. He took me to a lovely little restaurant on the ocean, and he took care of ordering. He's one of those men who knows all about wines and foods and I just love that in a man. He seemed interested in everything about me—what I did, how I felt about things, what I liked. I talked and talked and he just sat there, gazing at me with those electric eyes, absorbing everything I

said. After dinner we went back to my place and listened to music together, and then I seduced *him*. He was too much of a gentleman. I loved that about him. Of course, it was terrific with him sexually, and that was it. I felt closer to him than I ever had to any man before in my life.

Bob was 40, working as a sales representative for a clothing manufacturer. He told Laura he had been divorced the year before. Within the first month of their relationship, he and Laura moved in together and he began to talk about getting married. When he introduced her to his two young children, they all hit it off immediately. Bob's obvious devotion to his children made Laura feel even closer to him.

Jackie and Mark's romance started out as a blind date. It became a serious involvement that very first night. As Jackie described it to me:

I opened my door and saw this incredibly handsome man standing there. He just smiled at me. The first words out of his mouth were, "Can I use your phone?" I blinked and said yes, and he walked over to the phone and called the guy who had introduced us and said, "John, you were right. She's everything you said she was." That was only the beginning of the evening!

Jackie was a petite, vivacious 30-year-old when she and Mark met. She was working as a teacher in an elementary school, supporting her two children from a previous marriage, while trying to get her doctorate. Mark was 38 and had recently run for public office. Jackie remembered seeing his picture on billboards around town. She was very impressed with him and extremely flattered by his attentions to her.

We were having dinner with John, who had introduced us, and his wife. She turned to me and said, "I know you two have just met but I've never seen two people look so right together." Then she took my hand and said, "You are going to marry this man." Mark nodded and said to me, "Pay attention to what she's saying. She's a very smart girl." Then he whispered to me, "You've got a problem and his name is Mark." I laughed and replied "Why, are you going to be around for a while?" "I certainly am," he said. Then, when he took me home that night, we were sitting in the car in front of my house and he kissed me and said, "I know this sounds crazy, but I'm in love with you." Now *that's* romantic.

The next morning, when he called me, I told him that I wouldn't hold him to anything he'd said the night before. His response was, "I'll repeat every word of it right now."

Jackie felt like she was on a magic carpet from that evening on. Mark's falling in love with her so quickly completely swept her off her feet.

We All Love Romance

Romance makes you feel wonderful. Your emotions and your sexual feelings are at fever pitch, and in the beginning the intensity can be truly overwhelming. The relationship can affect you like a euphoric drug; being on "cloud nine" is the way many people describe it. The body, in fact, is producing a tremendous number of chemicals that contribute to the "wonderful glow" people talk about.

The fantasy, of course, is that we're going to feel like that forever. We've been told all our lives that romantic love has magical powers to make us whole and happy as women. Literature, TV, and movies help to reinforce this belief. The paradox is that even the most destructive misogynistic relationship starts out filled with just this kind of excitement and expectation. Yet despite the good feelings experienced in the beginning, by the time Rosalind came in to see me she was a nervous wreck, and her previously thriving antiques business was on the verge of bankruptcy; Laura, the former account executive, became so demoralized that she was sure she was incapable of ever holding another job; and Jackie—who had successfully juggled teaching, graduate school, and raising two young children—found herself breaking down and sobbing over minor incidents. What had happened to the beautiful, exciting romance that had marked the beginnings of these relationships? Why were the women so hurt and disillusioned?

Whirlwind Courtships

I believe that when a romance moves as swiftly as these did, there's an underlying sense of danger in the air. The danger may actually add to the excitement and stimulation of the affair. When I ride my horse, a trot is very pleasant but not particularly interesting; the thrill lies in the gallop. Part of that thrill is the knowledge that something unexpected might happen—I might get thrown; I might get hurt. It's the same sense of thrill and danger we all experienced as children when we rode the roller-coaster. It's fast, it's exciting, and it feels risky.

Once the element of sexual intimacy has been added, the speed and intensity of the emotions becomes even greater. You don't go through the normal progression of discovery with your new lover because there has not been enough time. Your new partner has many qualities that are going to affect your life—qualities that cannot be seen immediately. It takes time for both partners to develop the openness, trust, and honesty that are needed for a solid relationship. A whirlwind courtship, thrilling as it may be, tends to provide only pseudo-intimacy, which is then mistaken for genuine closeness.

Romantic Blinders

In order to see who our new partner truly is, the relationship has to move more slowly. It takes time to see others realistically so that we can recognize and accept both their virtues and their shortcomings. In a whirlwind courtship the emotional currents are so swift and strong that they overwhelm both partners' perceptions. Anything that interferes with the picture of the new love as "ideal" is ignored or blocked out. It's as if both partners are wearing blinders. We become intensely focused on how the other person is making us *feel* rather than on who the other person really is. The logic goes: since he makes me *feel* wonderful, he must *be* wonderful.

Laura and Bob were swept up by the spellbinding chemistry they felt between them in their first meetings. This chemistry had very little to do with who each of them was as a person. The rapture that Laura described related not to Bob's character but to his eyes, the way he moved, and how he ordered wine in the restaurant. Never did she say, "He was a decent, honest man." Bob was fulfilling for her the role of the perfect romantic lover, and both of them were caught up in the seduction and infatuation of the moment.

The first indication Laura had that there might be trouble came soon after she and Bob had begun living together.

> We were out together and he said, "I have something to tell you. I'm not divorced yet." I nearly fell off my chair, because by that time we were making wedding plans! He said, "I *felt* divorced, so I really didn't think it made that much difference." I was so shocked I couldn't talk. I just kept staring at him. Then he told me the divorce was in the works and he was taking care of it and I shouldn't worry. I realized that he'd lied to me from the beginning—I mean, he'd given me dates and all that sort of thing—but it just didn't seem that important then. Then, the important thing wasn't that he had lied but that he actually was getting the divorce.

Bob's deceptiveness should have been a warning to Laura that she needed to take a closer look at him, but she didn't *want* to see. She wanted to believe that Bob was the man of her dreams.

Jackie also received an early warning. In the beginning of her relationship with Mark, he told her a great deal about himself and his attitudes toward women, but his information was cloaked in flattery, so Jackie had not been alerted by it.

> He told me that all the other women he'd been involved with only wanted to know, "What can *you* give me?" But what he found so special about me was that I was interested in what I could give to him. He said it was as if I had been born, shaped, and existed only to take care of him. All the other women had been taking and taking, all gimme gimme gimme, there for the good times but running from the bad ones. I was different.

Jackie could have heard that Mark lumped all women together and categorized them as greedy, selfish, and untrustworthy. But she chose instead to see his statements as further proof that she was the special one who would make his life better.

A warning that there might be trouble ahead came early for Rosalind, too, but she failed to notice the signal for what it was.

> That first date, when he came over to my apartment for dinner, we went to bed together. He had a lot of trouble in that department, staying hard. It was disappointing, but I told myself that a lot of men have trouble like that with someone new and it didn't mean anything. Then the next morning we made love again and it was a little better, but still I could see that he had problems. I figured I could help him overcome this, and I told myself that sex wasn't that important. What was so overpowering to me about Jim was how close I felt to him and how much he responded to me as a person.

Rosalind did what so many of us do: she ignored everything that did not fit into her romantic picture. Jim made her feel so good about herself that she discounted what turned out to be a long-term sexual problem that seriously affected their relationship.

Without realizing it, many women divide the emotional landscape of their relationships into a *foreground* and a *background*. In the foreground are all the wonderful characteristics that the man possesses. These are the traits that are focused on, maximized, and idealized. Any hint of trouble gets pushed into the background as unimportant.

An extreme example of foreground and background manipulation is the case of the woman who falls in love with a convicted murderer. She will tell you he is the most wonderful man in the world. No one understands him but her. The murder has fallen into the "unimportant" background while the murderer's surface charm takes center stage.

The phrases people use to describe this process in the early stages of a romantic relationship are very telling:

- I just *couldn't see* his faults.
- I chose *not to look* at his problems.
- I just *shut my eyes* and hoped it would be different for us.
- I must have been *blind* not to see it before.

It's easy *not to see* clues about someone's past relationships, problems, and irresponsibilities when that person makes you feel terrific. Blinders serve the function of eliminating from your vision any information that might cloud or spoil your romantic picture.

Desperation and Fusion

Another recurring theme in the early stages of a misogynistic relationship is the sense of underlying desperation in both partners, each of whom has a frantic need to bind the other person to him.

Mark told me, "The reason I came on so strong to Jackie was that I was afraid I would lose her if I didn't." In Mark's statement there is more than just love for Jackie: there is a sense of panic. He added:

> On our second date I just laid it all out. I told her what kind of life I wanted and I told her we were going to get married. I asked her if she was seeing anybody else, and when she said she was I told her to end it because she wouldn't be able to see anyone else but me now. I knew this was it and I wanted her to believe it too.

In Jackie's eyes, Mark's intensity was proof of his willingness to commit fully to their relationship.

Laura experienced a different sort of desperation. Her thirty-fifth birthday was two months away when she met Bob, and her traditional Italian family was putting a great deal of pressure on her to marry and have children. When Bob began pushing for marriage during the first month of their relationship, she was not only flattered but relieved.

A casual observer of these whirlwind relationships might say: "What's the rush?" Obviously, when people meet, fall in love, move in together, and start making wedding plans all within a few weeks, what is going on is more than just two people caring about and wanting to be with each other.

What these people are experiencing is a heightened, almost unbearable need to melt into or "fuse" with the other person as quickly as possible. The separate sense of self becomes secondary to the relationship. They begin to feel each other's feelings. Every change of mood is contagious. Often, work, friendships and other activities fall by the wayside. A tremendous amount of energy now goes into loving, being loved, gaining approval, and psychologically melting into one another.

It is this need for instant oneness that appears to be the major force propelling these relationships forward.

Rescuing

Rescuing is another important ingredient in the "Crazy Glue" of misogynistic relationships. It creates a particular bond that makes a woman feel both needed and heroic.

Much of Jackie's excitement early in her relationship with Mark came from the abundance of maternal emotions she felt for him. She was going to provide for him what no one else had, and her love would make up for all the hardships in his life. He would become the successful, responsible man that she knew was there underneath. She explained:

> The second time I saw him he told me all about his financial situation, and I was so flattered that he was being so honest about it that I made it all right with myself that he was 38 years old and didn't have a job. After all, he'd just run for office, and *someone* has to lose an election. He painted such a glorious picture of his future prospects, and he was so suave and charming and winning that I was sure, with just a little help from me, he'd be all right in no time. I decided that I was going to provide him with the love and support he needed to get back on his feet.

Jackie believed that she would magically transform Mark through the power of her love. For many women, this belief is a very strong aphrodisiac. It enables a woman to see herself as a goddess, an earth-mother, and a healer. Her love can cure him, whether his problem is financial, drug or alcohol abuse, or unsatisfactory prior relationships. By giving, helping, and providing, she also creates an illusion of power and strength for herself. There is a sense of heroism in this for her: she becomes ennobled through rescuing, because with her help he will become a different man.

There is a big difference, however, between *helping* and *rescuing*. We all need help over the rough spots in life from time to time. To assist financially if you are able to, to be compassionate, and to offer support lets your partner know you are on his team. But I am referring here to the man who has a track record of being able to take care of himself. His trouble is just temporary. *Helping* him is an occasional thing. It is not a constant.

Rescuing, on the other hand, is a repetitive behavior. This man always needs your help and is usually in difficulties. He has an extensive pattern of instability in both his professional and his personal life. He also consistently blames others for his failures.

Compare, for example, these two men:

- Man #1 has always worked hard and been financially responsible. The company he works for is sold and his job is phased out. He needs to borrow some money until he gets back to work. He is actively looking for a job, and when he finds one he starts paying you back.
- Man #2 has had long periods of financial chaos in his life and is constantly coming to you to bail him out. No job is good enough for him, and he has a history of not getting along with his bosses. When he does get work, he makes little or no effort to pay you back for your help.

Rosalind had noticed Jim's financial problems the first evening they met, and she immediately began to help out by inviting him to dinner for their first real date. Within weeks, she had suggested that he and his two teen-aged children come to live with her until he could get a regular job with a band. "He said I was the most wonderful woman in the world and now that he knew me, things were going to be different in his life." It wasn't long before she was supporting all of them on a permanent basis.

Initially, Jim's gratitude to Rosalind intensified his feelings for her. If he was in love with her before, he was insane about her once she started taking care of them all. For Jim, as for so many misogynists, her helping became proof that she really cared.

Many women bask in the glow of their partners' gratitude; it makes them feel truly needed and wanted. And yes, it is exciting to help your mate and to feel that your love and your giving make a difference in his life. His effusive gratitude may feel so wonderful that you begin to accept it as sufficient repayment.

Obviously, not all misogynists need rescuing. Many are stable both professionally and financially. In fact, the more successful the misogynist is, the more he may insist that the woman in his life be totally dependent on *him*. It is the misogynist who has serious patterns of instability who is in need of being rescued. His instability can show itself in a variety of ways: problems with money, substance abuse, chaotic relationships, gambling, or inability to hold a job. This man is sending out distress signals for someone to save him. Many women, especially those with a career of their own, rush in all too quickly with a life preserver, only to get pulled down by the undertow themselves.

Not every high-pitched romance involves a misogynist. Certainly a relationship that starts out with a great deal of excitement can turn out just fine. But if, in addition to the romantic excitement, you find some of the other elements I have described coming into play—rescuing, a sense of panic and desperation, a too-quick bonding or fusion, and a kind of purposeful blindness—then you may be headed for some very rough waters.

2 | *The End of the Honeymoon*

The first warning that Prince Charming has a dark side usually occurs during a seemingly insignificant incident. What makes it so confusing to the woman is that suddenly her partner's charm has turned to rage and she is subjected to an unreasonable attack on her character.

For Laura, the first incident occurred on Christmas Eve, after she and Bob had been living together for four months. As she described it:

> I was wrapping presents late that night and he said he was going to bed and wanted me to come in with him. I told him I'd be in as soon as I finished and he just flew off the handle. He said he wanted me in there *now*. We'd already made love that evening, so I knew he wasn't asking me because of that. But I'd never seen him angry like that. Before I knew it, he was screaming at me, calling me a selfish bitch. Then he slammed the door to the bedroom so hard that the whole

apartment shook. I just sat there, totally shaken. I didn't
know what to think. I chalked it off to the holidays and pressure and things like that.

Laura was so enthralled with the way Bob made her feel most of
the time that she did not want to see his temper tantrum as the danger signal it really was. If she had not been so swept away by her romantic feelings, she might have been able to step back for a moment
and realize that Bob had a problem with his anger. This was very
important information, and it had a tremendous effect on her life.
But instead of seeing his explosion as a warning that her lover was
capable of childish and intimidating outbursts, Laura explained it
away to herself.

Rationalizing His Behavior

Rationalization is what we do when we smooth over any insight that
interferes with our good feelings. It's a way of making the unacceptable acceptable. By giving "good reasons" for what would otherwise distress us, we make sense out of confusing and even
frightening situations. It is different from the blindness I discussed
in chapter I in that we do *see* and acknowledge the unpleasantness,
but instead of denying to ourselves that it exists, we *relabel* it.

Rosalind began rationalizing much of Jim's irresponsible behavior shortly after he moved in with her. She told me:

Jim could only get paying music jobs occasionally. He tried
a lot of different bands, but so many bandleaders don't know
anything about jazz. Musically I know Jim was right, but for
financial reasons I wish he'd been a little more tolerant.

Rosalind found good excuses for Jim's inability to keep a steady
job with a band. As it turned out, Jim had a nasty temper and would
fight with any authority figure on any job. But she chose each time

to interpret it as the bandleader's lack of musical knowledge rather than as Jim's personality problem.

Here are some statements I've heard from women who are trying to explain away their partner's past and present behavior:

- Yes, he's been married three times, but nobody understood him before the way I do.
- I know he's had several business failures, but he had a lot of dishonest partners who really took him to the cleaners.
- He says terrible things about his ex-wife, but I can't blame him because she was incredibly greedy and selfish.
- I know he drinks too much, but he's in the middle of a big case and as soon as it's over I know he'll stop.
- He really scared me when he yelled at me, but he's just under pressure right now.
- He got so angry when I disagreed with his opinion, but then nobody likes being disagreed with.
- I can't really blame him for losing his temper when he had such an unhappy childhood.

Any woman who says, *He only did it because* . . . about such things as tantrums or violent outbursts is rationalizing.

No one is nice all the time, and we shouldn't expect it of ourselves or of others. And of course there are times when we need to be understanding and to accept the fact that someone we love is under stress or is particularly sensitive to certain issues. I am not talking here about the man who is basically kind and respectful but who loses his temper on occasion. This man will take responsibility later for his outburst, and he will feel genuine remorse for having taken out his frustrations on someone he loves.

The misogynist is different: he will not feel any remorse for his tantrums. In addition, the woman in his life will find herself justifying and trying to explain away his nasty outbursts more and more frequently.

Rationalization is a very human reaction and does not necessarily indicate a serious problem. It becomes one when you find yourself excusing your partner's unacceptable behavior on a regular basis. As his outbursts become more frequent, you will need increasingly to rationalize just to be able to cope.

Jekyll and Hyde-ing

If the misogynist were angry and critical all the time, any woman's rationalizations would soon wear thin. But between his outbursts he's liable to be as charming and lovable as he was when you first met. Unfortunately, the good times support your mistaken belief that the ugly times are somehow just a bad dream—not the "real him." His loving behavior encourages you to continue hoping that things will be wonderful from now on. But there is no way of knowing how he will react to anything, because his reactions are liable to be different each time. This kind of behavior mirrors so completely the classic Robert L. Stevenson story about the dark and light side of human nature that I have come to call it *Jekyll and Hyde-ing*.

Laura found herself totally at a loss when Bob, soon after his Christmas Eve outburst, began switching back and forth. He could still be charming and ardent, but his Jekyll and Hyde-ing became more of a pattern in their relationship.

> One night we had a terrific fight. I'd had a grueling day and I just wanted to sleep, but he wanted to make love. I told him I was too exhausted but he wouldn't accept that. He took it personally. He thought I was rejecting him and playing with him. He got so angry that he jumped out of the bed and punched a hole in the closet door. I was terrified. I told him I couldn't take any more of this kind of thing. Then he started to cry. He threw himself at my feet and sobbed. He told me he would change. He was just under pressure. He begged me to understand what a hard time he was having. I was so confused by all this that I didn't know what to do. Here he was, sobbing into my lap and swearing that he loved

me more than any woman he'd ever known. I just put my arms around him and tried to soothe him. Naturally we wound up making up in bed. I decided we'd gone through the worst part of our relationship and from now on things were going to be wonderful.

Laura was caught on an emotional seesaw with Bob. She was constantly being bounced between his loving behavior and his un-predictable outbursts of rage.

There is nothing more confusing or bewildering than this kind of switching back and forth. It creates an enormous amount of ten-sion, because you never know what to expect. It's very much like the pattern of people who are addicted to gambling: they get what they want some of the time but not most of the time. Their anxiety level is sky high. But the promise of the "good stuff" keeps them hanging in there and playing.

In a similar way, Bob's loving behavior kept Laura assured that his bad behavior was only temporary and not the "real" him. The duality of his actions and the constantly changing sources of his anger served as a powerful hook.

We have been focusing up until now on the misogynist's behav-ior, but the woman's participation becomes a crucial element at this point. Once she accepts an attack on her self-worth and permits herself to be demeaned, she has opened the door for future assaults. Contrast Laura's behavior with the self-protective behavior of Katie, a young friend of mine:

I had an experience with a man I went to Mexico with. One day he's Mr. Wonderful and we're having a great time together, and then all of a sudden he turns into a monster. He decided I'd tipped the cabdriver too much and started screaming at me in the middle of the street. I don't know why he thought he could get away with that kind of stuff, but he picked the wrong girl when he pulled it on me. I told him I wasn't going to put up with that kind of treatment and that if he pulled that again I was going to leave. Well, then he was sweet as pie for a day or two, and then he did it again. So I left.

Unlike Katie, Laura was effectively teaching Bob how much abuse she would tolerate. Bob's apologies and protestations appeased Laura; she believed they were expressions of genuine remorse. And probably, for that moment, he *was* sorry. If his future behavior had supported his protestations, she would not have had a problem. But his remorse lasted only long enough to "rehook" her. Another outburst was sure to follow.

Once you have accepted Jekyll and Hyde-ing, from attack to apology, from rage to charm, you are setting yourself up for an even more painful phase.

Blaming Yourself

The logic goes like this: *If he has the capacity to be so wonderful, then it must be something I am doing that's making things go wrong.* The misogynist bolsters this belief by reminding you that he would always be nice if only you would stop this, or change that, or be more of this or a little less of that. This is very dangerous thinking.

Your new attempt to make sense of the confusion in your relationship represents a giant leap in the wrong direction. You've gone from recognizing that there are troublesome aspects to your partner's behavior, to attempting to justify them or explain them away, to now *internalizing and accepting the responsibility* for how he acts.

Laura recalled:

Anytime I didn't jump to his every command he'd say, "You're selfish. You don't know how to give in a relationship." He'd tell me I was 35 and had never been married, so what did I know about sharing or living with someone? He'd been married before and he knew all about sharing. I figured maybe he was right. Maybe I was being selfish. That's when I began doubting myself.

Bob shifted the blame to Laura by attacking her where he knew she was most vulnerable.

Not all misogynists are as explosively critical as Bob was. Some express their disappointment in quieter, more subtle—but equally devastating—ways. This was the case for another of my clients, a former commercial artist married to a psychologist.

Paula met Gerry when they were in college. In the course of their eighteen-year marriage they had four children together. When she came in to see me, she was in her early 40s, a pleasant-looking woman with dark hair, large expressive brown eyes, and a robust figure. She told me that Gerry had become critical of her soon after they became engaged, and that his switch from attentive boyfriend to harping critic had been very confusing to her.

Once, while we were engaged, we went to a fair where Chuck Berry was performing. I wanted to hear him, but Gerry just started picking at me: how terrible that music was, how primitive, how he couldn't understand how anyone with half a mind could possibly listen to it. He accused me of having no taste and no culture. He kept looking at me like I'd just crawled out from under a rock. I knew he was right and that I was still hung up listening to the same music I was into as an adolescent. It's true that I don't have much refinement or class compared with him. I've got the tastes of a hick.

Paula supported her claim that she was at fault by calling herself a "hick" and by idealizing Gerry's cultural background. And Gerry had never let her forget his claim to intellectual superiority. Laura had been just as quick to assure me that she was indeed "selfish, spoiled, and lacking in the ability to really give to another person."

When I suggested to Laura that she was being too hard on herself and asked her where she'd gotten these ideas, she said, "That's what Bob says, and he's right. I *am* selfish, and he's got the right to be angry."

Both Paula and Laura made "sense" of their partners' psychological abuse by blaming themselves. They were convinced that if they could just find "the magic key," those "right" behaviors or attitudes that would please their partners, they could get their partners to behave more lovingly toward them. It's as if Paula and Laura were saying, "Maybe all I have to do is to listen to what he says and try to behave accordingly and everything will be fine. If everything is my fault and he's the person who defines what my faults are, then it follows that he's the only one who can help me become a better person."

Unfortunately, the misogynist's signals are always changing. What pleases him one day may not please him the next. There is no way to know what will set him off. Trying to figure out how to please him may come to dominate your life.

Rosalind had been a sympathetic audience for Jim's complaints about insensitive band leaders, but soon he began to turn his rage on her.

> I asked him to tell me how to be better so he wouldn't get mad like that anymore. Naturally he was happy to oblige, but it didn't stop the temper tantrums because I was always doing something wrong.

Rosalind and Jim had discovered another bond that was to bind them very closely together: *They both blamed* her *for everything that went wrong.*

His Disappointment

When a honeymoon ends, it ends for both partners. One partner doesn't get to stay at Niagara Falls while the other goes home. So, while the woman has been feeling bewildered and confused by the changes in the relationship, her partner has been experiencing his own brand of disillusionment. Because he so idealized her in the beginning, it is inevitable that he will be disappointed. As Jackie recalled it:

> Mark said to me that if he was asked to draw a blue-print of a perfect woman, it would be me, without any changes or modifications. I was just perfect, without a flaw.

Mark's idealization of Jackie felt wonderful and exciting to her. It is easy to see why she didn't recognize the potential danger. The fact is that Mark wasn't seeing her as a human being with the same shortcomings, failures, and faults that we all have. Instead, he was deifying her: she was his goddess. And of course he expected her to be like that all the time.

YOU ARE SUPPOSED TO BE PERFECT

Nancy and Jeff, whom we met in the introduction, had been dating for six months when the following incident occurred:

> We had a wonderful evening at a concert. When it was over, we were sitting there waiting for the aisles to clear. When I stood up, he said, "What's your hurry?" And then he got so furious at me. He yelled, "We'll go when I say it's time to go! God, you're pushy!" He was so furious, and I couldn't understand it. Then he stalked out ahead of me to the car. And he wouldn't let up. He kept at me all the way home. It was horrible. I didn't know what to do. I figured I must have done something terribly wrong because nobody gets that mad over nothing.

But the misogynist *can* get very mad over virtually nothing. He explodes over the most insignificant events. He exaggerates, he maximizes—he makes mountains out of molehills. Perhaps his partner forgot to pick up the dry-cleaning, or the toast came out too dark, or maybe they ran out of toilet paper. He treats her momentary fall from grace as if it were a federal crime. Nancy's getting out of her seat ahead of Jeff at the end of the concert was all he needed to unleash his rage at her. But Nancy did just the opposite: she minimized. She accepted his irrational attack and reduced his responsibility for it. The paradox is that while he was exploding over her innocent act, she was maximizing her own culpability and minimizing his!

Nancy told me that Jeff was always letting her know, in no uncertain terms, that she was messing up their relationship. He told her he was disappointed. She wasn't who he had thought she was. He felt tricked. Where was the perfect woman he'd fallen in love with?

YOU ARE SUPPOSED TO READ HIS MIND

The misogynist expects his partner to know what he is thinking and feeling without his ever having to state it. He expects that she will somehow anticipate his every need and that meeting his needs will take priority over everything else in her life. She is supposed to know his wishes without having been told. One of the proofs of her love is her ability to read his mind. He will say things such as:

- If you really loved me, you would have known what I was thinking.
- If you weren't so wrapped up in yourself, you would have been able to tell what I wanted.
- If you really cared about me, you would have known I was tired.
- If my needs mattered to you, you would have known that I didn't want to go to the movies.

The phrase *you should have known* implies that you are expected to have the power to see into your partner's mind and know his every thought and wish. It's not his responsibility to express himself; it is your job to be clairvoyant. If a woman fails to have ESP, that becomes proof of her deficiencies. It is also further justification for him to attack her.

You Are Supposed to Be an Ever-Flowing Breast

The typical misogynist expects his partner to be a never-ending source of total, all-giving love, adoration, concern, approval, and nurturing. He enters into a relationship with a woman very much as a hungry, demanding infant does, with the unspoken expectation that she will be totally giving and will meet all his needs.

Soon after Jackie married Mark, she found out that he had lied to her about paying some important bills. He was supposed to have taken care of them but had not done so. When she questioned him about this, he became furious.

> He accused me of not loving him, of not understanding him. He said I wasn't on his team. He had friends who did a lot worse, who came home drunk every night and who really screwed up financially, and yet their wives never stopped loving and supporting them. How come I wasn't capable of that kind of love? Somehow he worked it out that I was the villain for daring to question him about not paying the bills.

From Mark's point of view, no matter what he did, Jackie was expected never to be upset, never to question him, and never to be anything less than totally giving and loving. He saw himself as loving, caring, and generous. He wanted to give all of this to the wonderful woman he'd found, but as soon as he saw that she was not an "ever-flowing breast," he felt betrayed and turned on her.

You Are Supposed to Be a Tower of Strength

Rosalind's partner, Jim, couldn't see her as another human being, separate from himself, who had needs and feelings of her own. He told me:

I thought she was so together, and then one time, early
on, she started blubbering like a baby. Jesus, what a goddamned disappointment that was. I just couldn't believe
this was the same woman I'd fallen so hard for.

The fact is that Rosalind was a strong, competent, effective
woman. However, like everyone else, she had her bad days. When
she dared to express her vulnerability, Jim was disgusted and contemptuous. As she told the story:

It was the first time he'd seen me break down at all, and
his reaction was shock. Like, "Who are you to break down
and cry like that? Who are you not to be strong all the time
and take care of everything?" That was the feeling I got. I
thought he was going to walk out on me. It ended up that
I apologized. I tried to make little of the whole situation, but
I couldn't get over that he wouldn't accept me as just another
human being.

Because of her tears, Rosalind's status as a perfect woman was
lowered. As far as Jim was concerned, she no longer deserved to be
treated well by him.

Idealization is a double-edged sword. It feels wonderful and flat-
tering, but it also blinds a woman to the fact that she's doomed to
fail. It is impossible to live on the pedestal the misogynist places her
on, because there's no margin for error. If she is in a bad mood or
displays any behavior that he doesn't like, he views it as a sign of her
deficiency. He hired a goddess, and she isn't living up to the job re-
quirements. His contempt and disillusionment with her is all the
permission he needs to stop expressing his love for her and to begin criticizing, accusing, and blaming.

The initial disappointment for the misogynist usually occurs
early in the relationship. However, because there is so much excitement and romance going on, the moment of flare-up is easily swept

under the rug. If there is a sense of shock for the woman, it is only a small sour note in a symphony of good feelings.

The early indications of the misogynist's quick temper are sporadic. The explosions don't become a way of life until some kind of commitment has been made. This can be a verbal commitment, moving in together, an engagement, or a marriage. Then, once he's sure he "has" her, the situation changes rapidly.

3 | How He Gains Control—Weapons

Toward the end of the honeymoon, when the misogynist first does something to attack his partner's self-respect, he is testing the waters. If he doesn't meet with any resistance to this initial outrage, then what she is doing, without realizing it, is giving him permission to continue such behavior.

I tell women all the time that you can't afford to give Hitler Poland.

The Love Contract

There is a great deal of testing going on early in the relationship. The misogynist is defining for himself—often without even realizing it—just how far he can go. Unfortunately, his partner believes that by not confronting or questioning his behavior when he hurts her feelings, she is expressing her love for him. Many women fall into this trap. We have been taught since we were little girls that *love is the answer*. It will make everything better; all we have to do is to get a man to love us and then life will be good and we will live happily ever after. We have also been taught that in the service of getting that love, certain behaviors are expected of us. Some of those are "smoothing things over," backing down, apologizing, and "making nice." As it turns out, these are the very behaviors that encourage the misogynist to mistreat his partner.

It is as if we've made both a spoken and an unspoken contract, or agreement, with the misogynist. The spoken agreement says: *I love you and I want to be with you.* The unspoken agreement, which comes from our deepseated needs and fears, is far more powerful and binding. Your part in the unspoken agreement is: *My emotional security depends on your love, and to get that I will be compliant and renounce my own needs and wishes.* His part of that agreement is: *My emotional security depends on my being in total control.*

He Must Be in Control

There are power struggles in all relationships. Couples disagree over money, how to raise the children, where to go on vacation, how often to see the in-laws, who has the nicer friends, and who they should spend time with. While these issues may cause conflict, they can usually be negotiated with caring and respect.

However, in the misogynistic relationship, negotiation and compromise are in short supply. Instead, the partnership is played out on a grim battlefield where *he* has to win and *she* has to lose. This power imbalance is the major theme of the relationship.

The misogynist must control how his partner thinks, feels, behaves, and with whom and what she involves herself. It is amazing how quickly even successful, competent women will disavow their own talents and power in order to gain their partners' love and approval.

Of course, total control is an elusive thing. It is impossible to totally control another human being. Therefore, the misogynist's quest is bound to fail. As a result, he is frustrated and angry much of the time. Sometimes he is able to successfully mask his hostility. But at other times it will manifest itself as psychological abuse.

Why I Use the Term "Abuse"

The current definition of *abuse* in the mental-health profession covers both psychological and physical violence. *Abuse is defined as any behavior that is designed to control and subjugate another human being through the use of fear, humiliation, and verbal or physical assaults.* In other words, you don't have to be hit to be abused.

In physical battering the weapons are fists; in psychological battering the weapons are words. The only difference between the two is the choice of weapons.

I do not use the term *abuse* loosely. I am not using it to describe an occasional bad mood or the expression of angry feelings that exist in any relationship. I am using it to describe *the systematic persecution of one partner by another*. Verbal abuse has not received the attention that it warrants, given how devastating it can be to a person's mental health over a period of time. Often women say to me, "At least he doesn't hit me." My reply to this disclaimer is, "The result is the same. You are just as scared, you feel just as helpless, and you are in just as much pain. What difference does it make whether the weapon is his fist or his words?"

Control Through Psychological Abuse

The misogynist has an extensive repertoire of scare tactics, insults, denigrating comments, and other intimidating behavior designed to make his partner feel inadequate and helpless.

His most obvious attacks involve yelling, threatening, temper tantrums, name calling, and constant criticism. Attacks like these are direct, out in the open. They have an aggressive, assaultive quality to them.

IMPLIED THREATS

One of the most frightening and therefore one of the most successful tactics the misogynist can use to gain control carries with it the implied threat of physical harm. Such threats characterized the marriage of Lorraine and Nate, the parents of Jackie.

Nate was a successful businessman who was genuinely loved and respected by his many employees. Lorraine was a quiet woman who worked at home raising their two children and keeping house. During their thirty-five-year marriage, Nate used some extremely frightening tactics to run Lorraine and the rest of his family—tactics that no one outside the home ever saw. Lorraine recalled:

> His sister lived next door to us and I was very close to her. We went to the movies together one night and I had on a new dress and a new hat. On the way back she and I missed our bus, so I got home almost half an hour later than I had told Nate to expect me. When I walked in he was pacing up and down. He didn't even give me a chance to explain. He just tore my dress off and took the new hat and cut it up with a pair of scissors. Then he threw my nice new things down the incinerator. I felt like I wanted to die. I was terrified.

This vicious outburst was not an isolated incident. Such scenes occurred whenever Nate felt even momentary displeasure with Lorraine's behavior.

I am not suggesting that men like Nate consciously plan their attacks. Much of even their cruelest and most abusive behavior is motivated by forces that are outside their conscious awareness. Nonetheless, adults need to take responsibility for their behavior, no matter what demons are raging inside them. As Lorraine told me:

I used to plead with him not to do things like that to me. It scared me to death. He told me he only got that way because he worried so much about me when I was late. It was because he loved me so much, he said. But then about a week after the incident where he cut up my new hat, I overcooked a roast and he broke all the glasses in the kitchen.

For Lorraine, Nate's attacks were only a hair's breadth away from physical violence. The implication clearly was, "Today the glasses, tomorrow your arm." He didn't have to physically batter her; the implied threat was enough to keep her under his thumb.

VERBAL ATTACKS

Not all assaults are as overtly violent as the ones Lorraine described. Many involve shouting, which, because of the volume and the intensity of the rage, can be terrifying. Most people have a very difficult time handling anger, even their own. When anger is directed at you, it creates an atmosphere of tremendous tension. With the misogynist, the shouting usually includes insults and attacks on you, which make the experience doubly painful. These verbal assaults can be as frightening and demoralizing as implied threats of physical violence.

For Jackie, who was struggling to maintain a household while teaching and trying to get an advanced degree, Mark's verbal attacks proved to be very damaging:

I was really exhausted trying to finish a paper for a course. We'd had about a week of exceptionally heavy rains, and without my knowing it the garage had gotten flooded. I was typing away and Mark came in and said he wanted to show me something. I followed him obediently out to the garage and saw that the water had soaked into some cartons of clothes I had stored out there for the Salvation Army. He started in on me with, "You goddamned thoughtless, liberated asshole! All you can do is sit at your fucking typewriter.

You don't care a damn about the house or me or how hard I'm working." By then he was screaming while I was trying to get the boxes out of the water. He continued to yell at me, saying, "You think you've got a platinum asshole. You're just too good to worry about the house, big shot!" I went back into the house once I'd gotten all the boxes out of the water, and he followed me in, screaming and yelling at me the whole time. I just couldn't get away from him. I was so upset I couldn't go back and finish my paper, my hands were shaking so badly.

Mark's verbal assaults on Jackie's character were every bit as vicious as Nate's attacks on Lorraine, although in Jackie's case there was no threat of physical violence.

Unrelenting Criticism

Some misogynists do not resort to the obvious cruelty of scare tactics and screamed insults to gain control of their partners. Instead of raising their voices, they wear down their partners through unrelenting criticism and fault-finding. This type of psychological abuse is particularly insidious because it is often disguised as a way of teaching the woman how to be a better person.

Paula, the commercial artist we met in chapter 2, was always impeccably dressed when I saw her: she had that knack of being able to take the simplest clothes and coordinate them into a stunning outfit. Despite this, her psychologist husband, Gerry, constantly belittled her taste and appearance, as well as her character. She told me:

He hates for me to wear blue jeans, even around the house. He says, "Your colors aren't even coordinated and you don't look fancy." Once I started to cry when he'd been picking at me all afternoon and he said, "What's the matter with you? I'm just telling you for your own good!" He's at me about everything, though. I like old movies and he says

that's not deep enough. He says I'm not thoughtful enough,
I don't read the right things, I'm not helpful enough, I'm not
supportive enough. I'm trying very hard to be who he wants
me to be, but nothing I do pleases him.

Paula admired Gerry's intellectual and cultural knowledge. In
the beginning of their relationship she was very excited at the
prospect of his "making her over" into a sophisticated and worldly
woman: a worthy partner for him. She readily accepted that he was
smarter and better educated than she, and the idea that he was willing to share these treasures with her delighted her. The fact that
much of his advice was valid and rational further reduced her ability to see how unrelenting his criticisms were.

The "Professor Henry Higgins" type of misogynist—the one
who offers to help a woman to become a better person by making
her over—is liable to be in an advisory profession that is held in
great esteem or even awe by many people. These men are often
physicians, attorneys, professors, or, like Gerry, psychologists. The
prestige of their job provides these men with additional credibility
as critics and mentors.

This type of misogynist sets himself up as his partner's teacher
and guru, but no matter how much she shifts and changes to suit his
demands, she is inevitably in the wrong.

Criticism of this sort works in much the same way as water on a
rock: the first few drops are not damaging, but the cumulative effect
over time makes deep and lasting crevices. Similarly, the misogynist's constant criticism and picking eats away at his partner's self-
confidence and sense of self-worth.

The types of psychological abuse that I have just discussed are
recognizable, once you've learned what to look for. But there are
other behaviors, which are far more subtle, that can effectively
erode your ability to think and evaluate clearly. These hard-to-spot
manipulative techniques, which I call *gaslighting*, begin to make
you doubt your own perceptions and even your sanity.

Gaslighting Techniques

If you enjoy old movies, you've probably seen *Gaslight*, with Charles Boyer and Ingrid Bergman. Boyer plays a husband who appears to be loving and devoted to his wife, but who begins to tear down her sanity, using a variety of insidious techniques. He hides her jewelry and then convinces her that she lost or misplaced it; he takes a picture off the wall and insists that she moved it. These attacks on his wife's mind almost succeed in convincing her that she is insane. *Gaslighting* has come to mean just this kind of subtle manipulation of another person. The movie provides a classic example of how much power one partner can wield over another. The man in the movie did these things deliberately and methodically in order to gain a treasure that was hidden in the house where he and his wife lived. The misogynist, however, is after a different prize, and, unlike the Boyer character, his behavior is not the result of deliberate planning. But that does not make him any less oppressive.

DENIAL

There are many ways in which a person can be made to question the accuracy and validity of her own memory and perceptions. The most primitive and blatant of these tactics is *denial*. The misogynist convinces his partner that the incident just didn't happen.

Remember Jackie's story about the water on the floor of the garage and how abusive Mark had been to her? When Mark came in to see me shortly afterward, at my request, I asked him about that episode. He replied:

> I don't remember that. I don't know what she's talking about. I honestly don't remember these episodes that apparently mean more to her than all the wonderful times we've had together. You know, it's incredible how she only remembers the bad things.

From Mark's point of view, if he didn't remember an incident it simply didn't happen.

This type of convenient forgetfulness is even more apparent in a misogynist who used alcohol or drugs, which lower inhibitions and strip away the civilized veneer. When people are drunk or high on drugs, they are often explosive and cruel. Yet, they have an uncanny ability to forget their actions the next day. "Boy, I was so drunk last night that I don't remember a thing that happened" is a standard form of denial.

What is so distressing about the use of denial as a tactic is that you are left with nothing to deal with. It creates a sense of desperate frustration. There is no way to resolve a problem with someone who denies the existence of certain events and who insists that what you know to be real never happened.

REWRITING HISTORY

With this tactic, an episode is not denied but is reshaped to fit the misogynist's version of it. No two people remember an incident in exactly the same way, but the misogynist makes dramatic and extensive alterations to facts in order to validate his version of the story. Laura related the following incident, which took place the night before her wedding to Bob:

> We'd arranged for me to spend that last night at our friends' house, which was where the wedding was going to take place the next day. He and I had talked it out, it was all set, and our friends were expecting me. When Bob came home and saw my overnight bag, he asked me where I was going. I told him I was going to stay with Joe and Betty, like we'd planned. He looked at me like I was crazy. "I never agreed to that!" he said. "Who decided this?" And I told him we both had. Then he went into, "I'm really worried about you if you think I said such a thing, because I never would have agreed to this. It's our last night together before

we're married!" By the time he got done twisting and turning it, I felt pretty shaky. Could I really have misunderstood so totally?

This story reminds me of George Orwell's classic *1984*. There, the forces of totalitarianism gathered up all the history books and rewrote everything to support their version of past events. For Bob, as for many misogynists, facts are like clay, to be molded and shaped to justify their moods or needs at the moment.

Shifting the Blame

In tandem with the gaslighting techniques is the misogynist's contention that if he's behaving badly, it is only because he is responding to some crime of yours. Such men sincerely and convincingly argue that their outrageous behavior is an understandable reaction to some terrible deficiency or provocation on your part. By doing this, the misogynist avoids having to consider the possibility that he has some serious shortcomings. By shifting the blame to you, he protects himself in two important ways: he absolves himself of the discomfort of recognizing his role in the problem, and he convinces you that your character deficiencies are the real reason why you are having trouble together. Any criticism or questioning of him is immediately turned back on you as further proof of your inadequacies.

This process of shifting the blame to you starts early in the relationship and never lets up. In Laura's marriage to Bob, his inability to find a job quickly became her fault.

After we'd been married a couple of months he lost his job and he didn't actively look for another one for a long time. Finally he got an interview for something that sounded very promising. When he came home that afternoon I asked him, "Did you get the job?" He said, "Yes, but I didn't take it because you're a money-hungry bitch and it didn't pay enough to satisfy you." He told me I placed more value on money than on him. Of course, I was the one who was working all the time, but he told me I didn't stand by him, I didn't support him, and I wasn't there for him. By the time he got done I felt like a character out of an old Joan Crawford movie.

Bob exonerated himself while making Laura feel miserable. He didn't have to feel inadequate when the reason why he couldn't take a job was that nothing would satisfy his vicious, materialistic wife.

An extreme example of blame-shifting occurred in Paula's marriage when she discovered that Gerry had a pattern of having sexual relations with his female patients, under the guise of helping them work through their sexual inhibitions. When one of his patients finally reported him, the licensing board revoked Gerry's license to practice. However, Paula not only stuck by him and went back to work to support their family, she also accepted the blame for his criminal behavior. She told me:

> It was my fault when he lost his license, because if I'd been more of a woman he wouldn't have needed all those others. I just wasn't warm or loving enough.

I couldn't believe my ears when Paula said this. Gerry had behaved atrociously, had damaged many lives, and Paula was blaming herself! Of course, Paula was only repeating to me what Gerry had said about her, but she fully believed it.

Remember, in misogynistic relationships, both partners blame the woman for everything that goes wrong. What set Paula up to accept Gerry's shifting of guilt onto her was that the issue at hand—sexuality—was for her an area of extreme vulnerability, insecurity, and self-hatred. As a child, Paula had been physically and sexually abused by her father, and these traumatic experiences had left her with a deep sense of shame and guilt. In adulthood she harbored a view of herself as both damaged and inadequate. Therefore, when the man she loved attacked her on these grounds, accusing her of not being womanly enough, she was preprogrammed to accept it.

Paula was no more to blame for Gerry's losing his license than Laura was for Bob's inability to get a job. But both Bob and Gerry had learned how to use their wives' areas of vulnerability to their own advantage. By shifting the blame, they saved themselves from seeing any inadequacies in themselves. Unfortunately for Laura and Paula, their acceptance of the blame became "proof" of their love. In a situation like this, the problem becomes: there is no way to prove your love enough.

YOU ARE NOT ALLOWED TO SAY "OUCH"

Further proof of your love involves giving up your right to react to what your partner does. If you cry or get upset when he is abusive, his response usually is to get even angrier. He sees your reaction as an attack on him and as further proof of your inadequacies. Nancy, the former fashion coordinator whom we met in the introduction, told me:

> I'd say to him when he was yelling about something, "Please stop yelling at me because it makes me feel terrible." Then if I started crying he'd get even madder and start in on me with stuff like, "That's right. Just turn it around and make it my fault so you won't have to hear any criticism." He just twists it so that if I'm miserable, I get it even more.

As far as Jeff was concerned, the best defense was a good offense. By switching the situation around, Jeff was able to make Nancy the villain and himself the victim.

Many misogynists use this method of turning the tables to deflect blame from themselves. They may say: "You are too sensitive"; "You're overreacting"; "You just can't take any criticism"; or simply, "You're crazy." They are switching the situation around so that they never have to accept any responsibility for how they make their partners feel. Unpleasant as it might be to accept, the fact is that the misogynist is more concerned with deflecting blame from himself than with recognizing the pain he is causing his partner.

When a woman is attacked for showing pain or sadness over her partner's treatment of her, she must repress her normal feelings. But feelings need to be ventilated and expressed. When a direct outlet for expression is cut off, these feelings find other ways to manifest themselves—often unpleasant and harmful ways, such as physical illness, low energy, lack of motivation, and depression (see chapter 8).

Control Through Physical Abuse

Because of the intensity of the feelings involved, violence between people who are intimate with each other tends to be more brutal and more unpredictable than violence between strangers. The misogynist can become brutal under certain conditions. One of the most important of these is the use of alcohol, which decreases impulse control and raises the potential for acting out. Being drunk also provides an excuse for these men to vent their rage physically.

The risk of wife-battering also rises whenever the family is in turmoil or change. Stressful events such as a pregnancy, the death of a parent, the loss of a job, moving, physical illness, or a change in financial circumstances can trigger physical violence.

If the misogynist feels threatened that he is going to lose something that is important to him and therefore be humiliated, it is quite likely to tip the scales toward brutality. For instance, if a woman gets a job after having been at home for a number of years, or if she returns to school or makes new friends who make him feel threatened or left out, he might try to control her by bullying and threatening. If that is not successful, he may resort to physical violence, thinking that he can hold on to her more firmly if she is frightened of him.

HOW CAN YOU TELL IF PSYCHOLOGICAL ABUSE IS ABOUT TO ESCALATE INTO PHYSICAL ABUSE?

Extreme jealousy and extreme possessiveness always spell danger. If you are subjected to constant accusations, constant watching, spying, interrogation, or overreactions to such minor infractions as being late—be on your guard. If you talk to another man at a party and your partner overreacts with anger far out of proportion to the event, beware. This type of suspiciousness is a signal that the possibility of physical violence exists.

Threats of violence, even if violence has not occurred before, should always be taken seriously. Plans for getting even, for revenge, and attempts to control you through threats of brute force are a clear sign that you need to have a backup plan for yourself. As difficult as it is to admit that violence might occur, it is essential that you line up some basic resources, including:

- some available money
- a safe place for yourself and the children to go
- a way of getting there at any hour.

Hopefully, you will have family or friends to call on for support. But whatever your resources, all experts in the field concur on this point: if there is physical violence, *you must get out*, even if it means leaving a beautiful home and going to a battered-women's shelter.

There is a final control device that demands, as proof of her love, that a woman give up those things that make her unique and that are an important part of who she is: the misogynist demands that his partner narrow her world to keep the peace between them.

Narrowing Your World

This process often begins in a subtle, indirect, benign way, which may even be experienced as flattery. For instance, suppose you have been taking a class one night a week. Your partner lets you know how he counts the hours until you come home and how lonely and miserable he is while you are gone. This can sound like an expression of true love—he needs you with him all the time! But it's only a short hop from that kind of "devotion" to possessiveness over many aspects of your life. Of course, you can give up your class, but in all likelihood there will soon be some other activity that's meaningful to you but a threat to him. How much of yourself must you renounce in order to prove your love?

There is an insatiable, demanding quality to the misogynist's love; no matter how much you give, or give up, it is never enough. He is never convinced that you care about him as much as he cares about you. He will constantly invent new tests of your devotion. It's very much like having a final exam every week for a course you can never pass.

Laura thought it was wonderful when Bob finally found an excellent job and offered to "take care" of her. She'd worked since she was 19 and was delighted with the chance to stay home and fix up the apartment.

> He'd started to make really good money, and he asked me to quit working. He wanted me to just stay home and take it easy, something I'd never had the luxury of doing. But the next thing I knew he didn't want me to see any of my friends anymore. He even started getting upset when I called my family. It was like he was supporting me so he owned me.

What came in the guise of love and devotion on Bob's part wound up as a prison of control for Laura.

The misogynist uses either direct control or indirect control to gain his objective. He may directly state, plead, or demand that you give up a job, a class, or a friendship, *or* he may begin to attack indirectly those areas that are threatening to him, making it so miserable for you to continue with them that you give them up just to keep the peace. But, no matter what method your partner uses, the result is the same: *You have seriously limited your world to suit his needs.*

Nicki, a policewoman, was 24 when she met Ed. Ed, a 27-year-old officer with the department, was very taken with Nicki's intelligence, breeding, and physical ability both as a policewoman and as an athlete. Nicki found Ed's macho behavior and blond good looks exciting. They fell in love very quickly and were married. Within a short time, though, Ed's temper and jealousy became a problem. They had been together for two years when Nicki came to see me.

> He has to know everything I do. Anything I don't clear with him first he uses as a weapon to prove that I'm untrustworthy. He'll call in to my department or even my patrol car three or four times a day, checking up on me—where I am, who I'm with. It's embarrassing. If I'm not where he expects me to be, he throws a tantrum. Last week I went out to lunch with a woman officer and when I got back he was standing at my desk, all red in the face. He pulled me into another room and started screaming at me, how I'd betrayed him and he couldn't trust me. He scares me to death when he's like that.

Nicki had decided that Ed's outbursts were so embarrassing and frightening that it wasn't worth the trouble to cross him. She gave up what little freedom she had, even in her job.

This kind of jealousy and possessiveness is not limited to the traditional fear of your becoming romantically involved with another man; rather, it extends into all aspects of your life. Anything you do that is out of the misogynist's control or is seen as a threat to him must be abolished.

4 | *Where He Gains Control—Arenas*

One of the most unusual reasons for coming into therapy was given to me by a 43-year-old woman who couldn't get her husband to pay for her dental work. As I talked with her, what emerged was that her husband, a millionaire industrialist, was giving her a grand total of fifteen dollars a week for a five-thousand-dollar dental bill. I also learned that she was working for her husband's company without being paid a salary and was regularly being humiliated by him in front of his other employees. Obviously, there was a lot more going on than his reluctance to pay her dental bill.

I usually find that the specific problem that brings a person in for therapy is only the tip of the iceberg. Issues concerning money, sexual problems, vocational instability, and conflicts over the children are often merely smokescreens that cover a troubled relationship.

Control in the Bedroom

No sexual relationship can sustain the electricity of the honeymoon period. Sexual relationships, by their nature, ebb and flow as people mature together. With the misogynist, however, to whom power and control are the dominant themes, the sexual arena becomes one of major conflict.

It takes a concerted effort on the part of both partners to bring sexual feelings and preferences out into the open. When the element of negotiation is lacking, the sensitivity required for an open discussion of sexual desires and needs is usually missing as well.

Women tend to be particularly timid about expressing sexual needs and desires because it is often such an emotionally loaded issue for us. We have been taught all our lives that a great deal of our self-worth is tied into our being sexually desirable and responsive. Our vulnerability about our sexuality leaves us open to the misogynist's methods. His criticism, denigrating remarks, and consistent rejection or brutality can slam shut doors that were barely open in the first place.

As the relationship enters its post-honeymoon phase, the misogynist may feel that his disillusionment gives him license to attack. What started off as romantic and sexually exciting may begin to change once he feels "disappointed" in his partner. The considerate lover of the early days may become not only less considerate but actively cruel.

In a good relationship, the intense sexual feelings are supplemented by friendship, respect, and caring. Even if the sexual excitement has diminished or changed with time, there is still sensitivity to the other person's feelings. But the opposite takes place with the misogynist: *The longer the partnership continues, the less caring and concern there is about her feelings, and the more he's liable to criticize her desirability as a woman.*

SEXUAL CRITICISM

We all tend to believe criticism more than we believe praise. One cruel statement can have much more impact than twenty positive ones. We hear negative comments more sharply and clearly than positive ones, and we take them as truer, more honest views of ourselves. For this reason, even the most sexually secure woman can be thrown off balance by her partner's consistent negative remarks about her appearance or her sexual performance or by continual comparisons to other women.

Nicki, the young policewoman, told me:

> I always felt pretty good about the way I looked until Ed
> started cutting ads out of magazines as examples of how I
> should look. He'd point out how much prettier some
> model's hair was than mine. He'd tell me he wanted me to
> look more like this one or that one because then I'd be more
> attractive and more of a turn-on to him. I began to feel really
> unattractive.

Ed's picking at Nicki set up an imbalance in their sexual relationship. He had made himself the arbiter of how Nicki should look, which automatically put her in the lesser position.

As attacks become more vicious, their effects become more devastating. Paula, whose psychologist husband had been having affairs with his patients, related the following:

> Gerry said that because I'm not blond I couldn't possibly
> meet his needs. And then he'd say how ugly and flabby my
> body was and how my breasts sagged. He'd point to the
> scars I have from having our four children and say how ugly
> they were and how my butt wasn't high enough. It got to the
> point where I was ashamed to get undressed in front of him.
> Then he'd say, "If you were a real woman it wouldn't bother
> you."

Gerry made Paula feel that she had some terrible deficiency. His verbal assaults annihilated her already shaky self-esteem.

Even in the best of relationships, people sometimes want to change or modify some aspect of their partner's appearance. It's the *way* in which these wishes are expressed that makes the difference. If remarks are made kindly and with good will, there's no damage done. But the misogynist is *not* acting out of good will, because he is not sincerely after change. He's after *control*, and he does not hesitate to use continual, belittling criticism to get it.

The climate of intimacy and closeness that surrounds sexual contact, in which we are both physically and emotionally naked, leaves us susceptible to attack. Our defenses are down. We are sharing the most secret parts of ourselves. It is not a time when we can protect ourselves against remarks about performance. Jackie's mother, Lorraine, began to feel as though she was on trial every time she and Nate had sexual relations. She told me:

> I know I'm not the most passionate person, but I try to respond and be what he wants. But every time we do it he says something that just about kills me, like, "Even a two-dollar whore would put on a better show than you do." I just freeze up.

Lorraine and Nate were caught in a vicious circle: the more he put her down, the more sexually closed off she became, which then set off more put-downs by him and more withdrawals by her. Nate, like so many misogynists, believed that criticizing his wife was not only his right but his responsibility. His belief that he had to "shape her up" was all the justification he needed to continue, even though it worked against him and obviously did not help her.

SEXUAL SELFISHNESS

Sexual relations with a misogynist are liable to occur only when and how he chooses. If he's sexually selfish, only his needs will be important, and only those forms of lovemaking that are pleasing to him will be acceptable.

One of the first changes that many women report is that sex has become mechanical; the attention and affection that went with love-making in the beginning of the relationship has slipped away. The misogynist has stopped giving his partner time to become aroused, and her joy in touching, hugging, and kissing has diminished. Nancy described it this way:

> We hadn't been together too long before Jeff just stopped doing anything like what you could call "foreplay." He'd just hop on, do it, and get off. I didn't know what to say about it. He'd paid so much attention in the beginning to how I felt, but after a short time that part was all over.

Nancy's experience is not unusual. Like many misogynists, Jeff saw affection and caressing as time-consuming and unnecessary once he'd "won" his woman. Foreplay became something to rush through to prepare Nancy for the main event—intercourse. For Jeff, the rest was unimportant. But for Nancy, foreplay *was* the main event.

Women have been left with an unfortunate legacy that dictates that there is only one *right* way to have an orgasm—through intercourse. It has only been in recent years that studies have proved what many of us have known for a long time: that the majority of women need manual and/or oral stimulation to have orgasms. The misogynist is able to use the myth of "satisfaction only through intercourse" for himself and against his partner.

When Rosalind attempted to tell Jim what she needed from him sexually, he attacked her verbally. According to her:

> He didn't know word one about women, their anatomy, nothing. I'd try to explain but he'd start sulking. It was a put-down to him if I wanted anything other than intercourse. That's all he'd do. If I asked him to touch me until I came,

he'd leave the room. It was disgusting, he'd say. He made me
feel dirty about my body.

Jim used Rosalind's sexual desires as weapons against her. Because her needs were different from his, he labeled them "disgusting," thereby keeping her from asking anything of him that he didn't
want to participate in. Blame and punishment are standard reactions of the misogynist to sexual preferences that differ from his.

Paula, too, found that her husband experienced her sexual needs
as demanding and repulsive. Gerry let her know this in a harsh and
cruel way:

> The mention of oral sex made him grimace. He'd say, "It
> looks nasty, it smells nasty, and it tastes nasty." Another time
> he said, "Your idea of a good time is for me to spend the
> night with my head between your legs."

Gerry's contempt and revulsion made Paula feel enormously
self-conscious about her body and her sexuality. But there is more
than just a put-down in Gerry's remarks: there is a deep aversion
toward women's bodies. Gerry's unwillingness to have oral sex is
not in itself an indication that he's a misogynist. It is the hatred and
repulsion expressed in his statements that are the important signals,
not his sexual preferences.

Other misogynists take a less direct route to express their hostility and to gain control. These are the *sexual withholders*, who punish their partners by denigrating and humiliating them if they want
sexual contact. Rosalind experienced it this way:

> Every time we'd have an argument, he wouldn't touch me
> for two or three weeks. That was how he punished me. If I
> tried to initiate anything, he'd call me aggressive and tell me
> I was acting like an animal. He'd say all I wanted to do was
> screw and that nothing was more of a turn-off than a woman
> who was asking for sex all the time.

Jim blamed his recurring bouts of impotence on Rosalind. He took no responsibility for his sexual problems, even though he'd had them long before he'd met Rosalind. His attitude was that if he had problems sexually, it was because she wasn't behaving in the right way.

Both partners may bring sexual problems to their relationship, but in the misogynistic relationship these problems, whether they originate with him or with her, are consistently used as weapons with which to blame and humiliate the woman. Sex therapists have long recognized that when one partner has major sexual problems, *both* partners need help if treatment is to be effective. Blaming, showing anger, and punishing only worsen whatever sexual problems already exist.

However, blame, punishment, and rage are the misogynist's standard tactics whenever his partner doesn't go along with his wishes. In this way, he makes himself the only one to judge what is *right* and what is *wrong* in the bedroom.

A standard line used by misogynists is, "Don't tell me what to do." As far as Ed, the policeman, was concerned, his right to dominate extended even to Nicki's body; if she responded to his advances with anything less than total receptiveness, he experienced it as rejection. Nicki explained:

> He'd say to me, if I tried to tell him what I liked or wanted sexually, "Even in sex you're trying to take over." If I sat on his lap to cuddle, he'd immediately start to grab my breasts, and if I'd say, "I don't want to be touched like that right now, I just want to be held," he'd get angry and tell me, "These are my toys and I can do with them whatever I want."

Many misogynists use their perceived rejection as justification for further abuse. Nate carried the scare tactics he used in other areas of their life into the bedroom. Although Lorraine had initially been responsive to Nate's sexual attentions, as the years wore on she found that his abusiveness drove her away from him. She said:

He'd call me a cold bitch if I wasn't responsive the way he
wanted me to be. Then he'd start yelling, "Get out, get out,"
and kick me out of bed with his feet.

Even a woman who is energetic sexually can be gradually shut
down by a partner who is selfish and who lacks concern for her
feelings and needs.

All of the above are no-win situations. If a woman withdraws sexually because she has been made to feel inadequate, she may be attacked as "rejecting." If she has begun to shut down sexually
because of how she is being treated, she may be labeled as "withholding," "frigid," a "princess," "cold," or a "cock teaser." On the
other hand, attempts on the woman's part to initiate sexual contact
may result in her being called "demanding," "insatiable," an "ani-
mal," "too aggressive," or a "nympho."

SEXUAL BRUTALITY

Other misogynists take out their hostilities toward women in a
more active, brutal manner sexually. Nancy provided the following
example:

I was very tense one night. I asked Jeff to rub my back. We
would do things like that for each other. I was on my stomach and all of a sudden and with no warning at all he jabbed
his penis into my rectum. He really hurt me. I got mad and
pulled away from him. Then he rolled over on his back and
stared up at the ceiling. He had his fists clenched and his jaw
set. He said through his teeth, "How are you going to make
this up to me?"

Jeff reacted to Nancy's expression of pain by assuming the role of
the victim. Oblivious to the fact that he'd hurt her, he became furious and blamed her for what had happened.

This incident was one of many in which Jeff brutalized
Nancy sexually. These were not isolated episodes of thoughtless-

ness; they were part of an overall style of relating in a hurtful, hostile way.

Other misogynists work out their hostilities by inflicting physical pain through sex. They may pinch, bite, or ram with the intent to hurt the woman. I am not referring here to sexual behavior that both partners enjoy. I am referring to sexual activities that are unpleasant for the woman but which the misogynist persists in doing, despite the fact that they cause her pain, discomfort, or a feeling of degradation. It's as if he is saying: "Your body exists for my pleasure, and I expect you to go along with whatever activities I choose." Any woman who continues to permit sexual activities that are either repulsive or painful to her, who allows herself to be pushed into patterns of sexual sacrifice in which her partner's needs take precedence over hers, will inevitably get turned off to sex.

Sexaholics

There tends to be a dominant way of behaving in a sexual relationship. In other words, if you are with a partner whose style is withholding, that's probably the way it will remain; his style is not liable to change suddenly to overdemanding.

Some styles of sexual behavior are oppressive, particularly when the man makes such constant sexual demands on his partner that he exhausts her and eventually turns her off. I am not referring to those delicious times in a relationship when both partners crave a great deal of lovemaking; I'm talking about a pattern in which the man demands that his partner be available to him for sex as often as two or three times a day, as a matter of course. Such was the case with Laura and Bob:

> In the beginning I used to adore making love with him but it became such a turn-off! It became an obligation. He never gave me a chance to be spontaneous with him. I never had a moment to have a desire. If you're having sex two or

three times a day plus being pressured about it all the time, when can you have that yearning to make love? It was always being forced on me. He was a wonderful lover but it didn't matter how good he was after a while.

Bob's sexual neediness soon tainted what for Laura had been a very special part of their relationship. Bob was using sex to alleviate his fears and tensions, the way some people use drugs or alcohol. This compulsive pattern of driven, insatiable sexuality has recently been recognized as a serious emotional disorder, called *sexaholism*.

A sexaholic is essentially no different from any other kind of addict: he uses sex to narcotize deepseated anxieties. Sex provides for him a momentary respite from his tensions. Lorraine found that this was the case with her husband, Nate:

> He'd say, "I've got a big meeting to handle this morning so I need to have sex." It had nothing to do with me. Sometimes he'd come home and just grab me and start right in cold and say things like, "I had a rough day and I need this."

Instead of handling his problems in a mature, direct manner, Nate chose to temporarily deaden his anxieties with sex.

One of the most powerful examples of how the sexaholic uses sex for reassurance and control is shown in the statement that Bob made to Laura on several occasions: "The only time I feel I have you is when I'm in you." All of the sexaholic's desperate neediness is expressed in this remark.

Charlie, an engineer in his early 40s, who came in to therapy after three marriages and several relationships had failed, told me:

> I was screwing three or four women a day because, "God, it was a tough morning," or whatever. Now I hate to realize it, but I saw them all as toys. They were playthings that helped me feel less miserable.

If a woman protested the frequency of Charlie's sexual demands, he would turn on her in a rage. He would call her frigid or repressed, tell her she was withholding, and accuse her of not really caring about him. He explained:

> We could have had sex ten times that week, but if the eleventh time she'd say "no," I'd feel rejected and get mad at her. I know now it wasn't fair, but all I saw then was that my "fix" was pulling away from me.

If you are involved with a sexaholic, you will eventually begin to feel like an object that exists only for his release; the sexual contact between you will have very little to do with who you are. Laura found that with Bob, everything was secondary to his drive for sexual fulfillment, no matter what her needs were. She related the following incident:

> My grandfather died and I was really miserable about it. Bob and I were at the funeral together and all during the service he was pestering me to go. It was like the man hadn't had sex in twenty years! He just kept wanting to go home "for something." I knew exactly what he wanted. He became such a pest that I wanted to kill him. But I went home with him from that funeral. I was so aggravated with myself that the only way I could shut him up was to "do it" with him. Then afterwards we went back to my aunt's house and I hated myself for having given in to him. To have to leave my grandfather's funeral in the middle of the service! It was disgusting, but I just didn't want to hear what he had to say anymore about "his needs."

Sometimes women acquiesce to the demands of their sexaholic partners because sexual contact creates an atmosphere of calm and receptivity that simply doesn't exist outside the bedroom. Laura explained:

The only time we could talk was in bed. It was the only time I felt heard at all. I found myself giving in just to get him to listen to me. It was like a barter that went on between us. But then what made me crazy was if we'd discuss something in bed that was important to me, he'd forget the whole conversation. It was like it never even happened.

For the few moments of genuine closeness Laura felt during lovemaking, she put aside her feelings of being used and her resentment of Bob's incessant demands. However, Bob's moments of tenderness and receptivity did not carry over into the rest of their life. Their relationship outside of bed was still riddled with his outbursts of rage and accusation.

The Mask of Good Sex

The greater the gulf between the misogynist's behavior in the bedroom and his behavior out of the bedroom, the greater the confusion is for his partner. She asks herself: "If he wants me so much, can anything really be wrong between us?" For some women involved with misogynists, sex is the one area where their partners are *not* abusive or controlling. As Jackie said:

Mark was so loving in bed, so how could it have been so bad? I just didn't get it. He was never brutal, he was rarely insensitive, and it was never a quicky. I simply couldn't believe that someone who could be so wonderful and so giving in bed could be so appalling outside. I think if we could have just stayed in bed all the time everything would have been fine.

Had there been tension and conflict in their sexual relationship, it would have been easier for Jackie to see clearly how unacceptable Mark's treatment of her was. But, because of his ardor, she was convinced that they had a wonderful relationship. She used the pleas-urable intensity of their sexual relationship as a barometer of their marriage.

If you have a good sexual relationship with a partner who is abu-sive in other ways, you might want to ask yourself this: *Is he consis-tently nice to me only in the bedroom?*

A satisfying sexual relationship can cause women to ignore how badly they are treated the rest of the time. Terrific sex can be a pow-erful hook, lulling women into a false view of the relationship as loving even when other factors warn them that it is not.

Sex is only one part of a partnership. It may be the part that is go-ing well for you. But, if you are with a misogynist, you may be sure that his need for control and dominance will show itself in other areas.

Financial Control

Money can have enormous emotional and symbolic meaning. How money is managed often indicates the degree of trust in a relation-ship, because the one who earns it, doles it out, and decides how it is spent is generally the one who holds the power. It is far more than currency or a means of exchange. Money can symbolize compe-tence, adequacy, and freedom. It can also represent the amount of love in a relationship, because the giving or withholding of money can be parallel to the giving or withholding of affection. Often I have heard: "If he spends a lot of money on me, it shows how much he loves me." Many people think that their lovableness is defined by how much someone gives them or spends on them.

Attitudes and feelings about money start early in childhood. They are shaped and molded by our parents; and when we grow up we carry them into our adult relationships, sometimes allowing them to become the source of much conflict and contention.

Because money can be an emotionally loaded area, some people are secretive about it. In fact, often they are more reluctant to discuss financial conflicts than sexual conflicts. Therefore, it is difficult for many of us to air our financial woes and to get feedback and help in this area.

There are basically two types of misogynists when it comes to money issues: the *"good provider,"* who is financially stable, and the *"tragic hero,"* who sees himself as an innocent victim of other people's chicanery and who has an extensive history of unemployment and financial chaos; he often has to be supported by his partner. But whether the misogynist is earning most of the money, or both of you are contributing equally, or you are supporting him, *he* will take charge of how the money is spent!

THE "GOOD PROVIDER"

"I'm working hard and bringing home the money, I have a lot of pressure and responsibility, therefore I'm the boss and what I say goes." This is a traditional attitude held by many men; again, it is the degree of psychological abuse that goes with it that defines the misogynist. He knows how to use his earning power as a weapon to control his partner.

Lorraine never worked outside the home. In her thirty-five years with Nate, he handled all matters regarding money. He did this in the same abusive way as he handled other aspects of their life together. Lorraine explained:

> I had to defer to him for everything. If I wanted to buy
> something to wear I had to get the money and his permission
> first. I had to tell him where I was going to buy it, what it was
> going to cost, and afterwards I had to show him the bill. I felt
> like an incompetent child. He also kept me off balance on financial issues by his unpredictable reactions to insignificant
> purchases. I remember one time I went out and bought three
> hats without his permission. I was afraid he'd have a fit, but
> he didn't say anything; he just smiled. I was so surprised; but
> then two days later I bought a new leash for the dog and he
> blew up at me. I never knew what was coming.

The degree to which a misogynist needs to have control over money was brought home to me by a woman who called my radio program with the following problem:

> I had been a career woman, but when we got married he urged me to give up my job so I did. That worked for about six months, and then I realized I had no access to any funds. I was like a prisoner. He's a surgeon and makes lots of money, but his pay all goes into a separate account to which I have no access. He'll pay bills and groceries, but I haven't got twenty-five cents in my pocket. So finally I took some money I had saved from before our marriage and I started a little business of my own. Well, it's hardly solvent yet, but if I need a pair of pantyhose he says, "You've got the business. You buy it." It's ridiculous. He's not supportive of the business, either. He's always putting it down and making fun of me. Naturally I can't ask him for help if I have a bad month. I'm so frustrated. I love him, he's a good person, but he's controlling me to the point that I'm ready to steal the silver and sell it!

This caller's husband, having taken control by getting her to quit her job, was manipulating her by pulling the pursestrings as tightly as he could. She was earning a small income for herself, but it was not sufficient to provide financial freedom from her husband's dominance.

The misogynist's underlying suspiciousness seems to come from a fear that women are "only out for what they can get." He believes that by behaving as he does, he is protecting himself from his partner's innate greediness. To do this he withholds not only money but information about money. He may be secretive about what he earns or what his assets are, or he may hide money in secret bank accounts. To justify this behavior, he will relate how he was treated by an ex-wife or lover who bled him dry and was untrustworthy.

While the misogynist is withholding money from his partner, he is liable to be spending lavishly on himself, but his partner is forbidden to question this. As Nancy explained:

Jeff kept me penniless, but he'd spend anything on himself—a boat, new skis, new cars, the best tennis rackets, the best running shoes, custom-made suits and shirts. Meantime, I drove an old wreck of a car. If I needed new shoes, he'd blow his stack and say I was sucking him dry. I kept thinking he should have been ashamed to have anyone see me in that car, but he just blamed me and said it was my fault for not keeping it up properly.

Jeff's double standard strengthened his domination of Nancy, because his behavior implied: "I am a good person, so I deserve these things; you are not a good person, so you don't."

Of course, not all misogynists are tightwads. Many of them can be quite free with money, as long as it is on *their* terms.

THE "TRAGIC HERO"

This man has a distorted view of himself as honorable, hardworking, and noble. Unable to recognize how he orchestrates his own disasters, he sees the woman who is supporting him as the enemy. This man has had financial problems throughout his adult life and deals with money, whether it's his or yours, in an adolescent way. He is eager to explain that his difficulties are the result of what other people have done to him. His "enemies list" may include his parents, who never gave him enough, a business partner who cheated or betrayed him, an ex-wife who "took him to the cleaners," or a boss who fired him for no reason. It's only a matter of time before this misogynist's financial condition becomes his partner's fault.

When I interviewed Jackie's husband, Mark, he had been unable to complete a business deal in more than seven years. From his perspective, he was doing his best against tremendous odds, which included a nagging wife. He said:

I'm sick and tired of knocking myself out all day trying to put these land deals together. She never lets up! I keep telling her it's only going to take one deal for the dam to break and then we'll be on easy street, but I feel like I'm fighting the whole world and her too. The minute I walk in the door she starts on me: "We're overdrawn at the bank, I had three creditors call today, did you put the deal together yet?" Nag nag nag. She never lets me forget that she's bringing in the money. What she refuses to realize is that there's no way to put these deals together without my being able to pick up a check once in a while. I've got to look like I've got a few bucks in the bank, but you should see the expression on her face if I pick up the tab for a prospective client. She's just like every other woman: they love you when it's going good, but boy, hit a bump in the road and all of a sudden you're being treated like a child!

What Mark called a "bump in the road" was seven stressful years in which he was unable to earn any money. In that time, his speculative ventures had brought the family to the brink of bankruptcy, yet he refused to see his responsibility in their financial problems.

Jackie supported Mark and her two children during those seven years and often had to bail Mark out of his various misadventures, yet he continued to see her as a shrew, calling her unsupportive and demanding when she questioned his schemes.

Some couples decide mutually that the woman will earn the bulk of the family income while the man fulfills other roles and responsibilities. However, in the misogynistic partnership, the woman is punished for her position; her support of the family becomes another weapon in the misogynist's arsenal. Filled with anger and resentment of her efforts, once again he rewrites history, distorts reality, and skillfully shifts over to her the blame for his failures.

Rosalind found that while initially her efforts to rescue Jim made her feel strong, capable, and giving, within a few years she felt very different. She explained:

> In the first year we were together my antiques business did so well that I was able to borrow ten thousand dollars from the bank for new stock and was able to pay it back at

the end of the second year without a problem. I was very proud of myself. Then Jim hounded me to borrow twenty thousand at the end of the second year. I knew there was no way for the business to pay back that much, but he wanted to get involved in the business and he insisted. But then he wouldn't do anything. He'd had a furniture-refinishing thing on the side, so I thought how nice it would be if we could work together. I had the back of the shop extended so he could work there, but he still wouldn't do anything. I opened a second shop so we could have more income but that just spread me too thin. He wouldn't sit in the shop or work on the furniture, so I had to hire someone else to come in and mind the other shop. Then Jim started taking money out of the cash register. When I told him he couldn't just take money out of the register like that, he blew up and called me a selfish bitch. I couldn't understand why nothing was working out, why he wasn't doing the pieces he said he wanted to do. But I was going broke in the meantime, and the more broke I got the more resentful he got. I was running two shops, doing buying trips, doing shows, plus cooking and cleaning and supporting me, him, my son, and his two kids. All he did was practice drums and talk on the phone. I felt trapped and suffocated. My debts were incredible and my credit was ruined. Before I knew it my business was on the verge of bankruptcy.

No matter what Rosalind did, it was not enough to satisfy Jim. The "Tragic Hero" typically behaves in an infantile and destructive way. He will lie without compunction. He may tell his partner that he's paid bills when in fact he hasn't; he may run up enormous credit charges although neither he nor his partner can pay for them. When confronted, he will lash out at his partner for doubting him. He expects that someone will always be there to catch him if he falls. That someone is invariably the woman who loves him.

No matter what his style, the misogynist will *always* stake out the financial arena as a prime source of power and control. The struggle for dominance in this area can be more intense if the woman is working outside the home and is the only source of income. It is not his earning ability but his ability to manipulate his partner that determines his power.

Control Over Social Life

In order to feel safe, the misogynist must control your thoughts, your opinions, your feelings, and your behavior. Therefore, only those friends or family members that support his view of himself or his version of reality will be welcome in your lives. Anyone who may show you a different view of things will probably not be acceptable to him.

The misogynist may use a variety of tactics to constrict and narrow your world. One method is to make social contact with other people so unpleasant that you prefer to stay home. Nancy described how Jeff accomplished this:

> When we went out with other people, he'd spend the entire time checking on how I was acting. I'd be a nervous wreck. Was he getting mad at me for something I said to someone else? We'd get home and he'd say things like, "You were staticking again." That's his term for small talk of any kind or anything he didn't approve of. "That was a load of bullshit you were throwing around," he'd say. It was like being under a microscope.

Another control tactic in this area is the use of rages, tantrums, and insults to coerce you into giving up the people with whom he doesn't feel comfortable. Jackie told me that Mark was particularly nasty about her women friends.

> I went for a conference with some of my women friends and he accused me of being a latent homosexual! He was so

jealous of my friends that he'd humiliate me in public. He'd
call my friends sob-sisters and dingalings.

Most couples have friends of both genders and some separate activities. They can enjoy their time together but there is not an
atmosphere of suffocation and oppressive closeness. In a misogynistic relationship, however, separation of any kind must be
avoided.

Paula found that battling her husband, Gerry, in order to have
some friends and activities that did not include him became such an
enormous effort that she just gave up.

> It got to the point where I was not seeing anyone but him.
> If I said I was going to see my own friends, he'd be aston-
> ished. Why should I want to spend time with these stupid
> women when he was so intelligent. "I have so much to offer
> and we have such wonderful conversations," he'd say. Or
> he'd say how this was *his* night and *his* time. I had to fight
> for anyone I saw outside of him. After a while I just stopped
> fighting.

Many women make this kind of compromise to keep the peace at
home. Occasionally surrendering or backing down is part of the
compromise necessary in any working relationship. But when a
woman repeatedly gives in to her partner so that her needs take second place to his, she cannot maintain her self-esteem. Many women
give up the battle for activities and friends of their own because they
feel so drained by the bigger battles in the relationship; this one
doesn't seem worth the effort. But it *is* a battle worth fighting, because it is one of the more subtle ways in which the woman can become isolated. What makes it so subtle is that initially she may feel
flattered. It may appear that her partner is so in love with her that he
doesn't want to share her with anyone else. In reality, however, he is
gradually making her renounce the people and activities that are important in her life.

The misogynist may make a different sort of ordeal out of those occasions when he and his partner socialize together as a couple. He may be charming and gregarious in public, but the moment he is alone with his partner he launches into tirades about her ridiculous friends, using her choice of them to further point out her inadequacies as a person. If, at the end of every social event, a woman is faced with her partner's criticism and anger, she may find that going out with him is more painful than it is worth.

Another tactic the misogynist may use to isolate his partner is to actively humiliate her in public. Rosalind found that Jim carried into their social life many of the insulting and denigrating behaviors he used against her in private. She told me:

> I started cutting off friends because I never knew how he was going to behave. He'd insult me in front of people and say things like, "Oh, don't listen to her. She's dumb." He humiliated me so often that it just became too painful to have friends over. I was ashamed for them to see me taking it.

Rosalind's self-esteem had already been shaken by Jim's attacks on her when they were alone. Hearing him insult her intelligence and character in front of her friends was more than she could handle. When this sort of thing happens frequently, many women, like Rosalind, look for ways to avoid functioning socially as a couple.

Some misogynists will insult their partners by openly flirting with other women in front of them. This behavior is designed to hurt, punish, and humiliate. When a man uses social events as opportunities to make sexual overtures to other women, while blatantly neglecting his partner, he is expressing hostility. His partner, understandably, will soon come to dread going out with him.

Control of Contact with Your Family

If his partner's friends and outside activities are a problem for the misogynist, her family may be seen as an even greater threat. He may feel that her strong emotional connections to them may dilute his control over her. Nicki found this to be the case with her husband, Ed.

> He'd check over the phone bill to see if I'd called my family. They lived out of state, and if he found I had, he'd go into one of his rages and accuse me of all sorts of devious stuff. After a while I was afraid to even get a letter from my mother for fear of setting him off.

Nicki's fear of Ed's increasingly violent tantrums was so great that she stopped contact with her family rather than have to confront him on this issue.

Another way the misogynist makes relations with your family difficult is to demean them to you, which is actually a way of insulting you secondhand. Gerry constantly reminded Paula that her family and background were inferior to his. He told her that because his father was a professor and hers was an electrician, she was low-class and he wasn't. He couldn't stand to spend time with her family because they were such "uncultured, ignorant people." Since he implied that she was an extension of them, it was another way for him to wear her down and humiliate her.

Most of us are sensitive and defensive about our families, whether we are close to them or not. Just as the misogynist limits his partner's friends and activities, he makes contact with her family equally unpleasant.

How He Uses the Children

The misogynist may view children as powerful rivals for your affection. It makes no difference whether they are your children from a previous marriage, his children, or children you've had together. Just as he may resent the time you spend at your job, with your friends, or with any other interest or activity that doesn't involve him, he may resent and be jealous of your relationship with your children.

His license to use the children in his quest for control is based on his belief that in his home he can act in any way he chooses, regardless of how his behavior affects others.

No matter how many children there are, he gets to be the Number-One Kid.

JEALOUSY OF THE CHILDREN

Paula found that her husband, Gerry, was irrationally jealous of their children from the moment they were born. When their first child was an infant, Gerry berated her for the time and energy she invested in the baby. Later, when there were more children, his jealous rages escalated until even the smallest incident would set him off.

> I didn't dare run out of cheese and his special crackers and his special wine because there'd be hell to pay. One night when he came home early and there was no cheese, he started screaming. My mother was there and she couldn't believe it. She said, "Gerry, you're screaming over a little bit of cheese!" Then he started cursing me: "That bitch never has anything in this house to please me. Everything is for the kids. That's all she cares about, the goddamned kids. She doesn't care if I come home tired from work supporting their lazy butts and find no cheese in the house!"

Gerry saw the children not as dependent, helpless babies in need of both his and his wife's protection, but as competitors for his wife's attentions. The time Paula gave to them was viewed as proof that she didn't care enough about Gerry.

The sad truth is that there is *never enough*. There is never enough love, enough caring, or enough support to suit the misogynist. He is an insatiable, bottomless pit; he cannot be filled up. It is a fantasy to believe that you can ever reassure him sufficiently or make him feel truly secure.

ATTACKING YOU AS A MOTHER

Most of us are very sensitive about our roles as mothers. If the misogynist feels his partner is betraying him for the sake of the children, he may begin to attack her adequacy as a mother. However, her maternal adequacy is rarely the real issue. The children are simply scapegoats for his anger. He is simply exploiting his partner's *fears* of inadequacy to get her to acquiesce to his demands. Jackie told me how Mark used her two children as triggers for his attacks on her:

> I was sick in bed after an operation and on Christmas morning the kids woke up early and raced downstairs to open their presents. This was Mark's first Christmas with us and he went into a tirade that lasted all day long. He yelled about how selfish they were, how greedy, how they didn't think about anybody but themselves. He was talking about children eight and ten years old, mind you. They were ruining Christmas for him, he screamed. He wasn't going to come upstairs to see me; he would talk to me when I learned how to raise these damned kids. What the hell kind of mother was I to raise a couple of animals with no manners. There was no discipline, they were out of control. He just kept yelling at me from downstairs. He ruined the entire Christmas day for all of us, yet I ended up apologizing to him, like I always did.

Mark had found that whenever he attacked Jackie's children, she immediately capitulated. Apologizing was her way of keeping his rage from spilling over onto her children. She thought she was protecting her children from his outbursts, but actually what she was doing was giving him permission to use them in his war against her. By giving in and apologizing, she was rewarding him for his tantrums. Rather than deflecting his anger from the children, she was encouraging it.

TRIANGLING

When a woman is unable to resolve her conflicts with her husband, sometimes she will enlist her children's sympathy, using them as confidants and allies. In this way, children can become directly involved in their parents' war.

After telling me about Mark and the children, Jackie remembered how overwhelmed she had felt by her own mother's confessions to her when she was little:

> My mother would complain to me about my father. She'd tell me she didn't really love him, and I used to panic, thinking that somehow the family was threatened. If she didn't love him, then what did that mean about my life? I worried about it all changing suddenly. I didn't want to know that she didn't love him because then I had to take sides. I suddenly had divided loyalties. As cruel as he was, I began to feel sorry for him. I began to dream of rescuing him. I'd make up all sorts of fantasies about how I'd get my mother to love him again so we'd all be happy and stay together and then I'd be safe.

Burdened with information about her mother's secret feelings against her father, Jackie was being made part of an unhealthy triangle that threatened her sense of security. She was caught up in an adult conspiracy. This type of situation creates tension and guilt for a young child. It also damages the child's relationship with both parents.

Fathers, too, sometimes draw the children into an unhealthy triangle. A misogynist may try to turn the children against their mother by telling them how incompetent, selfish, or unloving she is. He may enlist them as allies in denigrating her, as Paula's eldest daughter reported:

> One day Mom and I pulled into the driveway while Dad was hosing the lawn. He turned the hose on the car as a joke

and started to laugh. We were coming back from a long day of errands and both Mom and I were exhausted, so she started to roll up the window so we wouldn't get wet. Then he started screaming. He said she was the ugliest fucking bitch he'd ever seen. He started telling me, "Your mother's face looks like an eighty-year-old woman's. Just look at her. What a pig!" I was so embarrassed for her, but he kept on yelling so all the neighbors could hear him. He said how glad he was that he was going away for a few days so he didn't have to look at her ugly face, and on and on. He kept trying to get me to join in with him, but I just got out of the car and ran into the house.

Gerry, like many misogynists, was fond of ridiculing his wife in front of the children. This puts a child in a terrible no-win position. No matter what the child's reaction is, she will be betraying one of the two most important people in her life.

Physical Brutality

Unfortunately, some misogynists cannot be prevented from physically brutalizing their children. Children may not be damaged by an occasional swat on the behind, even though I personally don't believe in any form of physical punishment. But ongoing punishment that involves inflicting physical pain and emotional terror is *always* damaging. In this way, the bully maintains control over everyone in the family.

For the last ten years I have specialized in working with adults who were victims of various forms of abuse as children. I have found that no other life event so scars people's self-esteem or sets them up for major emotional difficulties in adulthood.

When I first began working in this area, I was startled to learn that while people who were physically abused by their fathers or father-figures were angry at their abusers, they were often far angrier at their mothers for not protecting them and for allowing the abuse to continue. They saw themselves as sacrificial lambs, and their mothers as passive, weak, and unwilling to take a stand against the abuser on their children's behalf.

Many women in such situations comfort themselves by saying, "I didn't do anything, so how can I be guilty?" However, when a woman stands by or looks the other way when her children are being brutalized, she becomes a *silent partner* in the abusive behavior. Her children come to view her as an accomplice to the crime being committed against them. Any physical violence against children *is* a crime.

THE EFFECTS ON THE CHILDREN

Children in misogynistic households experience tremendous rage, tension, and frustration. When they see their mothers victimized either psychologically or physically, they become frightened and angry. Unfortunately, they have no more outlet for their anger than their mothers have for theirs.

Typically, such children express their feelings in self-defeating ways: psychosomatic complaints, difficulties at school, and depressions. Bedwetting and nightmares are common reactions among younger children. The older child may express his feelings through fighting with his peers, indiscriminate sexual activity, substance abuse, or other forms of antisocial behavior. If a child is also a victim of physical and/or sexual abuse, the symptoms of distress will be much greater.

The children of a misogynistic marriage witness a great deal of blaming and attacking between adults; they don't see grownups treating each other with compassion or respect. Therefore, these children are quite likely to reenact the same sort of family drama in their own relationships when they grow up.

The misogynist's control over his partner is like the roots of a plant: it spreads into many areas of her life. Her work, her interests, her friends, her children, and even her thoughts and feelings can be affected by his control. Her self-confidence and self-esteem can be so damaged as to bring about significant changes in the way she feels about herself and how she relates to the rest of the world. Yet, despite such devastating consequences, many women continue to insist that nothing is wrong with their relationships. The next chapter explores the powerful emotional hooks that make this paradoxical belief possible.

5 | *What Keeps Women Hooked?*

Whenever a client tells me that her partner abuses her, I ask, "Why do you put up with it?" Often the answer is, "Because I love him," or, "Because I'm afraid to leave him." Some say simply, "Put up with what?" indicating that they do not make any connection between their unhappiness and their partner's behavior. Or, as Jackie told me after ten years of marriage, "I know he yells at me sometimes but underneath it all we're really crazy about each other." All of these answers indicate the same thing: the woman is hooked into a relationship in which she is being mistreated.

A relationship with a misogynist is very intense and confusing. Many powerful emotional forces are at work, which makes it difficult for the woman to see clearly what is happening. However, once we learn what these forces are and how they keep the woman hooked, the reasons why she tolerates her partner's mistreatment become more understandable.

The Love Hook

Jackie minimized Mark's outbursts because at other times their relationship still fulfilled her. She and Mark still made love, laughed together, shared confidences, and felt intimate with each other. Her feelings for Mark were the most intense she'd ever known.

But good feelings, no matter how intense, are only half the story. The dark side of a misogynistic partnership is that in order to experience the good times a woman must also tolerate a great deal of pain. Any woman who is trapped in an emotionally abusive relationship but holds on because of the intensity of her feelings is in an addictive love relationship.

ADDICTIVE LOVE AND DEPENDENCY

Addictive love works like any other addiction, whether it is to alcohol, drugs, gambling, or food. There is a compulsive, driven need for the other person. When a woman is in an addictive love relationship, she experiences intense pain and suffering when she is deprived of her partner; she feels that she cannot live without him. The relationship provides a "high" that nothing else matches—and in order to get those highs she will tolerate a great deal of abusive treatment.

This sort of addiction makes the woman fiercely dependent on her partner. The more she sees him as the primary source of her good feelings, the more she will need him to be the center of her life. Remember, the misogynist's jealousy and possessiveness have already seriously limited her world, which further enhances his importance to her. It is a vicious cycle. The more dependent she becomes, the more important he becomes. The more important he is, the more she is willing to give up for him, so that there is less left in her life that is free of him. This keeps her hooked in very firmly.

THE PARADOX OF THE POWERFUL WOMAN

Many women who become emotionally dependent on their misogynistic partners are extremely *independent* in other areas of their lives. When I suggested to Rosalind that she had become far too dependent on Jim, she became very angry with me. "I'm not dependent," she replied. "I run two businesses and I bring all the money into our home. I'm supporting him and all three kids from both marriages." But Rosalind *was* dependent on Jim—her good feelings about herself depended on his moods. When he was angry at her, he annihilated all her feelings of competency and effectiveness.

This kind of dependency makes a woman believe that she cannot exist emotionally without her partner's love. Her sense of self-worth is tied to his assessment of her, no matter what other accomplishments she has achieved in her life. Laura provided an excellent example of this paradox:

> It was incredible how different I felt at work than I did at home. At work, people respected me and I had such a sense of my intelligence and competence. But the minute I walked in the front door I fell to pieces. Suddenly I couldn't do anything right. Bob would start on me right away about all the things I was doing wrong, how ineffective and stupid I was. It got so that I dreaded coming through that front door. I found myself looking for excuses to stay late at work.

What makes a woman vulnerable to mistreatment at home, no matter how well she functions outside, is the belief that her need for her partner's love is the most important thing in her life. The prizes of success, financial gain, status, and prestige pale in comparison to that need. In addition, our true natures and weaknesses generally become obvious only in our intimate relationships. The faces we put on for the outside world may have little to do with how we feel about ourselves, how we expect to be treated, and what we will accept from our partners.

Mistreatment and Addictive Love

Most people expect that a woman who is being mistreated by her partner will pull away from him. However, in a misogynistic partnership, just the opposite happens. *Nothing bonds a woman to a misogynist more addictively than his swings back and forth between love and abuse.*

Most of us have played a slot machine at one time or another. Remember how difficult it was to move away once you had started playing? One reason giving up the play is so hard is that you become convinced that the pay-off will come at any minute. The anticipation creates tension and excitement. The pay-offs come sporadically and in varying degrees, but they come often enough to keep your hopes up. The same effect is created by the sometimes-he's-nice-sometimes-he's-nasty quality of the misogynistic relationship. The mixture of not knowing when she is going to get his love and when he's going to be abusive keeps a woman hooked in and off balance.

I want to reiterate what I said in the introduction: I am not talking here about women's masochism. Any time love and pain are both operative, as they are in these relationships, the inevitable question arises: "Doesn't she really enjoy it? Isn't that really the way she wants it to be?" The answer is *no*. There is overwhelming behavioral evidence that what the woman is doing is searching for ways to get her partner to be kinder and more loving. Masochism is defined as a state in which a person gets pleasure from pain. The woman who is hooked in to a misogynist relationship is actually trying frantically to *avoid* being hurt.

Looking for the Magic Key

The misogynist's on-and-off behavior creates a belief in his partner that it is up to *her* to fix whatever is wrong. Without realizing it, she may have begun to barter for her partner's love and approval. Nicki, the young policewoman, told me:

> Sometimes I feel like I can control the way he treats me if I just act the way he wants me to act and do what he tells me to do.

Nicki had embarked on a quest for the magic key: the right way to behave so that Ed would consistently be loving. She believed that by going along with whatever he wanted she could keep his good moods and avoid his bad ones. Ed, like any misogynist, supported this belief: he often reminded her that he would always be nice if only she would stop this or change that.

Unfortunately, there is no magic key. The misogynist's outbursts as well as his tenderness generally have little to do with how his partner is behaving. He is driven by his own inner demons. (Chapter 6 will explore these in detail.) Therefore, there is no way to guarantee his good moods or eliminate his angry ones.

Nancy told me:

> I used to sit in the bedroom and rehearse ways to say things to him so he wouldn't get mad at me. I'd practice saying the same thing ten or twelve different ways until I thought I'd hit on the exact approach that would not upset him.

What Nancy found was that no matter how she said things to Jeff, he was just as liable to blow up as to kiss her.

Paula, too, believed that there was a magic key, and she was willing to barter away her dignity in an attempt to get her husband to be more loving:

> Gerry told me, "If you'd just cringe and cry a little now and then, I'd stop yelling at you." I actually tried cringing and crying, but that didn't work either.

When a woman believes that there is a magic key, she is likely to expend all her energy in the fruitless task of trying to find it, and in the process she relinquishes her right to good treatment. Because her emotional well-being is tied to her partner's mercurial moods, she loses her ability to act in her own best interests, to be assertive, and to have confidence in her decisions.

The Hope Hook

The fervent hope of every woman who is in a misogynistic relationship is that *something will happen and he will change.* The fantasy is that he'll take her into his arms and say, "I know I've been terrible to you. Please forgive me. I love you and I'll never yell at you again. From now on things will be different." The woman may use the smallest ray of light to foster this hope.

Laura recalled such feelings after she and Bob had had their big fight the night before their wedding:

> He called me at six in the morning and started apologizing. He said he was under stress, it would never happen again. He told me how much he loved and needed me, how upset he was that he'd behaved so badly, that he'd made a mistake. He apologized so beautifully and was so loving and wonderful that he just melted me. I was convinced that the worst that could happen was now over and from now on everything was going to be wonderful between us.

Throughout their marriage, this pattern of fighting and making up colored Laura's hopes. Bob's outbursts were usually followed by apologies, flowers, and tears. Not only was this tremendously exciting for Laura, but she experienced it as proof that Bob really was going to change. Of course, his changes were only temporary.

Apologies like this are strong addictive hooks: they encourage the hope that things will be better in the future. But hope must be directed where it will be effective. To hope that the misogynist will magically change is futile. (See Part II to learn how to redirect your hopes from changing *him* to changing the *relationship*.)

The hope that he'll change, the search for the magic key, and the intensity of her love all combine to place the woman in a very vulnerable position. Her acceptance of her partner's insults, humiliations, and scare tactics has given him enormous power over her: he can now control her behavior and feelings by the mere switch of a mood. This can be a terrifying position for her.

The Fear Hook

Fear in intimate relationships operates on several levels. On one level there are the *survival fears*—fear of making it financially on your own, fear of being poor, fear of being the sole provider and nurturer for your children, and fear of being alone—which keep women from leaving abusive relationships. (See chapter 15 for an in-depth discussion of these fears and the ways in which they can be handled.) But fear is present in the misogynistic relationship long before the woman begins to think of leaving. These fears result simply from the *interaction* between the woman and her partner.

FEAR OF HOW HE MAKES HER FEEL

When the misogynist yells at his partner, she gets the message that she has lost his love for that moment. Because she has become so dependent on his love and approval for her emotional well-being, when he withdraws his love she feels as if her world has been shattered. As Rosalind described it:

> When Jim is in a bad mood and starts to withdraw from me, I feel heat starting in my stomach and then spreading all over me. My skin feels tight and prickly and my legs get weak. I feel like I can't even walk. I get nauseous, I'm trembling, my head starts to pound, and my heart flutters. It's the worst thing I've ever felt. It's sheer terror.

Such incapacitating fears are not unusual for women in misogynistic relationships. The physical and emotional distress that result from incurring the misogynist's displeasure can be so painful that women will do virtually anything to avoid it, including tolerate their partners' irrational behavior.

It's important to remember that no matter how much distress a woman is in, her partner views her pain as *her* fault. She is not allowed to say "ouch" when he hurts her, especially if her pain is a reaction to his behavior.

FEAR OF WHAT HE MIGHT DO

Coupled with the woman's fear of losing her partner's love and being hurt emotionally is the fear of what he might *do* if she really upsets him. Misogynists can be very frightening when they are angry, and there is always the fear that their anger might escalate into physical abuse, even if they have never actually hit their partners. Lorraine described how Nate managed to keep her intimidated and scared:

> Nate's face would get beet red, the veins stood out in his neck, and his whole expression distorted. He was always breaking something and screaming. I was terrified of him.

Although Nate never actually hit Lorraine, his temper was so explosive that the air between them was always charged with the potential for violence.

In addition to threatening to physically harm his partner, the misogynist may threaten to harm himself or his children. He may threaten to cut off all the money, or he may threaten to find someone else and leave if his partner doesn't do what he wants her to. The more a woman gives in to these threats and intimidations, the less power she has in the relationship. Once she feels helpless, her fears become even more overwhelming.

To avoid having to live in a state of such painful, intense fear, many women will begin to do some very complex psychological maneuvers. Because the woman's sense of emotional well-being depends on her partner's good moods, she cannot afford to see him as cruel and irrational; she must see him as loving. To do this, she must alter her beliefs about herself and her perceptions of him so that she does not see anything wrong in the relationship. Her next step—and the most dangerous one—is to *convince herself that she actually deserves his bad treatment of her*.

The Collusion Hook

While the love hook and the fear hook are strong psychological bonds, a woman may still retain her ability to perceive clearly what is happening to her. The statement "I know he's being mean but I love him" shows that she is not distorting reality; she sees that her partner is acting badly, but accepts it as an unpleasant condition of his love. Similarly, the woman who says, "I put up with his bad behavior because I'm afraid of him" also knows she is being mistreated, but she is paralyzed by her fears.

Unfortunately, the misogynist has other tactics to keep his partner hooked in, one of which is to make her believe that she is at fault for everything that goes wrong between them.

Once she believes his version of the relationship—that he is "good" and she is "bad," that he is "right" and she is "wrong," that her deficiencies are the cause of his blow-ups, and that he is acting this way only because he is trying to help her become a better person—she has stepped into a dangerous twilight zone of distorted perceptions. Accepting his version of reality means she must give up hers. It's Alice in Wonderland time. She may still know that she is being mistreated, but she invents "good reasons" to explain it away. What makes this transition so destructive to her is that she actually has begun to *help him to abuse her*. She suspends her own good judgment, joins him in his persecution of her, and finds explanations to justify his behavior. I call this process *collusion*. Collusion reinforces and solidifies all the other hooks.

"He's Good and I'm Bad"

A woman who called in on my radio program opened by saying to me: "I want to work on my jealousy." As I questioned her, it turned out that her husband, who had accused her of being jealous, always ignored her at parties. He would flirt with every woman there and act as if he were single. "Work on your jealousy?" I said to her. "How about working on his lousy behavior?" She assured me that what he was doing was fine; *she* was the one with the problem. He had convinced her that if she could stop being so jealous and possessive, everything would be all right. She knew she disliked his behavior, but to make sense of it she had to view herself as the villain; she had to accept the blame for her partner's bad behavior. In reality, of course, she had every reason to feel jealous and to confront him about it. His behavior toward her in public was insulting and denigrating. But she had long ago accepted the role of "the bad one" in their marriage. She had learned from past experience that if she felt bad, it was *her* fault. No other conclusion was allowed. Like many women caught in misogynistic relationships, it was easier for her to blame herself than to see her partner as anything but loving.

"He's Only Doing It to Make Me a Better Person"

When a woman defends her partner's behavior on the grounds that he's teaching her how to become a better person by yelling at her, constantly criticizing her, and calling her names, she is rationalizing. Jackie fell into this trap more than once with Mark.

> He was supposed to get a big fee for a deal he put together, but as so often happened he didn't manage to get it all on paper. Instead of getting the ten thousand dollars they'd agreed to, his partner paid for a weekend for the two of us in some rundown resort. When we were shown to our rooms I just felt sick. I said how miserable it was that Mark had been taken by this guy. Mark turned and looked at me like I'd just crawled out from under a rock. Then he started

lecturing me about how ungrateful and greedy and demanding I was. He told me I had no faith in humanity, I was lacking in any kind of spiritual center, and that if I could just learn to be less materialistic I might be a decent human being. By the time he got through I was convinced that he was right. I was a terrible person and spiritually deficient. I also felt sure that only Mark could show me how to be the kind of good person he could be proud of.

One of the ways a misogynist avoids taking responsibility for his abusive behavior is to set up an elusive ideal of how his partner should be. In Jackie's marriage, her character deficiencies were the recurrent theme. Mark set himself up as the ultimate judge of her behavior. What made this so destructive for Jackie was that she had come to believe his negative evaluations of her. Having done this, it was now her job to renovate herself to meet his standards. Once he'd attacked Jackie's character, Mark's poor business judgment was totally out of the picture.

Statements such as "I'm trying to improve," "He's only helping me to behave better," "He's trying to get me to recognize my faults," and "I'm trying to live up to his expectations of me," show that the woman's perceptions have been distorted by her partner's attacks; she is not only defending his bad treatment of her but is blaming herself for causing it.

The Stockholm Syndrome

Ascribing good motives to people who are harming you is not limited to those in misogynistic relationships. Sociologists first described this behavior and named it the *Stockholm Syndrome* after analyzing events that took place during a bank robbery in Sweden. Instead of hating the holdup men who had taken them hostage, the captives began to defend them. They projected positive motives onto their captors in an attempt to find safety in a hostile, life-threatening situation. Several of the people who had been held hostage by the robbers began to exhibit a combination of love and pity toward them. This phenomenon is becoming more widely seen and discussed with the rise of international terrorism.

I am convinced that for many women in misogynistic relationships the Stockholm Syndrome is in operation. It shows up most often in the area of jealousy and possessiveness. It is as if the man owned his partner's freedom, and could dole it out to her in bits and pieces, as he saw fit. Certainly this was the case with Carol, who came in to see me after she and her husband, Ben, had participated in a marriage-encounter weekend and realized that their twenty-seven-year marriage was troubled. Carol spoke of Ben as if he were a benevolent jailer:

> I really want to take this class in flower arranging. It's something I've always wanted to do, but he won't let me because he can't stand to have me out of his sight. The last time I wanted to take a class, I decided to just go ahead and take it, no matter what he said. But he got furious and took my car keys away from me. But I guess I shouldn't be complaining. He's only like this because he loves me so much.

Carol had begun unconsciously to identify with her oppressive husband. She not only defended his irrational possessiveness, but reinterpreted his control as being "loving" toward her.

Of all the ineffective things that a woman does, both consciously and unconsciously, to make her relationship with her partner less painful to her, *collusion* is both the most subtle and the most destructive to her. Once a woman starts colluding with her partner, she *must* lose sight of what is actually going on between them. Her distortion of reality to fit her partner's view of it indicates that her perceptions are severely out of focus.

6 | *How Men Learn to Hate Women*

I've been very emphatic in my judgment of the misogynist. I've called his behavior insensitive, abusive, unacceptable, and cruel. All this is true—but now it is time to make his portrait more complete. Once we begin to examine the forces that drive the misogynist, we find that much of his abusive behavior is a cover-up for his tremendous anxiety about women. He is caught in the conflict between his need for the woman's love and his deep-seated fears of her.

This man needs, as we all do, to feel emotionally taken care of, to be loved, and to feel safe. As adults we fulfill these yearnings through physical intimacy, emotional sharing, and parenting. But the misogynist finds these yearnings terribly frightening. His normal needs to be close to a woman are mixed with fears that she can annihilate him emotionally. He harbors a hidden belief that if he loves a woman, she will then have the power to hurt him, to deprive him, to engulf him, and to abandon him. Once he has invested her with these awesome and mythical powers, she becomes a fearful figure for him.

In an effort to assuage these fears, the misogynist sets out, usually unconsciously, to make the woman in his life less powerful. He operates from the secret belief that if he can strip her of her self-confidence, she will be as dependent on him as he is on her. By making her weak so that she cannot leave him, he calms some of his own fears of being abandoned.

All these intense, conflicting emotions make the misogynist's partner not only an object of love and passion but the focal point of his rage, his panic, his fears, and inevitably his hatred.

I realize that my use of the word *hatred* in the context of an intimate relationship is both explosive and controversial. It is a word most people don't like to use. But it is the only word that sufficiently describes the combination of hostility, aggression, contempt, and cruelty that the misogynist exhibits in his behavior toward his partner.

When we examine the childhood experiences that gave rise to the misogynist's underlying fears, we begin to understand why he behaves the way he does. The ways in which his parents related to each other and to him provide us with important insights into how he became a woman-hater.

The Important Balance Between Mother and Father

While both parents work together to raise their son, they also have separate jobs. Mother is the nurturer and the boy's primary source of comfort, while Father helps him to pull away from Mother so that he does not become overly dependent on her. However, in the family backgrounds of misogynists, just the opposite occurs. The father is either too frightening or too passive to pull the boy away from the mother, so that the boy has no other option than to make Mother the center of his universe.

Both parents set up this situation. Mother, instead of meeting her son's needs for comfort and nurturing, is liable to try to get her son to meet *her* needs. Women in troubled marriages frequently try to work out their problems through their children. Whether a woman does this through the extremes of overwhelming demands, severe rejection, or smothering control, the results are the same: the boy becomes too dependent on her.

Without realizing it, in adulthood he transfers this dependency, as well as the conflicts and fears that go with it, onto the woman in his life. The misogynist saw his mother as having the power to frustrate him, to withhold love from him, to smother him, to make him feel weak, or to make insatiable demands on him—and he now views his partner as having those same powers.

The father who doesn't provide his son with any alternative to his mother's influence leaves the boy alone with his fears and his panicky feelings of vulnerability and neediness.

When Father Is a Misogynist

When Nicki came into counseling to try to save her marriage to Ed, I told her that we could move much more quickly and effectively if Ed was willing to participate in the therapy. Ed was very resistant; he viewed the need for therapy as a sign of weakness. However, his fear of losing Nicki eventually won out. What emerged in the course of Ed's therapy was that he had been reenacting with Nicki the same kind of relationship his military-officer father had had with his mother.

Ed's mother was a timid Southern girl from a working-class family. She'd met Ed's father when he was stationed at an army base near her home. They were married after a brief courtship, and from the beginning, Ed's father was extremely possessive and overbearing with his wife. He had very set ideas about women's and men's roles. As Ed remembered it, his father's favorite line was, "Somebody has to be in charge and that somebody is *me*."

"YOU'LL ONLY BE SAFE IF YOU ARE LIKE FATHER"

Ed, the older of two boys, grew up with a keen awareness that his father was the unquestioned authority at home. His father was physically abusive both to his wife and to his sons. He was obsessive about cleanliness and held white-glove inspections every evening when he came home. Ed recalled:

> Jesus, he was tough. He'd come in, and if there was any dirt, dust, dishes lying around, he'd let you have it. Nobody was exempt from punishment, not even Mother. If she messed up, he'd slap her. Nobody talked back and nobody questioned him. You just did as you were told. He was a real bastard, but he got things done the way he wanted them. . . . There was one way to do everything—*his way*. You could forget about having a "discussion" about some idea or something, because he seemed to know everything, even what the schools taught us. If I came home with some newfangled idea about politics, he'd just shoot me down.

The only safety Ed could find as a child was in parroting his frightening father in every way. He promised himself, "When I grow up I'll get to scream and yell at everyone and treat people the way *I* want to, because that's what men get to do."

Like so many children whose fathers are tyrants, Ed could see only two options: he could be like his mother, which meant being weak, helpless, and a victim (Ed's younger brother did so; he became an extremely timid and sickly child, has never held a job, and now in his thirties he still lives with his mother), or he could be like his father and have some sense of power and control. Ed took the latter option. By identifying with his father, he learned to tyrannize and abuse people.

"FATHER'S WAY IS THE ONLY WAY"

A boy raised in this kind of household learns about the world only through his father's narrow, rigid system. He isn't taught to explore new ideas or to form his own opinions and attitudes about life, nor is he permitted to make simple mistakes. When Ed tried to develop a sense of himself that was different from his father's, he was severely punished. If he was different from his father, it meant that he was *bad*. His father saw any differences as tantamount to betrayal by his son. "You'll learn," he remembers his father saying. "I will win. I'm a better general. I fight better, and I have more strategy."

A tyrannical father will establish a minidictatorship in which only *he* is allowed to express himself. Much of that expression is likely to be angry and punitive toward anyone in his domain who dares to disagree with him. There will simply be no room for a child to express his thoughts or feelings if they differ from his father's in any way. This kind of oppressive system inevitably creates a great deal of anger for the child, which is never allowed to be expressed. This anger is then stored internally.

"THE ONLY WAY TO CONTROL WOMEN IS TO ABUSE THEM"

Coupled with the strong prohibition against being angry at or different from Father is the tyrannical father's role model of how men relate to women. Ed told me:

> My poor mother just couldn't stand up to him. If he wanted it some way or other, that's how it was. And if she didn't comply, he'd beat her. Once he threw her out. I always felt sorry for her because she was just no match for him.

The messages Ed received as a child were that *mistreating women is acceptable* and that *men are powerful while women are helpless*. As painful as it was for Ed to watch his mother being abused by his father, he was also developing a secret contempt for her because she was unable to defend and take care of herself.

A man who is raised by a misogynistic father can absorb his father's contempt for women very early in life. The boy learns that a man must always be in control of women and that the way to get that control is to scare them, hurt them, and demean them. At the same time, he learns that the one sure way to get his father's approval is to behave as his father does.

When Mother Is a Victim

A woman who submits to her husband's abusive treatment is living out the role of victim and behaving more like a helpless child than an adult. She relinquishes the entire adult field to her husband, leaving her children with only one grown-up to deal with: Father. As we have seen, Father can be a very scary person. When Mother abdicates her adult role, she not only deprives her children of a strong maternal figure, but she leaves them with no one to protect them from their father.

"WOMEN'S NEEDS ARE OVERWHELMING"

> I remember her kneeling next to me and sobbing onto my chest. I couldn't have been more than six or seven. She'd cry and cry about how mean Father had been to her and how unhappy she was. It really tore me up inside. She'd tell me how I was her whole life and the only one who really loved her. I swore to myself that I'd do anything I could to make her happy.

This statement from Ed shows how his mother was *reversing roles* with him. *She* became the needy, frightened child, and Ed was expected to become the nurturing parent.

But how could this little boy possibly deal with the adult problems his mother was putting on his shoulders? He tried, as any
child would, to be what his mother wanted him to be. He developed
grandiose fantasies in which he was able to rescue her from her terrible life. But when he was unable to alleviate her sufferings he was
left with a tremendous sense of guilt and failure. In the face of his
mother's overwhelming neediness, there was no other way for Ed to
feel but inadequate.

By reversing roles with her son, a mother communicates to him
that he is supposed to comfort, protect, and take care of her. She
may express this to the child in a variety of ways: she may suffer in
martyred silence but make it very clear to her child that she feels
trapped and miserable; she may tell her son that she can't take care
of herself and that without his love she has nothing left to live for;
she may get ill often or be chronically depressed, drink heavily, or
become involved in some other form of self-destructive behavior.
No matter how she shows her suffering, the result is the same: the
young boy feels it is his responsibility to make her happy. He believes that he is expected to rescue his mother. By shoving her son
into a role he is not equipped to handle, this mother helps to create
in him deep resentments that will later turn into anger at women.

"MOTHER CAN'T EXIST WITHOUT ME"

Ed is still taking care of his dependent, helpless mother. His father
left her for another woman when Ed was 12. This created tremendous emotional and financial burdens for the family and forced Ed
into assuming the role his father had abandoned. To this day she
still depends on Ed to rescue her and her younger son. Without realizing it, Ed let me know how angry he was with her:

> Somebody's got to take care of them. If my father hadn't
> left, things would have been different, but she never has got-
> ten over that, so I have to help. What gripes me is that she
> won't learn even the simple stuff like handling her own fi-
> nances. I'm always having to go out there and make sure the

electricity doesn't get turned off, or the bank calls me and says she's been bouncing checks again and then I have to go down there and take care of it.

Although Ed was transferring much of his rage at his mother onto Nicki, he became very defensive when I suggested that his mother was the real source of his rage. To acknowledge this would have caused him to feel very guilty. It was safer for him to be angry at Nicki. Nicki confirmed this:

> I dread his having to go out there and see her because within an hour after he's back there's a blow-up about some-thing. Of course I can't mention that maybe he's really mad at her and not me, or that maybe he ought to let her solve her own problems, because then he'll carry on even more.

Being his mother's rescuer enabled Ed to feel some power and importance as a child and later as an adult. Managing everyone, in-cluding his wife, became his way of trying to compensate for his deep feelings of inadequacy and helplessness.

When a mother leans on her son in this way, she is setting him up to feel frightened and overwhelmed by women's needs later in his life. If a woman expresses any kind of pain or need of him, he is likely to react with disgust, anger, and contempt, because she will remind him of the overwhelmingly needy mother who made him feel inadequate.

"No Woman Can Ever Love Me Enough"

Because so much of the needy mother's energies go into her own suffering, she has little left over for her children's needs. Her son doesn't get the constant maternal support, care, protection, guidance, and validation that he requires.

All children yearn to feel safe, protected, and loved by their par-ents. They also need permission to grow up and become inde-pendent people. Paradoxically, *people can become independent adults only when their own dependency needs were met in childhood.* If their dependency needs were not met, there is an aching emptiness created inside them, and this feeling is carried into adulthood.

Initially Ed saw his mother as the only possible source of nurturing, as any child would. He expected her to fulfill all his needs. He couldn't go to his father to get these needs met because his father was too frightening a figure to approach. When Ed was unable to get what he needed from either parent, he didn't just forget about those needs: he took them into his adult life and particularly into his relationships with women. As an adult he expected women to meet his desperate need to be mothered in a way he never was as a child.

There was no way Nicki—or any other woman—could possibly give Ed enough to satisfy these old needs. But, because his emotional growth had been stunted, he could not understand this, and he felt angry, frustrated, and disappointed in her. For him, these feelings justified much of his abusive behavior toward her.

An even darker side to the behavior of the needy, victim mother is that she may use her son as a sacrificial lamb. In addition to not protecting him from his abusive father, she may actually place him between herself and her husband in order to deflect some of his wrath away from her.

The Making of a Misogynist

Charlie came into therapy after the break-up of his third marriage. He and his three siblings had been raised in eastern Tennessee. His father was a driven, ambitious man who had worked his way up from carpenter to a partnership in a successful contracting firm. Charlie's mother, born in a rural area to a very poor family, had managed to put herself through two years of college. She became an accountant, then quit working when she married. Her husband terrified her and treated her like a child. Over the years she became more and more disturbed and began to use her children as a shield to ward off her husband's attacks on her.

"You Cant Trust Women"

My father was a very brutal man. He used to do things like sit at the dinner table with a broom close to him, and if you hadn't done what you were supposed to that day you would get the broom handle across the face. Then, what was worse, he'd tell Mother to have us do things and she would forget. Father would come home and want to know why it hadn't been done. We'd say we didn't know it was supposed to be done, and then he'd turn to Mother and say, "Did you tell them?" and she'd say, "Of course I told them!" Then he'd beat us for not doing it and also for calling our mother a liar. She really betrayed me. She set me up to be brutalized by him and she didn't protect me. Later she started stealing money from me when I was working because she was afraid Father would get mad at her for not staying within her budget. She was like a helpless kid. I was more a parent to her than she was to me.

Not only did Charlie have to take care of his childish and unstable mother, but she betrayed him as well. By lying to protect herself, she caused much of the physical abuse Charlie suffered at his father's hands. From this he received the message that *women are treacherous, helpless, and not to be trusted.* He had deep resentments and a bottomless pit of unexpressed rage toward her.

Children expect different things from each parent. Traditionally, the mother is expected to protect and defend the children, while the father is seen as head of the household, primary wage earner, problem solver, and disciplinarian—roles that often seem to entitle him to respect and devotion no matter how he behaves. Many abused children blame their mothers as much as or even more than they blame their fathers for the abuse they experienced. A boy's additional need to identify with his father makes it even harder for him to find fault with his father, even if the father is brutal. But the boy is free to get angry at Mother when she does not protect him from abuse, because she is expected to be the fountainhead of all love and comfort.

In adulthood Charlie found himself drawn to helpless, waiflike women who were very much like his mother. Without realizing it, he was attempting to accomplish as an adult what he could not do as a child: to rescue his inadequate, disturbed mother. However, his need to rescue was accompanied by an equally strong need to retaliate for the injuries his mother caused him when he was little. Now, as an adult, he could fulfill his hidden need to make it "come out better" because now he could not only rescue a woman, he could control her, as well:

> When I met my third wife she was five feet ten inches tall and weighed maybe a hundred pounds. She was nervous, scared, and trembling all the time. I figured all she needed was some self-confidence and she'd be okay. So I was going to give her those things. I was going to rescue her and then she'd be grateful and love me forever and life would be beautiful.

Charlie's deep rage and resentment toward his mother, coupled with his neediness, were transferred onto the women with whom he became involved. These ambivalent feelings heated up whenever a woman threatened to pull away from him:

> When she didn't do what I expected her to or when she tried to pull back from me, I'd make her feel guilty by saying stuff like, "I've invested all this in you, in helping you. How could you pull away from me, you stupid bitch!" I'd really start hating her. I'd say, "Here I've done all this for you and you're a goddamned ingrate. You're just a sniveling piece of crap." I didn't hit her, but I know how to burrow in and get to those soft spots. I know all the weak places where I can hurt them and break them down. I know how to make a woman feel small and helpless so she can never get away from me.

Charlie, believing that any woman he needed had the same powers as his mother had to hurt, betray, and deprive him, felt justified in using any method to get back at a woman and to reassert his control over her. Charlie's father had demonstrated a gross distortion of male behavior. As Charlie put it:

> By the time I was eighteen and got married for the first time, my view of marriage was that men were controlling and brutal while women whimpered and made promises and demands.

When Mother Is Suffocating

It's easy to see how a boy learns to be a misogynist when his father is a misogynist. Interestingly, however, boys from families in which the father is passive and the mother is dominating and controlling may also become misogynists. Following his father's example is not the only way in which a boy can learn to be contemptuous of women. It is just as likely that he will turn out to be a misogynist if his mother suffocates him with overcontrol and overprotection.

While the victim mother doesn't provide enough protection, the suffocating mother provides too much. This type of woman needs to control everyone and everything in her family. She does this by intruding into everyone's business and convincing them that only she knows how to handle or solve problems. She cannot let go of her children, even when they are grown up. She is likely to remain present and overinvolved in their adult lives, too, as was the case with Ben's mother. Ben, Carol's husband, is a successful accountant in his early 50s. His father, a pattern cutter in the garment industry, was a quiet and rather depressed person. By far the most powerful force in Ben's early life was his mother. Disgusted with and bitter about her own marriage, she became engrossed in her young son's life. To make sure that he would not grow away from her, she tried to control him even into his middle age! Carol told me:

She calls us at least once a day, sometimes three or four times. She expects us over to her house every Sunday, and one way or another she gets to know everything that's going on in our lives. Ben never tells her to butt out.

Unlike a girl, who can stay close to her mother while she finds her own identity, a young boy must pull away from his mother in order to grow up as a healthy adult. Parental love is the only kind of love in which the ultimate goal *must* be separation. The mother who validates her son's striving for independence and encourages him to separate from her when he needs to, gives him some very important tools with which to deal with life. When the mother is willing to let her son establish his own identity, by permitting him to take risks on his own and by allowing him to make mistakes, yet being there for him should he need her, she helps to build a man who is confident about himself and his abilities.

The suffocating mother, on the other hand, restrains and constricts her son's development by overcontrolling him and by making him feel inadequate and helpless.

"A CONTROLLING WOMAN MAKES ME FEEL INADEQUATE"

At my request, Mark came in to see me while I was working with his wife, Jackie. He reported that his relationship with his mother had been a struggle for freedom and independence from the beginning. While Mark's father, an engineer, traveled often on business, Mark's mother doted on her young son. He explained:

When I was a kid I couldn't breathe without her telling me how I could do it better if I did it *her* way. The minute I got home from school I had to practice the violin. If I wanted to go out and play, it was too cold or too hot. When I did go out, she'd follow me down the street with a sweater or my gloves in her hand, waving them after me. She'd embarrass the hell out of me. I can still hear that voice: "Marky, you for-

got your sweater. Marky, you didn't practice yet. Marky
Marky Marky," everywhere I went.

After a few meetings with Mark, it became apparent to me that
his mother was more than a concerned parent or a harmless nag.
She had invaded every area of her son's life, trying to live his life
for him.

When Mark had other children come to his house to play, his
mother insisted on being present all the time and organized all their
games; she hovered over them and supervised their every move.
She also decided what Mark would wear, what he would eat, who
his friends would be, and what books he would read. She continued
to make all the decisions that affected his life until he left home to
go to college. Whenever Mark tried to do anything that went against
his mother's wishes, he was faced with long lectures or martyred
disapproval:

> She'd say, "You ungrateful boy. After all I've done for
> you." It wasn't just a case of "mother knows best." It was
> more like "mother knows *all*"!

By being so controlling, Mark's mother was preventing him from
developing a sense of mastery over his own life. He never had a
chance to see himself as competent and effective because his
mother, by rushing in and taking charge, took those chances away
from him.

Even very young children need to be given the room to make
mistakes, to try new experiences, and to explore the world around
them at their own pace. Mark's confidence in himself became shaky
as a result of his mother's dominance over him. As an adult, he
viewed all women as frightening and malevolent creatures, out to
control him and to rob him of his masculinity. Consequently, his relationships with women were always power struggles.

"I'M ENTITLED TO HAVE EVERYTHING MY WAY"

Frustrations are an inevitable part of life, and learning to deal with them in manageable doses helps us to develop a solid sense of ourselves and of reality. Our parents teach us how to handle frustrations by setting reasonable degrees of restriction for us. This enables us to relinquish the magical expectation that every need or wish we have will always be met. When a child is faced with a disappointment and his parent tells him that "life is full of frustrations but we all have to learn to live with them," the parent is helping the child to learn to cope with reality.

The suffocating mother, who swoops down to fix everything in her son's life, thwarts this learning process. The boy doesn't get to experience the necessary doses of frustration that will enable him to deal with life's bigger disappointments later on. In one of his sessions Mark told me:

> My mother used to say, "It's not your fault, you didn't do anything wrong," even before she'd heard the story. She'd jump in right away and say, "What did they do? They started it, didn't they?" I think if I'd shot someone she'd have said it was their fault for getting in the way of the bullet.

When a child isn't allowed to deal with his frustrations on his own—to cry, for instance, then to handle the situation, and then to go on playing—because his mother is always there to intervene and rescue him from any discomfort, in adulthood he will be unable to handle even the most minor setbacks.

The mother who consistently rescues her son from all of life's little unpleasantnesses is giving him the following messages:

- You don't have to stand frustration.
- Whatever goes wrong, someone will always be there to fix it for you.
- You are entitled to a life without any irritations.

Unhealthy, self-centered messages like these give a young boy an enormous sense of entitlement: he comes to expect that he can always get what he wants when he wants it.

This type of mothering may sound as though it is comforting to the child, but in fact it is very frightening. When the mother binds her child to her by overcontrolling him and constantly rescuing him, she sets him up to believe that he cannot survive without a woman. This creates in the boy an enormous sense of dependency. Later on he'll see his partner as having the same power to frustrate him, to withhold love from him, to smother him, and, most important, to make him feel weak, helpless, and dependent.

If a boy has a strong and effective father figure upon whom to model himself, he may develop the confidence to break away from even a very dominating mother, but, as we know, dominating women tend to link up with passive, weak men who can rarely offer their sons any alternative to Mother's rule.

When Father is Passive

Just as the tyrannical father sent his son to his mother's arms by frightening him, the passive father sends his son back to Mother by being withdrawn and unavailable to him. Neither father is able to offer his son the help he needs in the difficult task of separating from Mother.

The passive father tries to blend into the background of the family's emotional life and retreats into his own world at the first sign of any trouble in the family.

"MEN CAN'T STAND UP TO WOMEN"

When Mark was 8, his father stopped traveling on business. Mark was excited at the prospect of spending more time with him, now that he would be at home. When it became apparent that his father still had no time for him, Mark was bitterly disappointed and hurt.

He was either working all the time or he was up in his room alone. I think he must have retreated to that room at least once every day. Mother would get on him about something and he'd just give up and go upstairs. Sometimes he stayed there all evening. After she'd picked on him he just wouldn't talk to anyone.

By leaving whenever there was a conflict with his wife, Mark's father gave him the message that *when women are dominating men can't stand up to them.*

I am not referring here to the man whose basic nature is to be quiet and reserved; obviously a man can be gentle and soft-spoken and still be in close emotional contact with his family. The type of passivity I'm describing is that of the man who is a shadowy and remote figure; he doesn't interact with the other members of his family, and he withdraws from any conflict with his powerful wife.

Such passivity and withdrawal are not as benign as they may appear. Passivity can be a way of dealing with anger. The passive father often has a great deal of rage toward his wife, but instead of expressing it in a healthy way, he punishes her, and often the rest of his family as well, through silence, withholding, and avoidance. These tactics very effectively protect the passive person while simultaneously hurting the other members of the family. By refusing to interact, the passive man frustrates, angers, and upsets the person who is trying to connect with him.

The boy whose mother is suffocating and overcontrolling will inevitably look to his father to learn how to deal with her. A passive father, by refusing to confront his dominating wife, not only abdicates his role in his son's emotional development but reinforces the view that women are controlling and frightening. "After all," reasons the little boy, "if Dad can't stand up and defend himself against women, how am I supposed to?"

This message, added to the fact that the boy already feels inadequate and dependent, further colors his adult relationships with women. For both Mark and Ben, any display of power on the part of their wives threatened their sense of safety as men. They experienced even the most benign expressions of differences of opinion as attempts by the women to take over and control them.

It might seem that a man who had a suffocating mother and who feels the need to control women would be drawn to a partner who is the exact opposite of his mother. However, what often happens is that this man becomes magnetically attracted to a strong woman and then tries to weaken her. What he is doing is trying to rewrite the old family script to make it come out better. If he can control a powerful woman, he can prove to himself that he is more of a man than his father was. He will win the battle that his father was afraid to fight.

The passive father/smothering mother and the tyrannical father/victim mother are the types of families I have seen most frequently in the backgrounds of misogynists. However, there are other parenting styles that can strongly influence how a boy will later relate to women.

When Mother Is Abusive

A mother who terrorizes her son with abuse, coldness, and severe punishment keeps him feeling helpless, inadequate, and afraid.

"IF YOU NEED A WOMAN SHE WILL HURT YOU"

Lorraine remembered Nate's accounts of how his mother brutalized him when he was a child:

> He used to tell about the time his mother threw a knife at him because he had his feet up on the furniture. But he also would talk about the times when she would beat him with a belt for absolutely no reason. He'd get it if he left a book lying on the floor, or if he'd forgotten his sweater at school. I got the impression that he lived in mortal terror of her throughout his childhood.

No matter how cruel Nate's mother was to him, he was still dependent on her to fill all his childhood needs. As with any abused child, his mother's cruelty didn't push him away from her but rather bound him to her in a frantic search for her love and comfort.

Just as Father is the first man in a girl's life, Mother is the first woman in a boy's. If this needed and important woman is a source of terror for him, as Nate's mother was, he will develop both a deep hatred and an intense need of women.

When Mother Is Rejecting

The rejecting mother, who is both cold and withholding, is the opposite of the smothering mother, but the effects of both extremes are quite similar. The smothering mother doesn't permit her son to experience frustration, so he does not learn to deal with disappointments later in life. The rejecting mother frustrates her son to an unbearable degree, so that he, too, cannot cope with frustration when he reaches adulthood.

Paula gave me this perceptive account of her husband's background:

Gerry was a very sickly child. He had frequent bouts of pneumonia and asthma until he was well into his teens. He told me he was in bed for long periods of time, once for over a year. He required a great deal of special attention and care, but his mother only intermittently provided what he needed. He said he spent so much time alone in his bed that he got into the habit of fantasizing about his mother coming in and rescuing him, bringing him special treats, reading to him, that sort of thing. He was always saying how wonderful she was and how much she loved him, but it just didn't jell with the woman I met. She was terribly cold, even to her grandchildren. I couldn't picture her ever being the woman he described. And he seems to swing back and forth between romanticizing her and hating her for not giving him what he wanted. One minute he'll scream at me, "You're a cold, withholding bitch, just like my mother," and the next minute he tells me how she used to make special waffles for him on Sunday mornings. Eventually he told me that she used to stand by while his father beat him in alcoholic rages. She didn't try to protect him. Then when he was fifteen his younger sister was born and suddenly she claimed all of his mother's attentions, or that's how Gerry saw it anyway. He says he didn't know how or why but he'd lost his mother's love somewhere along the way. He tried very hard to get it back, but she was so cold to him and so uninterested in him that she didn't even send him a congratulations card when he finished graduate school. I know that hurt him very deeply.

The fantasy mother Gerry created blended with the real experiences of his childhood. As an adult he saw women as cold, treacherous, and withholding, while at the same time he idealized them as good, rescuing, and comforting. The "good" woman was someone who would focus all her attention on him. Anything less than total involvement and attention to his needs reactivated all his old feelings of neediness and deprivation.

In their marriage, when Paula attempted to fill her own needs and wishes, Gerry felt extremely threatened; if she paid attention to herself, it meant she was depriving him. Paula told me:

> I hadn't been home in over five years and my mother invited me. She was even paying my way. Gerry screamed all the way to the airport, "You're leaving me! You know how I feel about being left. You know when I was a little boy my mother used to leave all the time and it scared me, but you don't care about how I feel." I felt so guilty that I ended up not going.

As we saw in chapter 4, Gerry was also jealous of Paula's attentions to their children.

Because of Gerry's overwhelming neediness during his childhood, as an adult he was unable to tolerate even the most minor frustrations:

> Anything could set him off, and it was always my failure. Once he went out to start the car and it didn't start. He came in, threw the keys at me, and screamed, "You bitch! You did it! You didn't take proper care of this car." But the fact was I never drove that car. It was *his* car.

Gerry's rage had very little to do with the car. It had much more to do with the anger he felt toward his mother for all the deprivations and extreme frustrations of his childhood.

"IT IS SHAMEFUL TO BE VULNERABLE"

In addition to withholding love and attention and thereby frustrating her son, a cold, rejecting mother will often punish him for his normal needs of her. From this he gets the message that his *neediness is unacceptable and shameful*. He may begin trying to cover up his vulnerability whenever he can. Many misogynists use bullying and macho behavior toward women to defend against these unacceptable feelings of vulnerability.

The unfortunate logic that follows from this is that if the misogynist's needs are unacceptable, so are his partner's needs. They remind him too sharply of his own. Therefore, he must deny them. This explains in part why many misogynists are so insensitive to their partners' emotional and even physical suffering.

With the rejecting mother as well as with the abusive mother, there is overt cruelty and pain, which color the boy's entire childhood with neediness, rage, and humiliation. These types of mothers can be seen as clear and direct precursors of misogyny. If strong fathers were present to mitigate the punitive behavior of these women, the results might be very different. But this is not usually the case. Nate's father was a withdrawn man who had almost no involvement with his son; Gerry's father was a violent and unstable alcoholic. Gerry and Nate grew up with an aching sense of emptiness. As adults, they were constantly searching for the good, loving mothers they never had.

Angry Boys, Angry Men

Denying or repressing strong emotions doesn't eliminate them. Instead, they get displaced or stored up.

Charlie was later able to make some very direct connections between the anger he felt toward his mother when he was a child and the explosive outbursts he had with the women in his adult life:

> My mother was overprotective in some pretty crazy ways. I remember her making me sit in a chair without moving for hours on end. That was her way of watching me. She'd say, "Don't you dare move out of that chair." If I walked out onto the front porch, she'd start screaming, "I don't want you out of my sight!" So I'd sit in that chair and my stomach would be so tight it felt like it was made of concrete, and my head would start pounding so hard I thought it would fall right off.

Charlie redirected his angry feelings back onto himself and turned them into physical reactions. It was far more acceptable to him to have a headache or a stomachache than to be conscious of his anger at his mother. When he grew up, he continued to have physical reactions when he was enraged. Early in his therapy Charlie was excited to find the connection between the physical warning signs and his behavior:

> It's always the same feelings inside me. It's a tightness in my gut and the old pounding in my head. Just like I felt as a kid. Now, that's my signal that the demons are about to come out and I'm either going to say something rotten to her about

herself, scream at her, or do something to reestablish my
control over her and show her who's boss.

When Charlie became angry at his present partner, he lashed out
at her, just as he would have liked to at his mother. What he was doing was fighting an old battle with a new, and inappropriate, adversary.

The misogynist genuinely believes that his rage toward his partner is due to her deficiencies. It is easier for him to attack her than
to deal with the real sources of his rage. He feels justified in acting
out rage on women. Part of this justification may come from his experiences at home as a child, but a great deal of it comes directly
from our culture.

CULTURAL SUPPORT FOR MEN'S AGGRESSION TOWARD WOMEN

Our laws and institutions concerning women's rights and male
prerogatives are changing, but many men still believe that their masculine image depends on their ability to dominate and control women.

Our culture reinforces this idea by depicting women as appropriate targets for men's hostilities. In literature, movies, and television, women are used by men as shields, foils, and hostages. They
are raped, beaten, and shot with frightening regularity. Pornography
implies that a woman's inherent seductiveness justifies any sadistic
and/or sexual act a man wishes to commit against her.

For the misogynist, who comes into adulthood fearful of women
and of his strong feelings about them, these cultural messages seem
to give him further license to behave cruelly. A culture that has de-
picted women, from the Bible on, as evil, malignant, and sinister
gives misogynists even more reasons to hate, fear, and revile
women. As psychoanalyst Karen Horney said, "Man has never tired
of fashioning expressions for the violent forces by which he feels
himself drawn to the woman and, side by side, the dread that
through her he might die or be undone."

In addition to the picture of women as evil is the impossible cultural model of manliness that boys are expected to emulate. This model requires that a man be powerful, independent, invulnerable, in charge, and nonemotional. Certainly he must never be afraid of or dependent on women. No man can live up to this model because it doesn't allow for normal human emotions and needs. It is particularly unrealistic for the man whose childhood circumstances left him with a desperate neediness for a woman's love.

Extramarital Affairs

When Gerry grew up, his hunger for a woman's attentions resulted in very destructive and unethical behavior. In his work as a psychologist, he was able to gain power and control over many of his female patients by having sexual relations with them. This was one of the ways in which he attempted to deal with his longings for comfort from a woman.

Similarly, many misogynists engage in extramarital affairs in their never-ending quest to make up for what they didn't get as children.

Understanding why the misogynist has extramarital affairs does not provide much comfort to his partner, however. Nicki discovered that Ed was having an affair when she found a receipt for some expensive lingerie in his sportcoat. She told me:

> He was so insanely jealous of everything I did, of everyone I saw, and then I found out that *he* was having an affair, and that did it. I started packing. I didn't even want to talk to him.

Ed's jealousy and possessiveness are typical. Many misogynists who are having extramarital affairs will assume that their partners are doing the same. The more guilty the man feels, the more he will need to project that guilt onto his partner. By doing this he makes her the "bad" one. This also enables him to assume less responsibility for his behavior, because he thinks she is guilty also.

These affairs usually don't change the misogynist's desperate need to hold on to his partner.

> When Ed came home and saw I was serious about leaving him he went to pieces. Never in a million years would I have expected to see this big six-foot-plus cop bawling his eyes out like that. He begged and he pleaded and he sobbed. He was like a little kid. I found myself feeling so sorry for him. He swore he'd stop seeing this other woman if I'd just stay, if I'd just give him another chance. So I did. I stayed.

To Ed, Nicki still represented his mother. He couldn't let go of the woman whom he saw as his primary source of nurturing and love.

Ed did his best to keep his affair a secret from Nicki, but other misogynists make no such effort. Nate, for example, was very open and blatant about his infidelities with his female employees. Lorraine told me:

> I hated having to go with him to any company functions because I had to pretend I wasn't noticing how he was falling all over whoever his "favorite" was at the time. He'd leave me alone, with everyone staring at me, while he danced with these women and made obvious passes, right in front of me. It was horribly humiliating.

Nate used his extramarital affairs to punish and humiliate his wife as well as to fill his sexual and emotional needs.

Other misogynists may use extramarital affairs as a way of assuring themselves that they'll never have to be alone. They create a fallback position for themselves so that they don't have to worry about being without a woman.

There are many factors that go into the complex area of infidelity, and not all misogynists are unfaithful. But for those who are, affairs are often another area in which these men are working out their childhood fears, needs, and conflicts.

Dependency and the Fear of Abandonment

All of the men we've described come into their adult lives with deeply ambivalent feelings about women, based in large measure on their relationships with their mothers. We have also seen how they transfer these feelings onto the women with whom they become involved. Once a man has done this, he comes to believe that he is as dependent on his partner as he was on his mother.

Inherent in his fear of this dependency is the equally dreadful fear that she will leave him. His terrors of being alone, of being unable to cope, and of being overwhelmed by an insatiable neediness all grip him again. Chronologically he is an adult, but psychologically he is still a frightened child.

All of the controlling behaviors the misogynist uses against his partner come from his profound fear of abandonment. It is a fear that must be defended against at all costs. In an effort to quell his anxiety, he tries to gain control over his partner by destroying her self-confidence, so that she can never leave him and he will be safe.

7 | How Women Learn to Love Women-Haters

Jackie felt discouraged when she realized that despite her determination to do differently, her marriage to Mark was almost a carbon copy of her mother and father's relationship. She told me:

> I was determined to have a home where people were nice
> to each other and where there was some mutual respect. I
> wasn't going to live in the same kind of three-ring circus my
> parents had. But now I see that I've done the same thing
> they did.

When Jackie married Mark, she thought he was a charming and exciting man who would make a wonderful life partner for her. His positive qualities were the obvious reasons for her excitement about him; the less-obvious side of the attraction was hidden from her, rooted deep within her. Whatever reasons we may give ourselves for falling in love with a certain person, the reality is that many of the connections we form in intimate relationships are based on patterns we learned from our parents.

Once Jackie and I began to explore those old family patterns, she felt them losing their power over her. When she understood the connections between her choices as an adult and how she was raised as a child, she gained more control over her life and her feelings about herself.

Many people are frightened to take a look at the forces that shaped their characters and their backgrounds, believing that the past should be buried and that looking back might mean wallowing in self-pity and old wounds. But self-discovery can open up exciting new choices and options for us. The more we understand what shaped us as individuals, the more tools we have to free ourselves from behaviors that no longer work for us.

What Makes Families So Important

When we are children our families take care of our basic survival needs; they are also our first and most important sources of information about the world. It is from them that we learn how to think and feel about ourselves and what to expect from others. Our emotional foundations are created by the ways in which our parents treated us, the ways in which they treated each other, the kinds of messages their behavior communicated to us, and the ways in which we handled that information internally.

SELF-IMAGE

Young children believe that their powerful, important parents have a monopoly on truth and wisdom. Therefore, whatever a parent says must be right and true. When a parent makes a judgment about a child's basic worth, this opinion becomes fact in the child's impressionable mind. If parents let their children know that they are good, valuable, and lovable, they will develop a view of themselves that is positive and solid. They will expect good treatment from others because they will believe they deserve it.

But if a child's early treatment teaches her that she is bad, inadequate, worthless, and unlovable, she will find ways to set up her life that support this view.

The negative self-images that some children develop carry through into adulthood. As I looked for a common denominator among the women I worked with who were with misogynistic partners, I found that they all carried with them from childhood a profoundly negative view of themselves. It was this damaged self-image, more than any other factor, that set these women up to accept abusive treatment from their partners.

MODELING

While our self-images are developing, we are also learning, through identification with our mothers, what it means to be a woman and how women are supposed to behave with men. Our fathers, on the other hand, are our first references for how men behave and how they treat women. In addition, our parents' interactions with each other provide our first and most important picture of how couples behave together. No film, television program or school primer is a more powerful teacher than our daily exposure to our parents' marriage. As children we don't realize that there are many other ways of conducting a marriage. Our parents' marriage becomes the model on which our future views of male-female relationships are based.

MESSAGES

One of the ways we learn from our parents is by receiving messages from their behavior. The word *message* in this sense relates not to direct verbal communications between the parent and the child but to the child's interpretation of her parents' behavior and statements. For instance, a girl may never be told directly that her opinions don't matter, but if her parents constantly interrupt her or tell her to be quiet, she will quickly infer that what she has to say is of no importance.

The messages we receive as children become the core information we use about ourselves and our position in the world for the rest of our lives. Often, however, we do not consciously realize that this information even exists. One of the greatest benefits of reexamining our backgrounds is that we discover what messages we got from our parents. Although this discovery process is painful, it assists us in our efforts to change our current behavior and even our feelings about ourselves. Messages, after all, are learned; and anything we learned can be unlearned.

REPEATING PATTERNS

As children, because of our dependency, we experience a sense of being powerless in a world of powerful people. If our home environments are unpleasant or painful, we defend ourselves by secretly promising ourselves that when we grow up we will do things better than our parents did.

However, because we know only what we learned as children, as adults we continue to seek out experiences and relationships that offer the comfort of familiarity. So, despite our heroic promises to do things differently, we often end up duplicating our childhood situations and relationships. A good example of this is the case of the woman whose father was an alcoholic and who winds up marrying an alcoholic. She is reenacting what is familiar to her. She is also trying to convince herself that now, as an adult, she has the power to rewrite the old family script and make it come out with a happy ending. Once she suffered from the withdrawal of her father's love because of his drinking. Now she will try to win that love from another alcoholic man.

The drive to repeat the familiar combined with the equally powerful drive to make it come out better creates a trap into which many women fall. Despite their determination to have better relationships than their parents had, they wind up in partnerships that are very similar.

When Jackie and I began to explore her background and family history, we discovered many early-life patterns that were evident in her current problems with Mark. I was particularly fortunate in Jackie's case to be able to work not only with her and later with Mark, but with her mother, Lorraine, as well. Lorraine originally came in to help Jackie deal with some of her conflicts about the family, but stayed to do important work of her own. This gave me a valuable multigenerational view of the family patterns.

Jackie's Family History

Jackie's mother, Lorraine, was 17 when she met Nate. To him she seemed a delicate, beautiful, exotic flower growing in their poor urban neighborhood. She was interested in the arts, and even though her family was poor she was studying dance. Nate fell madly in love with her. He was a dashing young man with a flock of female admirers. He was driven, ambitious, and charismatic. Lorraine was extremely flattered by his immediate interest in her.

Nate had a ferocious sexual appetite, and Lorraine, sheltered and naïve, soon became pregnant. Her family forced her and Nate into a hasty marriage. Lorraine had to abandon her dreams of becoming a dancer; Nate had to quit high school and get a job, abandoning his dreams of becoming a doctor. They both felt cheated, as if their youth had been cut short.

The relationship was stormy from the day they married. Nate's adoration of his young wife soon turned into angry jealousy and possessiveness. He demanded to know every move she made and gained control over her by throwing tantrums and verbally attacking her. During periods of calm he was still the ardent lover, but his angry outbursts often drove her into long depressions and tearful withdrawals. The overwhelming responsibilities of marriage and a baby at the age of 18, coupled with Nate's volatile behavior, crushed what independent spirit Lorraine had. This was the marriage into which Jackie was born.

When Mother Models Submission

One of Jackie's earliest memories was of her father screaming at her mother because her mother had left a cupboard door open:

> He called her selfish, lazy, and a goddamned slob, and then he threw all the pots and pans all over the floor and made her pick them up. I could see my mother was trembling, and there were tears on her face, but she didn't say anything. She just did what he told her to do.

Lorraine did not try to fight back or stand up for herself. Later she would complain to Jackie about how unhappy she was and that there was nothing she could do about it. Whether Lorraine was aware of it or not, she was modeling very potent behavior for her daughter.

"RELATIONSHIP AT ANY PRICE"

The cupboard incident Jackie described represents the style of relating and the power imbalance in Lorraine and Nate's marriage. The message Jackie received when she saw her mother submit to Nate's mistreatment was that *the only way to deal with aggression from men is to submit and give in.* From her father's behavior she learned that *men are allowed to act any way they choose and women have to take it.*

Another powerful message implied in this scene was that *if Mother can't protect herself, she certainly can't protect me.* In other words, Jackie could not depend on her mother for help if her father turned his wrath against her.

While every parental behavior sends out a message of some kind, it is only the repetitive themes that form the child's picture of the world. If a girl sees her mother accepting physical abuse as well as psychological abuse, she learns that there are no limits to what a man is allowed to do to a woman. A battered woman demonstrates to her daughter that *a woman must tolerate anything in order to hold on to a man.*

When Lorraine continually submitted to Nate's abuse, she was communicating to Jackie that she couldn't survive without her husband. Jackie told me:

> I could never understand why my mother, who I saw as wonderful, stayed with my father when he treated her so miserably. Even as a young child I knew he didn't appreciate her for the special person I thought she was. I'd ask her why she stayed, especially when she was crying after he'd screamed at her, and she'd say, "Where would I go? What would I do? Who would take care of us?"

The messages that Jackie received from her parents' interactions—that *the world is a scary place for a woman without a man,* that *women are helpless and dependent on men,* and that *men have all the power in relationships and women have none*—were etched deeply into Jackie's attitudes and perceptions. She grew up firmly convinced that *a woman must have a relationship with a man at any price, even if that price is her dignity and sense of self-worth.*

Cultural Support for Women's Dependency

Society has traditionally reinforced the idea that girls are inferior to boys, that girls can't take care of themselves, and that women need men to take care of them. We've all seen men portrayed in the media as stronger, more competent, and smarter than women, while women are often portrayed as highly emotional, indecisive, scatterbrained, passive, illogical, manipulative, and even malevolent. Such stereotypes further damage a young girl's ability to see herself as a strong and worthwhile person.

Coupled with these views is the disparity between the accomplishments for which boys are admired and those for which girls are admired. While girls may be praised for their manners and appearance, boys are often praised for academic achievement and physical strength. Girls may also be discouraged from exploring and mastering life and encouraged instead to develop skills to manipulate others to negotiate in the world for them. What these girls are getting are *lessons in helplessness*.

Even after we grow up, many of us continue to believe that we have little control over our lives. We may see others as the decision-makers in our lives and come to view life as something that happens *to* us. This belief system, reinforced by childhood identification with mothers who model extreme dependency and helplessness, sets many women up for abusive marriages.

"Do What I Say, Not What I Do"

It is behavior, not words, that has the greatest impact on a child. When a mother tells her daughter not to allow a man to control her or abuse her and then models the opposite in her own relationship with her husband, the girl will respond only to the behavioral message, not to the verbal one.

Paula, who was a successful commercial artist before she married Gerry, told me that her mother had encouraged her in the pursuit of a career and had supported her emotionally as well as financially:

> My mother was an accomplished artist and was starting to have some financial success with her work. But my father picked on her about it constantly. He'd stand over her shoulder while she was painting and sneer, "You're no Picasso, dear." When I was 14, she quit painting altogether. When I asked her why, she said, "What's the point if Daddy doesn't like it?" Here she was, always telling me how important it was for me to have my own interests and to do the things I wanted, no matter what anyone said, and yet she was giving up her painting because Dad didn't approve. I was furious at her.

The message that Paula received was, It's important for you to be your own person and have a career and success, but I'm not allowed to do that. Later, in Paula's marriage to Gerry, she was quick to abandon her career when he became critical of her work. "I guess it was more important to have his approval than it was to continue," she told me. Despite her mother's verbal support for Paula's professional success, Paula responded to the more powerful effect of seeing her mother abandon her own career.

Even when a woman is able to free herself from this type of role modeling by her mother and to achieve financial independence, she may still view herself as inferior and allow herself to be subjected to psychological abuse by her partner. Both Rosalind and Laura provided good examples of this. As I pointed out in The Paradox of the Powerful Woman (p. 87), a woman may be a fully independent adult in her business or professional life, and still react as a helpless child in her most intimate relationship.

Dual Identification

It is a great tribute to the resiliency of children that from even the most conflicted family situations they will often internalize positive and useful characteristics to serve them in adulthood. Jackie, for example, internalized in a very positive way some of her father's aggressive characteristics, which gave her the tools she needed to reach her career goals. Most women whose fathers were tyrannical and whose mothers were passive make their primary gender identification with their mothers, but they may also take into their characters some of their fathers' aggressiveness. In families where one parent is obviously a lot more powerful than the other, a child often, without being aware of it, takes into his or her character many attributes of the more powerful parent, even though that parent may be of the opposite sex. But Jackie, like many of the women I've seen, believed she could use the power she took from her father only in her professional life. As we worked together, she was delighted to find out that she could tap in to that same effectiveness in her personal life. She already had the skills; it was a matter now of learning how to apply them to her relationship with Mark. (I will discuss how to use and redirect some of these skills in the second half of this book.)

The Fear of Losing Father's Love

When Jackie was 5 years old, Lorraine became pregnant again. Once again the timing was bad: Nate was working on commission and his income fluctuated sharply. Lorraine, for whom the pregnancy was difficult, dreaded the additional responsibilities of a second child. She struggled with bouts of depression and spent a great deal of time in bed. Jackie remembered that this period marked a significant shift in her father's treatment of her:

> When we were having dinner one night I spilled my milk. My father suddenly blew up at me and started screaming. He'd never yelled at me before. He got so angry I thought he was going to burst. His face got red and the veins stood out in his neck. I was terrified. He screamed that I was wrecking the whole goddamned household, how he'd worked his ass off for us and I was ruining everything. Then he made me clean it all up while he stood over me to make sure I got every drop, screaming and cursing at me the whole time. I was sobbing so hard I couldn't even see the floor. It felt like the end of the world, like I'd lost his love forever.

For the child who believes that she has lost her parent's love, the agony is very real. The fact that children tend not to see past the present moment intensifies their distress; they believe that the terrible feelings they are experiencing will go on forever.

Because children are totally dependent on their parents for their physical and emotional survival, their need for parental love is absolute. The normal need for bonding with the parent becomes more intense if the parent withdraws love and becomes a figure of fear and anxiety. The more frightening the parent, and the more he threatens to pull away, the more fiercely the child will cling to him in an effort to regain the parent's goodwill. To the confused child, the angry parent, who both loves and hurts, is a giant. This giant controls the child's life through the use of fear and the manipulation of love. The child must be constantly designing her behavior either to avoid the parent's wrath or to get the parent's approval.

Every father-daughter relationship has its share of conflicts and disagreements, but if the predominant tone of the relationship is affection and respect, the daughter will develop a sense of trust and safety about men. Because the father is the first man in her life, he becomes the model on which she will base her emerging expectations about men. His treatment of her will also determine much of her view of herself.

"If Daddy Says It, It Must Be True"

When Jackie's father called her names, she took them as true evaluations of who she was, not as the outbursts of an angry, critical man. His words were like physical blows, and they scarred her sense of self-worth as surely as if he had slapped or beaten her.

When a child is subjected to verbal attacks, she sees it not as something being done to her but as something she has caused by her own failings. Because children cannot conceive that their all-powerful godlike parents can do anything wrong, they believe what their parents say. The parent's negative opinion becomes the *fact* on which the child bases her self-image. If the messages the child gets about herself are primarily positive, her self-image will be healthy. But for many children the positive messages are constantly being canceled out by negative ones.

Nate's opinions of Jackie became part of who she believed she was. As an adult, when her husband attacked her in much the same way, it was easy for her to slip back into feeling like a "bad girl."

The child who is made to feel like a "bad" person will begin to accept blame for whatever goes wrong in her home.

Learning to Take the Blame

When Jackie was 6, her sister, Clare, was born. At this same time Nate became manager of a sporting-goods store. With the increase in income and the promise of a brighter future, the family moved to a larger apartment, and Lorraine began to take a delight in Clare that she had never been able to take in Jackie. Jackie soon became aware that Clare was the favored child. Clare came to symbolize the turnaround in the family's fortunes. Nate began to use Jackie's natural jealousy of her baby sister as further evidence of her unworthiness. He had also begun to blame her for whatever tensions or conflicts occurred in the family. Although he still verbally attacked Lorraine, he now found in Jackie another outlet for his rages. Whenever he became angry, he blamed Jackie for all his frustrations.

Nate's use of Jackie as a target put her in the position of being *the family scapegoat*. People like Nate, who cannot accept responsibility for their shortcomings and frustrations, traditionally find a less-powerful person to blame for their discomforts. Children are ideal candidates for this scapegoat role because of their dependency, their vulnerability, and their limited view of the world.

Because of the scapegoat role she was assigned in her family, Jackie was unable to give up the idea that *she was to blame for whatever went wrong in her life*.

Her sister, however, was not subjected to these kinds of accusations. This is not unusual. Often two children from the same family are treated very differently. As a result, they can end up with widely varying self-images, and there will be dramatic differences in their lives and in the relationships they create as adults.

"DADDY'S ONLY UPSET BECAUSE OF YOU"

When Lorraine began pointing out to Jackie all the things she was doing that upset her father, she was, without realizing it, reinforcing the idea that Jackie was to blame for the family's problems. "Daddy's only upset because . . ." Lorraine would tell her, and then any number of reasons for Nate's irrational behavior would follow.

> If I talked too loud or ate too fast, if I didn't greet Daddy just the right way when he came home, my mother would say that I was getting him upset. I spent an awful lot of time thinking, "What did I do? What did I say? Why can't I be good so Daddy will love me and not get angry?" I'd make a million promises to myself every day to be a better person so Daddy wouldn't get upset anymore.

Lorraine was deflecting some of Nate's anger from herself onto her daughter. Jackie accepted this responsibility and believed that when her father was upset it was up to her to appease him. As a result, the energy that should have been devoted to her emotional development was spent in her preoccupation with helping her mother to keep peace in the household. The motto "don't upset Daddy" became what both mother and daughter lived by.

"YOU CAN NEVER BE SURE HOW A MAN WILL MAKE YOU FEEL"

Nate's treatment of Jackie was not always abusive. When he chose to do so, he could make Jackie feel like the center of the universe— adored and very special. When he was loving toward her, Jackie saw him as heroic and wonderful and believed anew that she would always be his precious little girl.

> I had wanted a pair of ice-skates more than anything. Daddy had promised to get me a pair but I had unusually narrow feet, so finding me skates turned out to be quite a

task. The evening he planned to get them for me it was rain-
ing very hard, but he went out for them anyway. He had to
go to eight different stores before he found the right ones. It
was after ten o'clock when he got home and I was already in
bed. I woke up when he came into my room, and I'll never
forget the smile on his face when he brought in those skates
and placed them at the foot of my bed. I loved him so much
for that. I thought he was the best and bravest father in the
whole world to have done that for me.

The wonderful, giving father juxtaposed against the angry, tyrannical father created for young Jackie a man of mythical proportions.
Knowing that at times she could bask in the glow of his adoration
made his cruel outbursts all the more devastating for her.

"You Have to Love Him No Matter What"

The dilemma for Jackie was that when her powerful, adored father
was loving toward her she felt wonderful, but when he was cruel she
felt fear, rejection, and confusion.

In her marriage to Mark, Jackie found herself experiencing the
same pattern. There were the wonderful highs when Mark was loving
and the terrible lows when he withdrew his love and was cruel to her.
No matter how she felt, she was expected to give Mark all her loyalty
and devotion, just as she had been taught in childhood to give her
love and devotion to her father, even when he was mistreating her.

The powerful messages on which Jackie's behavior was based
were, *your feelings don't matter* and *even if a man treats you badly,
you still have to love him*.

Learning Not to Show Anger

Any child who is being mistreated experiences a tremendous
amount of anger. How can you be treated unfairly and not be angry?

How can you be treated as if your feelings don't matter and not be angry? Jackie was no exception. But, like many children, Jackie was not permitted to express her rage.

> Once I said something Dad didn't like during dinner and he said to me, "I hope you choke!" I felt the tears burn into my ears and I felt like I'd been stabbed. I ran from the table to my room and sobbed my eyes out. All I could think was, "I hope *you* choke. I hope you *die*." I was so hurt and so angry. Then my mother came into my room and said, "You better come back to the table because Daddy's really mad at you now." When I came back she whispered to me, "Tell him you're sorry." I always had to swallow this awful rage each time he humiliated me.

Anger is a normal human emotion and all children experience it to some degree, but many parents have difficulty dealing with it. Often they mistakenly see their children's anger as an indication of their failure as parents. When a child throws a tantrum, most parents believe that they have lost control, and they feel helpless. Children need to express their angry feelings, but within reasonable limits. They must be taught that the *feelings* of anger are all right but that this doesn't mean that the child may kick the dog, hit someone, or break things. When a parent teaches a child how to ventilate her feelings in appropriate ways, he teaches a very important lesson.

CULTURAL RESTRICTIONS ON GIRLS' ANGER

Boys are encouraged to siphon off a great deal of aggression and anger through contact sports, fighting, and overt competitiveness, but girls are given far fewer outlets. Girls are expected to be polite and sweet-tempered; it is not considered "ladylike" for them to express anger by yelling, fighting, or engaging in aggressive sports. Although some girls become tomboys, most girls learn to ventilate their anger through verbal aggression. Gossiping, name-calling, and sarcasm are the standard forms; other, less direct forms include sulking, pouting, and crying.

TURNING ANGER IN ON YOURSELF

When verbal aggression is not sufficient as a means of siphoning off anger, as was the case with Jackie, the angry feelings get buried alive. Unfortunately, when a strong emotion like anger is blocked from normal expression, it doesn't just disappear. It finds another outlet. For Jackie, as for so many mistreated children, the outlet became herself.

Jackie began to boomerang her angry feelings back onto herself. She began to feel guilty for having such strong and prohibited emotions and convinced herself that she was experiencing these terrible feelings because she was a terrible person. The anger, of course, turned into self-hatred.

Jackie then attempted to atone for her angry feelings by designing an elaborate group of behaviors to prove to everyone, including herself, that she really was good and lovable and, above all, not angry. She became overcompliant, overadaptive, and submissive. Many girls are taught to do just this. They then carry these same behaviors into their adult lives.

The problem with this set of defenses against anger is that it sets up a vicious cycle. The more compliant she is, the more her feelings and needs are ignored, the angrier the girl becomes, and then the more compliant she becomes in order to deal with the anger. This cycle is the track that every mistreated child runs.

"IF YOU FEEL BAD IT'S BECAUSE YOU ARE BAD"

When Jackie left the table in tears after her father had told her he hoped she would choke, she was drawing attention to his behavior. Everyone began acting as if it were Jackie who was the villain; it became Jackie who had behaved terribly. Nate's cruelty was never permitted to be the issue. So, not only was Jackie not permitted to vent her anger when her father wounded her, but she was not permitted to say "ouch."

When a child is not permitted to express her pain, one of the important, destructive messages she gets is that *if she is feeling bad it is due to her own deficiencies.* Coupled with this is likely to be the message that *if she needs comfort, then she is ugly and repulsive to others.* Jackie recalled:

> I'd be crying because of something my father had said, and right away he'd start making fun of me. He'd imitate the sound of my crying and he'd say, "Look at that ugly face. No one wants to see that." He'd tell me I was disgusting and to "stop sniveling."

As a result of this, Jackie carried into her adult life a sense of loneliness and isolation when things went wrong. Rather than seek comfort when she was in pain, she learned to berate herself, which further intensified her distress. After Jackie had described an incident in which her husband, Mark, had been cruel to her, she said:

> I'm really sick of how I react and how incapable I am. I just sat there sniveling like a baby. No wonder he finds me disgusting.

Jackie had fallen into the pattern of punishing herself when she felt emotional pain; she was picking up where her father had left off. She became her own worst enemy.

One destructive repercussion of this in Jackie's adult life was that she avoided at all costs any painful decisions or encounters. But some adult choices, such as renegotiating or ending a harmful relationship, necessarily involve emotional pain. If these choices are avoided, the pain is then compounded by self-indictment and self-punishment.

Drama as a Way of Life

What I remember the most strongly was the palpable tension in the air when my father was expected home. When it was my mother, my sister, and myself, it was easy and relaxed, but as soon as we heard that key in the door, everything changed. We all got tense because we never knew what kind of mood he was going to be in. There was always this sense of us scurrying around the house like little bugs, either to clean up in a hurry or to try to have something there at the door when he came in to appease him . . . a drink, his slippers, the newspaper, anything so he wouldn't blow up.

The tension that Jackie described above was a direct result of the chaos and unpredictability in the household. Everyone was fearful of Nate's unpredictable moods. There were always tears, pleading, screaming, and the threat of physical violence about to erupt, followed by periods of calm. Jackie recalled that many times when her father had a violent outburst, her mother's response was to cry, beg, and plead, and then a few moments later they kissed and made up. The climate of her parents' home was one of enormous tension combined with elements of love, kindness, and affection. The result was a huge emotional stew. Jackie received the message that *drama is an essential component of love.*

It is to be expected that children raised in such tempestuous households will learn to mistake uproar and chaos for love. As adults, they will have a need for these elements in their love relationships. They have developed what I call an addiction to high drama.

This kind of high drama can effectively mask—as any addiction masks—the destructive and infantile aspects of a relationship. Chaos keeps the participants in a state of such emotional turmoil that they cannot clearly evaluate the situation. Often both partners are so drained and exhausted from fighting that they cannot even think.

Children from high-drama households often grow up with the

idea that tension is an integral part of love. Therefore, the girl who grows up in a high-drama family is an ideal partner for the charismatic, explosive misogynist. The fighting, the tension, and the drama are "normal" and familiar to her. She views the swings from despair to joy, from love to hate, from abuse to intense lovemaking as proof of love.

Controlling Fathers and Adolescent Daughters

Here is an excerpt from a letter I asked Jackie to write to her father about their relationship during her adolescence.

> I loved and adored you so much, but I'd tremble with fear when you were angry with me. I did everything to try to please you, but no accomplishment ever seemed enough for you. You compared me to all my friends. This one was prettier, that one was smarter. Then if I achieved something you belittled it. If I didn't achieve what you wanted me to, you called me a failure. You constantly humiliated and degraded me in front of other people. I never knew what you wanted from me.

Instead of getting the support and help she needed during her adolescence, Jackie became even more persecuted by her father.

> I committed a terrible crime; I discovered boys. I became very popular, but because of that I think I lost my father forever. He seemed to go kind of crazy. He started fighting with me every time he saw me. He started doing things like withholding money, refusing to buy me clothes. I had to beg for anything I got. He was always inventing ways to get me to stay home if I had a date or was going somewhere with my friends. He began interrogating me every time I came in. I had to account for every minute I spent out of the house. He tried to squash any attempt at independence on my part.

It is not unusual for a father to feel uncomfortable with his adolescent daughter's blossoming sexuality and her need for independence. But Nate's behavior was extreme and harmful to Jackie. Nate dealt with his confusing and forbidden feelings of attraction to his daughter by simultaneously pushing her away and becoming extremely jealous and possessive. By creating fights, picking on her incessantly, and grounding her over the smallest incidents, he kept the two of them locked in a constant state of warfare.

Adolescence is the last stop before womanhood. All of a girl's experiences from her childhood begin to converge and to form who she will become as an adult. It is a time when she feels painfully unsure of herself. Her emotions seem to have a life of their own, wrenching her from one extreme reaction to another. For this reason, adolescence can be a taxing time for the entire family. The teenager needs both to become independent and to have her family's support as well.

Nate's treatment of Jackie at this delicate juncture convinced her that there was something wrong with her. He made her feel evil about her emerging womanhood and branded her normal strivings for independence as further proof of her unworthiness and her deficiencies. Naturally, this reinforcement of Jackie's view of herself as a "bad girl" further damaged her self-esteem.

Women who wind up with misogynists usually come from backgrounds quite similar to Jackie's: there is a tyrannical, controlling father and a passive, dependent mother. Some form of psychological abuse is always present. When there is physical and/or sexual abuse as well, the impact on the child's development and self-esteem is even more devastating.

The Effects of Physical and/or Sexual Abuse

When Nancy first came in to see me for her problems of depression and overweight, she was not even aware that she'd been a battered child. Her father's brutality toward her came out in the course of her therapy. Only then was she able to see the connection between Jeff's mistreatment of her and how she'd been treated as a child. Nancy had grown accustomed to being controlled through fear and severe beatings. As with all abused children, she'd learned to blame herself for the abuse to which she was subjected. When she found herself being labeled a "bad" person in her marriage, it felt very familiar to her.

When a girl is sexually abused, layers of secrecy and shame are added to her self-blame. The incestuous aggressor always projects the guilt for his crime onto the child he is molesting. The girl then learns to see herself as dirty and worthless. Having accepted humiliation, betrayal, and exploitation as the conditions of survival during childhood, the girl is likely to reenact that same abuser/victim relationship with men in her adult life.

The terrible crime of incest is finally getting the attention it deserves. In this country alone, at least one out of every ten girls will be molested by a trusted member of her family. These experiences wreak tremendous emotional damage on a young girl and severely distort her view of herself as a lovable woman.

8 | Madness for Two

The misogynistic relationship is not really satisfying to either the misogynist or his partner. However, as we have seen, it is the woman who suffers most. The tremendous power imbalance between them, which is so harmful to her, keeps both her and her partner locked together in what I call a "madness for two."

Whenever two people are in a close relationship there is bound to be some polarization and therefore some imbalance of power. In healthy relationships, the power shifts back and forth so that each partner at times has more power than the other. In misogynistic relationships, however, only the man has power; it never shifts to the woman.

Both the misogynist and his partner learned in childhood to see the world in terms of the powerful and the helpless, and to see themselves as weak and inadequate. Yet, in adulthood, the man appears strong, because he's aggressive, assaultive, and intimidating, while the woman appears weak, because she placates him and gives in to his demands. But what is showing externally is not necessarily what is going on under the surface.

Exchanging Forbidden Feelings

We are often drawn to partners who will act out for us those feelings that we are the most uncomfortable with. This is one of the ways that shame-filled impulses find expression. For this reason, many women are attracted to misogynists: they appear to be powerful, aggressive, dynamic, and able to ventilate anger whenever they want to.

If the woman has been afraid of and uncomfortable with her anger since childhood, she will see the misogynist as someone who can express for her some of her angry feelings.

He, on the other hand, feels a deep shame about his neediness. One of the reasons he's attracted to his partner is that she can express for him some of his vulnerable feelings.

These attractions and the vicarious exchanges of hidden feelings do not take place within the realm of conscious awareness. Yet, this unconscious exchange, which drives the misogynist and his partner to behave the way they do together, is a potent underlying force in their relationship.

THE DEPENDENCY EXCHANGE

The misogynist is very uncomfortable with feelings of sadness and helplessness because he is ashamed of these emotions; vulnerability does not fit in with his view of himself as a man. However, his feelings are still there, and like all strong emotions, they must find expression through some outlet. When his partner expresses these emotions, he gets to experience them *secondhand*. In addition, by controlling her, he gains a sense of mastery over the frightened little boy hidden within him.

This unsatisfactory exchange has two inherent drawbacks. First, the woman's expressions of emotional pain mirror that part of the man that he fears and hates the most. Therefore, although he needs her to show these vulnerabilities, he feels contemptuous of her for being "weak" or "sick." He gets her to express his shameful feelings for him, then he hates her for doing so.

Second, although he may have assuaged his fears of abandonment by making her too frightened to leave him, she may become so preoccupied with her own emotional distress that she can no longer meet his insatiable need to be nurtured. So he's liable to feel abandoned anyway—the very thing he was trying so hard to avoid.

THE ANGER EXCHANGE

Just as the misogynist siphons off some of his feelings of dependency through his partner's behavior, she siphons off some of her anger through his outbursts of temper.

Jackie told me that although Mark's tantrums were very painful and frightening to her, she was aware of being envious of his freedom to express his rage:

> I could never blow up like that. At least he knows how to get things off his chest. He doesn't sit on it, like I do.

Vicariously experiencing Mark's expressions of anger was not enough to help Jackie significantly with her own feelings of rage. Instead, because the bulk of Mark's anger was usually directed at her, his attacks added another layer to the anger she was still carrying around within her from childhood.

Like many women, Jackie had few socially acceptable outlets for her anger. She had to repress both her anger at Mark and her anger from her past. The pressure of all this unexpressed rage left Jackie terrified; she believed that if she allowed herself to get angry at all, she would lose control of herself. She felt that her anger was like a bottomless pit and that if she ever tapped into it the rage would never stop.

Anger and Suffering

We all need to say what we think and feel. When we block the normal channels of expression, the emotions find other ways to manifest themselves. Some of these manifestations can be very destructive.

When a woman in a misogynistic relationship disowns her angry feelings, they often return disguised as illnesses. For many women, *suffering is the only way they know to express their rage.*

I've heard women recite long lists of physical and emotional problems, yet they rarely make a connection between their bad feelings and their relationships with their partners. The following exchange on this subject is from one of my recent radio programs:

JENNIFER: I want to learn how to communicate better with my husband.

SUSAN: What does that mean?

JENNIFER: Well, he keeps getting mad at me all the time.

SUSAN: What does he get mad about?

JENNIFER: Oh, it could be anything. I can't seem to do anything right anymore.

SUSAN: What does he do when he gets mad?

JENNIFER: He's very domineering. He's always giving orders. He never asks. He just demands. He calls me lots of names, like stupid and ding-dong.

SUSAN: How does that make you feel?

JENNIFER: I feel terrible. I'm depressed all the time.

SUSAN: How long have you been feeling depressed?

JENNIFER: On and off for about fifteen years.

SUSAN: Don't you think there's some connection between how you are being treated and how you're feeling?

JENNIFER: Oh, look, he's not like that all the time. I must have given you the wrong impression. He's a very good provider and he's real sweet when he's not mad at me.

SUSAN: But when he *is* angry, he gets very critical and insulting, and look what it's doing to you. When people are treated this way, they usually feel angry. Aren't you angry, Jennifer?

JENNIFER: [she starts to cry] Yes, but I love him and know he loves me.

SUSAN: That may well be, but what you are doing with your

normal and appropriate anger is turning it in on yourself. It's turning into depression and self-blame. These are very typical ways for women to handle anger they can't express.

Jennifer had successfully isolated her distress from her relationship. As long as she kept her attentions focused on her depression and her "wrongness," she avoided having to confront the destructiveness of her relationship with her husband. Jennifer is not atypical. Many women turn their angry feelings into emotional and physical ills.

Stress and Anger

Repressed rage can be one of the major sources of stress to the body. In fact, it can actually begin to wear the body out. Rather than deal with their unacceptable rage at their partners, many women unconsciously redirect their anger inward, back onto themselves. The more a woman does this, the more internal damage she is likely to do to herself. The medical and psychiatric literature are filled with descriptions of illnesses that result from this inability to deal with emotional distress.

PHYSICAL MANIFESTATIONS OF STRESS

Family history, genetic predispositions, and various other personality and body characteristics determine how a woman will manifest physical symptoms of stress.

Stress may show up in the musculoskeletal system as backaches, muscle spasms, general body tightness, and/or tension headaches, or it may manifest in the digestive tract as ulcers, colitis, chronic indigestion, and various types of bowel disorders. Stress can also show up in the cardiovascular system in such ailments as vascular headaches and migraines, and it can be lethal when it finds expression in high blood pressure and coronary disease.

EMOTIONAL EXPRESSIONS OF STRESS

The most prevalent and damaging of these is *depression*, which can show itself in many ways. Occasional feelings of sadness, negativity, loneliness, or uncertainly are a normal part of being human. In a serious depression, however, these feelings become chronic and all-pervasive. Some depressed women may be aware only that they constantly feel tired and bored. They may complain of lacking energy and enthusiasm. For them, depression is experienced primarily as an inability to feel pleasure or joy. Other women withdraw into lethargy, sleeping long hours every day, with all feelings and responses blunted. Still other women experience the pain directly and acutely. They may cry a great deal of the time, bursting into tears at the slightest provocation. They may have suicidal fantasies and wishes as the depression deepens, and in some cases, these wishes may be carried out.

Few people want to admit they're depressed, falsely believing that it is a sign of weakness or deficiency. But even a few of the following symptoms may indicate the presence of depression:

- Constant fatigue
- Boredom
- Inability to enjoy former pleasures
- General feeling of sadness
- Sleep problems: either too much sleep or its opposite, insomnia
- Brooding over the past and how things have turned out
- Pessimism about the future
- Loss of interest in sex
- Overreaction to trivial events
- Trouble with concentration and/or memory
- Loss of interest in food; unusual weight loss
- Overeating; unusual weight gain
- Extreme irritability
- Neglect of appearance
- Frequent thoughts of death or dying

Stress may be the underlying factor in other emotional reactions as well. Attacks of anxiety and panic, sleep disturbances, and a wide range of mood swings can stem from the stress that results from the repression of anger.

I don't mean to imply that every psychological problem that befalls a woman is the direct result of her partner's treatment of her. As we have seen, many of the women who bond with misogynists have had difficult childhoods, and they may have pre-existing tendencies toward emotional problems such as depression. Also, some depressions and anxiety states are now known to be the result of imbalances in body chemistry. However, the pain, confusion, loss of confidence and repressed rage that exist in these relationships provide the perfect soil for physical and emotional illnesses to develop or intensify.

STRESS AND ADDICTIONS

Some women attempt to deal with stress through a variety of physical addictions. Excessive drinking, drug use, heavy smoking, and compulsive eating can temporarily mask unacceptable feelings and impulses. Addictions serve a dual purpose. They deaden pain and at the same time intensify the avoidance of dealing with the cause of that pain. They can make a chaotic relationship appear tolerable, while decreasing the discomfort that motivates change.

Whatever form the addiction takes, it represents a desperate attempt at psychological survival. But a woman in an unhealthy relationship seriously undermines her chances of improving her situation when she adds a physical addiction to the already overwhelming stress and conflict she faces. Addictions wear out the body and the mind and deepen the woman's sense of helplessness and self-hatred. She also provides her partner with further proof of her deficiency and further justification of his need to control her.

When I begin to work with anyone who has a physical addiction, I make it clear that I will treat them only if they also involve themself in some type of program or organization designed to help break their dependency.

The Hidden Pay-Offs of Suffering

The reactions listed above *punish* the woman for her unacceptable feelings; they may also constitute an unconscious wish that through her suffering she will also punish her partner. Through her physical symptoms she may be trying to send her partner the following messages:

- Aren't you ashamed of how awful you are making me feel?
- You are a bad person for doing this to me.
- It's up to you to make me feel better.
- See how I'm suffering? You have to pay attention to me and be nice to me.

A woman may believe that because she is suffering she has the right to be taken care of and to be pitied; most important, she may view it as justification for not taking any action to make her life better. However, suffering *doesn't change anything*. Backdoor, indirect attempts to communicate are never effective because they don't confront the issues. Also, the misogynist is rarely sensitive to his partner's feelings. If he does recognize that his partner is suffering, his attitude is liable to be that it has nothing to do with him. The woman's suffering is considered further evidence of her deficiencies. If she breaks down physically or emotionally, it may only add to his contempt for her weakness. In his eyes, she becomes pathetic as well as deficient.

Trying to Get Even Without Getting Angry

No matter how compliant a woman is, and no matter how much she turns her rage into suffering, her anger at her partner for his cruelty cannot be totally contained. Instead, it may slip out in a variety of subtle yet hostile ways.

DIRECT HOSTILITY

The woman in a misogynistic relationship may engage in covert verbal attacks and sniping in an attempt to retaliate and to siphon off some of her anger. Lorraine was furious about the way Nate treated her, but she had very few ways of expressing this. As Jackie remembered:

> My mother would compare my father with other men and let him know that he wasn't as handsome or as intellectual or as cultured. I remember her calling him a "crass merchant." She'd also tease him about being short, which was a real sore point for him. She'd make fun, in front of other people, of how he mispronounced words. It was her way of getting back at him.

As might be expected, Lorraine's hostile remarks merely gave Nate further justification for his cruelty to her.

INDIRECT HOSTILITY

Some women express their angry feelings by what they *don't* do. For instance, they may become forgetful about little things that matter to their partners, they may have difficulty making even the simplest decisions, or they may get into the irritating habit of always being late. Many women withhold and turn off sexually, which is a very powerful way of expressing anger. Or they become cold and distant, withdrawing into angry silence and sulking.

Whether direct or indirect, all of these expressions of anger are relatively feeble compared to the ongoing explosive assaults of the misogynist.

In the dependency-anger exchange, once again it is the woman who gets shortchanged. Despite the misogynist's conflicts and fears in regard to his neediness, he nevertheless feels free to release his anger. I believe that this is the major reason why these men seem to suffer so little.

The women, on the other hand, whether out of fear of retaliation, old family programming, or fear of falling apart or of losing their partners' love, do not enjoy this essential emotional freedom. They repress their rage and ultimately turn it back onto themselves.

A relationship in which one partner can express hostile feelings but the other cannot is based on a serious imbalance of power. Yet, the woman who sees herself as powerless in such a relationship is not seeing things as they really are. She actually has *more* power than her partner, because *he is far more dependent on her than she is on him*. She just doesn't realize it. His neediness, his fears of abandonment, his need to be in total control, his intense possessiveness, and his distorted view of reality make him a paper tiger. No matter how powerful he appears, he *feels* powerful only when he is subjugating and controlling her. These defenses give him a sense of safety but also keep him locked into a very rigid way of behaving.

In contrast, once the woman learns to accurately assess her real strengths, she is in a much better position than he is to change her behavior and her life.

PART II

The Women Who Love Them

How to Use the Second Part of This Book

The second part of this book is devoted to teaching you how to help yourself and to change your relationship with your partner. This journey of exploration and change requires you to participate in many of the exercises and assignments that I take my clients through.

My counseling style is very directive and I make extensive use of writing as a tool for unlocking and focusing on hidden or buried emotions. Often there is resistance to this kind of work; the temptation is to read through the exercises without doing the assignments. Certainly there is much to be gained just from reading about the processes I use and the information on renegotiating relationships. However, just as reading a diet book without going on the diet will not make you any thinner, reading the exercises without doing the assignments won't provide you with the tools that will enable you to change your unhappy relationship—or, when necessary, to end it.

I have included lists of questions for you to answer, letters for you to write, and other types of written exercises. I suggest that you keep a pencil and paper by your side as you read. You might even want to get a small notebook for this purpose, so that you can later review your work. In any case, please save your written assignments, because I'll be referring back to some of the exercises as we go along.

Even if you are not currently in a misogynistic relationship, some of the tools and skills I have designed can help you learn to be more assertive and to deal more effectively with any psychologically abusive people in your life.

If you are in a misogynistic relationship, the exercises I've designed may take you down some rocky paths. Some of this work is painful, but the rewards will be lasting and worth whatever discomfort you experience. Most important, these skills will help you to find much of the self-confidence you thought you had lost. Together, you and I will reclaim that self-confidence and reinstate it into your life.

9 | *How Are You Feeling?*

When my client Nancy first came to me she genuinely couldn't see that many of her problems stemmed from her marriage. Her husband, Jeff, had taken such complete control over their lives together that Nancy had lost all perspective on what was happening to her. She did not know what she was responsible for causing, how she felt, or what Jeff's treatment of her was doing to her. In order to regain control over her life, Nancy needed to define for herself what made sense and what was real, instead of continuing to accept Jeff's views.

Nancy's feelings, thoughts, and behavior, as well as Jeff's behavior, were the areas on which we needed to focus. Getting in touch with her true feelings was our first step.

The Importance of Feelings

Jeff's control over Nancy's life extended not only to how she should think and behave but how she should feel in order to get his love and approval:

He would say "Tell me how you feel. Please, I want to know. We have to communicate. Just tell me how you feel." So I would. I'd say something like, "I feel hurt by what you just said about me being too stupid to understand," and he'd snap, "Wrong, Nancy. Those are the wrong feelings. You shouldn't feel that way."

Jeff labeled "wrong" any feelings that displeased him. But feelings, unlike behavior, do not have moral ratings. There are no "right" or "wrong" feelings. No one has the right to judge how we feel or to devalue our feelings. Feelings simply exist, and we are entitled to them.

During Nancy's four-year marriage to Jeff she had so repressed her feelings that they had become unrecognizable to her. She had gained weight, developed an ulcer, become extremely depressed, and lost confidence in her abilities. When Jeff started judging and condemning her feelings, Nancy became confused about what she was "supposed" to feel. As a result of repressing those feelings that Jeff had labeled "wrong," she had begun to *disconnect from and to doubt* her emotions. By the time she came in to see me, the only thing she was sure of was that she was in pain.

Nancy's pain was a very clear signal that something was wrong. But, like many women, she believed that she was supposed to "tough it out" when she was hurting. Paying attention to her pain meant to her that she was "wallowing in self-pity."

TAKING EMOTIONAL INVENTORY

Our feelings are our best sources of information about ourselves. They are our greatest guides to who we are, what we need, and what is meaningful to us as individuals. To begin to understand what has been happening to you, you must first identify and take inventory of your feelings about yourself, your life, and your partner.

The following list of questions is designed to help you do just that. The feelings mentioned in the questions are the ones I hear most often from clients who are in misogynistic relationships.

Please answer each question with a *yes* or a *no*. You might also put a light checkmark next to the questions to which you answer *yes*. If you have other strong feelings that are not covered here, write them down.

1. Do you feel sad much of the time?
2. Do you feel afraid of your partner?
3. Do you feel hopeless and overwhelmed?
4. Do you feel enraged much of the time?
5. Do you feel confused and bewildered about how you are supposed to behave?
6. Do you feel overpowered by your partner?
7. Do you feel guilty and always in the wrong?
8. Do you feel self-hatred?
9. Do you feel frustrated?
10. Do you feel trapped?

If you have answered *yes* to six or more of these questions you are clearly in a great deal of emotional pain.

Many women who have been denying or minimizing the importance of their emotional distress are frightened of getting acquainted with their feelings. This is perfectly normal. There is no easy way to look inside ourselves. However, summoning the courage to do this kind of exploratory psychic probing is the first step toward making changes in your feelings and therefore in your life. Stay with me and we will deal with some of the emotions that may be surfacing for you.

In order to gain a sense of mastery over these strong emotions so that they don't overwhelm you, you must first understand where they come from. Feelings can be wonderful, but when they are out of control or are emanating primarily from fear and helplessness, they can interfere with both judgment and reason.

The Important Connection Between Thoughts and Feelings

Most of us are not aware that our feelings are a direct result of our thoughts. We tend to believe instead that our feelings are a result of external events. But *there has to be a thought before there can be a feeling*. Statements such as these show how people confuse their thoughts with their feelings:

- I feel that you are angry with me.
- I feel that my brother is a weak person.
- I feel that if I would only change, my husband would love me more.

All of these sentences express *thoughts, beliefs, and perceptions*, which then *result* in certain *feelings*. Let's look at the feelings that these thoughts create.

"I feel that you are angry with me." This is actually a perception, which, more accurately stated, would be: "I see you are angry with me, therefore I now *feel* scared, confused, sad, hurt, and angry."

"I *think* my brother is a weak person, therefore I *feel* contemptuous, superior, disappointed, sad, frustrated, and helpless."

"I *believe* that if I would only change, my husband would love me more, therefore I *feel* bad, inferior, unlovable, and bewildered."

These vital distinctions are not differences in semantics. Learning to distinguish your thoughts from your feelings is a very important step in your growth. *To gain control of your life, you must first take control of your thoughts.*

The following example shows how thoughts and feelings can get confused in a relationship. Imagine that you have fixed a nice dinner and have sat down at the table with your husband. Suddenly he criticizes you because you've folded the napkins wrong. He begins saying such things as: "You don't care enough to do it right"; "You don't care about anything and especially about me because you know how important it is for me to have the table looking good"; "You're thoughtless, selfish, and lazy."

Very likely all you would be aware of during this tirade is feeling scared, humiliated, guilty, and angry. The intensity of your feelings may be all that is real for you at the moment. But *it is vitally important for you to recognize that you have skipped a step in understanding what is happening to you.* Before you felt all those intense emotions, *you had thoughts.*

Isolating and recognizing those thoughts enables you eventually to *change your behavior and your reactions.* Between a tirade, such as the one described above, and your panicky reactions, the thoughts that sped by unnoticed may have included: "He's angry at me"; "I'm in danger"; "I have done something wrong"; "Why can't I ever defend myself against his criticism"; "I can never think of anything to say when he's angry at me"; "He never appreciates anything I try to do for him"; "I wish I could kill him." When you can recognize the crucial distinction between your thoughts and feelings, you can begin to exercise some control over your reactions.

UNDERSTANDING THE THINKING PROCESS

To help my clients in this area, I ask them to focus on their thoughts. Unlike feelings, *thoughts* do not have specific labels. For this reason, thoughts tend to be more general.

The following exercise is designed to help you to clarify the connection between your thinking process and your feelings. The feelings listed are the same as those contained in the questions you answered on p. 160, in the Emotional Inventory. See if some of the thoughts that go along with the feelings seem familiar to you.

FEELINGS	THOUGHTS
1. I feel sad much of the time.	Life is miserable. I wonder if everybody wouldn't be better off without me.
2. I feel afraid of my partner.	Something bad is going to happen to me. I don't know what he might do next. He might hurt me. He might leave me.
3. I feel hopeless and overwhelmed.	It's never going to change. There's no way out. I can't handle this. Nothing I can say or do will make a difference.
4. I feel enraged much of the time	I'd like to smack him in the face, if I weren't so scared.
5. I feel confused and bewildered about how I'm supposed to behave.	What did I do wrong? Why is he so upset with me again? How come he can be so loving sometimes and so awful at others?
6. I feel overpowered by my partner.	I can't ever win. Nothing I do works. He's stronger than I am in every way.
7. I feel guilty and always in the wrong.	It's all my fault. I've got to learn to become a better person.
8. I feel self-hatred.	I'm selfish. I'm weak. I'm contemptible, I'm inconsiderate, demanding, and a bad person.
9. I feel frustrated.	No matter what I say he doesn't listen to me. He won't take me seriously. Nothing I do makes any difference.
10. I feel trapped.	There's no way out. I have no place to go.

Now go back over your Emotional Inventory. See if you can figure out what thoughts preceded each of your feelings. Be as specific as you can. Try this exercise at least once a day. Take a few moments to connect your feelings (both positive and negative) to the thoughts that came before them. For example, let's say you just bought a birthday gift for a close friend. You feel a warm glow of satisfaction; you feel happy and good about yourself. Some of the *thoughts* that may have preceded these feelings are: "I'm a nice person"; "I'm kind"; "I'm generous"; "I like to make people I care about happy"; "My friend will love this gift."

Conversely, if giving the gift makes you feel tense and worried, the thoughts might have been: "Maybe my friend won't like this present"; "I spent too much money"; "I never know the right thing to buy for people"; "Am I only trying to buy my friend's love with this gift?"

Trying to find the connection between your thoughts and your feelings may seem awkward and mechanical at first. However, doing this exercise will help you to learn how to interrupt your automatic reactions, particularly to stressful situations. (Chapter 13 will give you more techniques for dealing with thoughts and feelings.)

THE BEHAVIOR COMPONENT

Since behavior is the result of both thinking and feeling, we must focus on it, too. The following exercise concerns what you have been *doing* as a result of your thoughts and feelings about your relationship. Please answer each question with a *yes* or a *no*. Then make a separate list of your own, describing other aspects of your behavior in your relationship.

How You've Been Behaving
- Do you apologize all the time?
- Do you willingly accept the blame for everything that goes wrong in your relationship?
- Do you "walk on eggs"? Do you watch every word you say, or

rehearse what you will say to your partner, so as not to set him off?

- Do you constantly tell the children to be careful so that they won't upset Daddy?
- Do you cry a lot more than you used to?
- Do you repress your feelings, especially your anger?
- Do you constantly try to figure out how to get your partner's approval? Do you twist yourself into a pretzel trying to suit his ever-changing demands?
- Have you given up interests, activities, and people that once were important to you?
- Have you let go of opinions, ideas, attitudes, hopes, and dreams you had for yourself?
- Do you hold yourself back in your educational or vocational advancement?
- Do you constantly excuse your partner's behavior to yourself or to others?
- Have you let yourself go physically? Have you gained or lost a great deal of weight? Are you paying less attention to your personal appearance than you used to? Do you find excuses not to leave the house?
- Is your life based on trying to please your partner so as to avoid his wrath or disapproval?

I understand all too well how distressing it is to see beneath the surface of a relationship that you would like to believe is loving or at least satisfactory. However, while denial can be comforting in the short run, ultimately there is nothing more harmful than this sort of self-deception.

When Nancy found herself answering *yes* to most of the questions listed above, she was very upset. This process was a real eye-opener for her. She had to face the fact that she'd renounced a flourishing career in fashion and given up many of her friends and outside activities in order to appease Jeff. She had also given up her right to make any decisions that didn't meet with Jeff's approval.

Most distressing of all for her was the realization that, by submitting to his abusive treatment, she had actually given him *license* to mistreat her.

The exercises you've just completed will pull back the curtain of clouded perceptions and wishful thinking. You can now see what has really been going on in your life and particularly in your relationship. I urge you to be honest with yourself and to tolerate some discomfort. Whatever pain you may experience as a result of this work can be used as a bridge toward understanding how all the elements in your life interact and affect you.

The last element we have to examine now is your partner's behavior. As before, answer the questions, then make up your own list, describing other aspects of your partner's behavior.

How Your Partner Has Been Behaving

- Does he insist on having control over your life, your thoughts, and your behavior?
- Is he unrelentingly critical of you and always finding fault?
- Does he intimidate you by yelling or by threatening to withdraw his love or to leave if you don't do as he wishes?
- Does he frighten you into submission by threats of physical violence?
- Does he switch from charm to anger without warning?
- Does he make derogatory comments about women in general and you in particular?
- Does he withdraw love, money, approval, or sex to punish you when you displease him?
- Does he project the blame for all his failures and shortcomings onto you or other people?
- Does he attack your character through insults and name-calling?
- Does he devalue your opinions and feelings?
- Does he accuse you of being too sensitive or of overreacting if you get upset when he attacks you?
- Does he confuse you by refusing to confront issues, by denial,

by changing the subject, by rewriting history, or by acting as if nothing has happened right after a big blow-up?

- Is he in competition with your children, or other important people in your life, for your attentions?
- Is he extremely jealous and possessive?
- Does he insist that you give up what is valuable and important to you to satisfy him?
- Does he constantly criticize the other important people in your life, such as your family and friends?
- Does he belittle your accomplishments?
- Does he belittle you sexually?
- Does he force you to participate in sexual acts that are unpleasant or painful for you?
- Does he have extramarital affairs?
- Is he inconsiderate of your sexual needs?
- Is he charming in public but apt to launch into a tirade when you are alone together?
- Does he humiliate you in front of others?

If you've answered *yes* to ten or more of these questions, you are in a misogynistic relationship.

Setting Our Course

Nancy told me that after she had completed the preceding exercises she felt flooded by emotions and was alarmed at how much seemed to be wrong in her relationship with Jeff. I had expected these reactions. This kind of stock-taking stirs up very strong feelings.

In my experience, people cannot change their painful feelings just by talking about them. They must experience them, examine them, and then attempt to modify them. Sometimes this can be very painful, but it is almost always effective.

I told Nancy that the intensity of her discomfort was not a sign that we were going in the wrong direction; rather, it indicated that the process was beginning to work. She was gaining painful but essential insights into her marriage. This was an excellent beginning. However, insights and understanding in themselves are not enough. Without actually *doing things differently*, insights and understanding are merely intellectual exercises.

Many of us know someone who has been in therapy or analysis for four or five years or even more. These people can give you a long list of reasons why they continue to act in self-defeating ways. In fact, the primary change after years of therapy is in their bank balance, not in their behavior. I have always considered it my job as a therapist to help people *to change their behavior as well as to gain insights into why they behave as they do*. When clients commit themselves to take on this task and to actually begin to *do* things differently, there is dramatic personal growth almost immediately.

It can be frightening even to contemplate doing things differently. But in order to change the quality of your life you must be willing to change your behavior and to take some real risks with that new behavior. One of the most rewarding things about being an adult is that there are so many avenues of change available to you. The pay-offs, in terms of self-confidence, are immediate. Increased self-esteem is also a natural result of any efforts to change. Once people begin to see that they can affect things, they actually begin to *feel* very different about themselves and their lives.

But change often doesn't feel comfortable in the beginning. This is the main reason that people resist behavioral changes with every fiber of their beings. Often they mistakenly believe that their feelings indicate how well they are doing in the change process. They assume that if they were doing things "right," they would feel better immediately. However, the reality is that most people feel frightened, anxious, and off balance when they first start to change their behavior.

Jackie said to me after our first three sessions together: "I thought therapy was supposed to make me feel better. I'm feeling worse now than I did before I started! How am I supposed to do new things when I feel so terrible?"

Jackie made a very typical mistake: she believed that she had to *feel different* before she could *behave differently*. I assured her that once she began to change her behavior, the good feelings would catch up.

However, I wasn't going to ask Jackie to behave any differently at this point. Instead, we would begin to build a foundation for behavior change, by first making some important shifts in her feelings and perceptions.

The initial shifts I will recommend to you are concerned primarily with your feelings, not with your head-on collisions with your partner. Through these shifts, you will learn to step back from your intense, distressing emotions so that you can better control them, rather than allow them to control you. Once you have your emotions under control, logic, instead of fear and anxiety, will dominate your life. You will begin to think clearly about yourself, your relationship, and where you are headed. When you reach this point, you are ready to make real behavioral changes.

The exercises that we've done so far are the first step in this process. The steps described in the next few chapters focus on judgment, reevaluating your view of yourself, discovering where many of the negative messages come from in your life and where your confidence and self-worth first were damaged, and managing that old devil, anger. You will learn ways to take better care of yourself so that when strong emotions arise you have some comfort available to you.

Once you've dealt with yourself, you'll be prepared to deal with your partner.

10 | Preparing for Change

Nancy was frightened by the dilemma she found herself facing, once she'd looked closely at her relationship with Jeff. What could she do about it, given how she feared him? She said to me:

> Can't I just leave the marriage alone and work on my ulcer and weight problem? At least I'm used to the way things are between us.

I told Nancy that, judging from her description of Jeff's behavior and from the information she'd revealed in the exercises, her relationship with Jeff was at the center of many of her problems. If she wanted to feel better she had to confront these problems directly.

Accepting the Status Quo

Nancy believed that to do nothing was the easiest and least threatening way to handle her relationship problems. She was, of course, assuming that the situation between her and Jeff would not get worse. She hoped that if she did nothing, things would at least stay the same, if not improve.

The status quo in a relationship cannot be maintained indefinitely. The situation will change even if we do nothing, because ultimately we are not in control of all the variables that can affect our relationships. I asked Nancy what she thought would happen to her marriage if Jeff's practice fell off, if she went back to work, if they had children, if there was a death in the family, or if either one of them got sick. Any of these events can create a shift in the balance of a relationship. My professional experience has shown that when an event disturbs the precarious equilibrium of a misogynistic partnership, the misogynist's abusive behavior toward his partner automatically escalates.

Therefore, while you might get by with accepting things the way they are right now, doing nothing in the long run is a dangerous game. It presupposes that nothing will ever happen to upset your lives.

The fervent hope of every woman I've treated in a misogynistic relationship is that somehow something will happen that will make it all better. Each woman wants to believe that one day her partner will come to his senses, take her in his arms, and say, "I know I've been terrible to you. Forgive me. I'll never hurt you again. I love you, and from now on things will be different."

In truth, your relationship is far more likely to get worse than to get better. People become more entrenched in their behaviors as they get older; they are less willing to change. By accepting the situation the way it is, you are renouncing your right to be treated with the respect and dignity to which you, and all of us, are entitled. You are making an active choice to stay in the victim position in your relationship.

If you have children, that choice affects them as well. As you have seen, misogynistic marriages generally teach young boys how to become abusive men and to teach young girls that they are of little value. Accepting the status quo may perpetuate the abuse behavior into the next generation.

Ask yourself whether it isn't worth trying to change the system rather than to accept it the way it is. Perhaps the questions you should ask yourself are: Haven't I already tried doing nothing? Haven't I in fact been more and more accepting? Has it done any good?

Many women become quite discouraged when they answer these questions. What they must realize is that a good relationship *is* possible for them. Understanding what makes a good relationship sets up a contrast to the misogynistic partnership and also helps women to set goals they can work toward.

What Makes a Good Relationship

Often when I ask clients to describe their partners' attributes I hear such things as: "He's a hard worker"; "He's a good provider"; "He's fun"; "He spends lots of time with the children"; "He's charming"; "He's handsome." Certainly these traits and behaviors are attractive. But they are not the underpinnings of a good relationship.

A good relationship is based on mutual respect and a relatively equal balance of power. It involves concern for and sensitivity to each other's feelings and needs, as well as an appreciation of the things that make each partner so special. Of course, within this ideal there is room for arguments, bad moods, differences of opinion, even anger. However, loving partners find effective ways of dealing with their differences; they do not view each encounter as a battle to be won or lost.

A good relationship, in other words, should enrich and add to your life, not narrow it by forcing you to give up those things that are integral to your character. We enter into relationships attracted to the qualities we see in our partners. If we are required to lose our best qualities in order to keep the peace, something is seriously wrong.

You Can Only Change Yourself

Early in Jackie's therapy she complained to me:

> Why do I have to learn to do things differently when if Mark would just stop being such a bully I wouldn't have any problems at home?

I told Jackie what I tell many of my clients: *You cannot change anyone else's behavior but your own.* The good news, however, is that once you begin to change your responses to your partner's behavior, the relationship itself must change along with you.

Jackie didn't want to give up her belief that if Mark could just see things her way he would stop being cruel to her. Nancy had a similar belief. She said, "I know that if Jeff knew how he was making me feel, he wouldn't act this way with me." However, the fact was that both men could know exactly how they were making their wives feel and still not change their behavior. In addition, their partners' understanding was something over which neither woman had any control. I told both Jackie and Nancy that trying to get their partners to "see" would ultimately be a tremendous waste of energy.

With this in mind, I am going to ask you to throw away contemporary buzz-words like "communication" and with them all the techniques for "letting the other person know how you feel." They don't apply to misogynistic relationships. There is no magic phrase that will unlock your partner's ability to *see* what he has been doing. He doesn't want to see and he doesn't want to communicate. *He wants it his way.* He hears your expression of hurt feelings as an attack on him, which means he will counterattack. Therefore, trying to communicate with a misogynist is fruitless. It's a lot like trying to teach a bull to sing. It doesn't work and it irritates the bull.

What this all boils down to is that *you* are the one who has to learn to do things differently.

But before you can begin to do things differently you must get some control over how you are feeling. The following strategies are designed to help you do just that.

STEP ONE: BECOME AN OBSERVER

One of the first distancing strategies I suggest to my clients is that they become observers of their reactions to their partners' attacks.

I told Nancy to say to herself after each confrontation with Jeff: "How interesting! Every time he's upset with me I feel . . ." (she was to fill in the blank with whatever emotion she felt). At our next session she reported:

> I had carried the groceries from the car into the kitchen when Jeff came in. Right away he started telling me how to put everything away and then yelling at me that I wasn't doing it right, what a slob I was, and how I didn't give a damn about doing anything right. He stood there barking orders and telling me how I was doing it all wrong. Afterwards, I sat down quietly and made up a list of what I had felt when Jeff was attacking me. It was the first time I ever noticed how my hands started to shake and how angry I got. Once I started watching how I was reacting, I could feel it.

Nancy's list of things that happened to her during each confrontation began with: "*Every time he's mad at me I feel . . .*" She soon found that Jeff's attacks left her feeling "angry, scared, shaky, hurt, outraged, defenseless, and overpowered."

Try doing this same exercise. The next time your partner attacks you, try to notice exactly what is happening to you. Afterward, sit down and make up a list of your reactions, both emotional and physical. Head your list "*Every time he attacks me I feel . . .*" and then list whatever you can recall.

Written lists provide you with clarity and focus. They enable you to organize your thoughts and to see how you have been reacting all along. Once you have learned to do this, you will have gained some distance from the turmoil itself, because observation automatically gives you distance. As a result, you will feel less overwhelmed by your emotions.

You'll notice from this exercise that there is a consistent pattern to your reactions. Identifying these reactions will diminish their intensity because they will become predictable. You won't be so panicked or surprised by them the next time there's an incident.

In addition to listing your reactions, take note of how long they last. Nancy reported that although her shakiness and fear subsided fairly quickly, some of her other emotional reactions hung on for several days. Her feelings of hurt and anger lasted the longest.

The more you are able to identify and clarify your feelings, the more predictable your reactions will be and the less off balance you will feel.

STEP TWO: CHOOSE TO CONTINUE TO BEHAVE EXACTLY AS YOU HAVE BEEN

Many of my clients are surprised that I don't ask them to change their behavior at this point. Instead, I ask them to do exactly what they have been doing, with one crucial difference: *recognize that the choice to behave as they do is now theirs.*

Once you choose to do something, it is no longer automatic or reflexive. It becomes conscious, planned, and within our control. You become *active* instead of *reactive*.

Interestingly, a behavior done out of fear or intimidation feels terrible, while that same behavior done out of choice feels significantly better. Although this may seem like a minor strategy, it is in fact a big step. Choosing the way in which you react will help you to *desensitize* your feelings of powerlessness in your relationship.

When Jackie began to make a conscious choice on the way she reacted to Mark's outbursts, she told me:

He always made me feel so scared and upset that the only thing I could do was try to stop him by apologizing and making nice. But once I took that extra second to *decide* to apologize, I felt less frightened and less like a puppet.

To help Jackie gain more sense of mastery and control, I had suggested that she *continue to apologize*, but that before she did so she was to say to herself, "I choose, as an effective adult, to apologize." This slight shift in attitude made a difference in the way she felt.

Try this relatively simple behavioral strategy. Most likely you will notice a decrease in your emotional distress.

In chapter 9 I discussed the difference between thinking and feeling. Jackie found that by making a conscious effort to change her thought patterns—from "I *must* apologize" to "I *choose to* apologize"—*although her behavior remained the same*, she was able to interrupt her automatic emotional reactions.

STEP THREE: WRITE DOWN ALL THE LABELS YOUR PARTNER HAS USED AGAINST YOU

This exercise has a practical written part and a creative, imaginative part. To start, buy a box of labels. Any kind of labels will do, even the ones used for addressing packages, but the self-adhesive labels found in stationery stores are the easiest to use. (If buying labels presents a problem, take a few sheets of paper and tear them into equal-size pieces. A little glue will do the rest of the work.)

I ask my clients to write a separate label for each negative name their partners have called them. Jackie's labels read: selfish, bitchy, stupid, inefficient, lazy, demanding, castrating, mean.

Make up as many labels as you need to cover every name your partner has called you. Then paste them down on a sheet of paper under the heading "*What he says I am.*"

By doing this, you are making *tangible* the labels that your partner has been affixing to you. The reason I suggest you use actual labels for this task, instead of just make up a list, is that by giving these names solid form and shape you will see more clearly that they are merely what have been *stuck onto you*, rather than realistic evalua-tions of who you are. These labels are symbols that represent how your partner has been treating you.

Very likely your partner has labeled your skills and your effec-tiveness as negative traits. He may have labeled your intelligence "being a wise-ass" or "being a know-it-all," or he may have called you a "smart alec" and said, "No man likes a smart-mouthed woman." Similarly, your competence or success may have been labeled "an ego trip," "self-centeredness," "ruthlessness," "ball-busting," "running a power trip," or "trying to be a man."

To help counteract these negative labels, make up a second group of labels. These will be the *positive* qualities you know you possess.

If you find yourself a little short on positive qualities, include the good things other people have said about you. Head a second sheet of paper *"What I really am"* and paste down all the positive labels you can come up with. I asked Jackie to make her positive labels a di-rect rebuttal to Mark's negative labels for her whenever she could. When she held the two pages next to each other they looked like this:

WHAT HE SAYS I AM	WHAT I REALLY AM
bitchy	gentle
selfish	considerate
stupid	smart
inefficient	competent
lazy	energetic
demanding	reasonable
castrating	supportive
mean	kind

This exercise will help you to begin rebuilding your self-confidence. Don't rush through it. Take time to think about these labels. Let the contrast between your partner's negative names and your real attributes become clear and distinct.

Once my clients have made up their lists of positive and negative labels, I ask them to get comfortable and relax so that they can do some important visualization exercises. The images they create help them to counter their partners' negative labels for them.

We all do visualizations when we daydream or fantasize. Without realizing it, we work through many different situations in life in this manner. We daydream about getting a job we want; we picture ourselves in a new outfit we've seen; we envision our children being graduated from school. An actor friend of mine told me that every time he goes to an audition, he pictures the director and the producer sitting on the toilet. "My anxiety level goes way down when I imagine this," he said, "because how much power can a person wield sitting on the john?" What my friend had done was to make formidable people more human in his imagination. This enabled him to relax and to appear more confident.

For my actor friend, visualization helped to desensitize an anxiety-producing situation. Just as visualizations can help us to attain goals, they can strengthen our images of ourselves. The following exercise is designed to reinforce your positive labels while diminishing the impact of the negative ones.

First, read over both your negative and your positive labels. Then picture yourself as a castle. Around the castle construct a wall made of your *positive labels*. Now imagine that the castle is under seige. Your partner's *negative labels* are arrows being shot at the castle. Picture the negative-label arrows hitting the protective wall of the castle and falling into the moat. They are ineffective against the strength of your positive labels.

The more relaxed you are when you do this visualization, the clearer and more potent the images will be. It is important to do this exercise at a time when you are free from distraction and can let your imagination work. It may take a while before you are able to envision the entire castle scene, but my clients have found that once they have constructed the picture they are able to return to it quite easily. I suggest you use the castle visualization after any attack by your partner that involves negative labeling.

Jackie reported:

> At first I felt silly, but then I figured I had nothing to lose.
> It was after Mark had called me a selfish bitch because I
> didn't want to visit his mother. He got me very upset, so
> I went into the bedroom and sat down and tried the castle
> thing. The first thing that happened was that I saw that he
> always called me selfish if I didn't do what he wanted, and
> then I realized that I didn't have to take what he said to
> heart.

Jackie had been defining herself according to Mark's labels for
her. The castle visualization helped her to see that his opinions of
her weren't necessarily fact and that she didn't have to be frightened
or wounded every time he attacked her character.

Exercises such as this will help to decrease the power of your
partner's attacks on your self-worth. They will also help to reinforce
your positive evaluations of your strengths.

STEP FOUR: PICTURE YOUR PARTNER BEHAVING AT HIS WORST WITH SOMEONE ELSE

In this exercise, visualize your partner screaming, criticizing, shifting blame—or whatever else he does when he's attacking you—but
picture him doing it with another woman. I tell clients to make that
other woman someone they care about, such as a sister, a daughter,
or a good friend.

When you begin running this scene in your mind, notice that
your partner's behavior doesn't change even though he's with
someone else. He has a very limited repertoire of behaviors, particularly with women he's involved with. No matter how charming he
can be at other times, in an intimate relationship he will behave with
any other woman the same way he behaves with you. It has very little to do with *who you are*.

When you visualize your partner behaving badly with another

woman, there are two major awarenesses that you will likely experience:

First: *His behavior is not okay.*

Second: *His behavior has very little to do with you.*

Now ask yourself the following:

Would you want somebody you value to be treated this way? If you saw your daughter (or friend, sister, or mother) being treated this way, what would you want her to do?

Why is it not okay for her to be treated this way but it is okay for you? Aren't you just as important as she is? Don't you have the same rights to good treatment and kindness?

These are extremely important points. Ask yourself these questions and take the time to answer them *often*, but particularly after an attack. Visualize your partner doing to someone else what he just did to you, and then ask yourself these questions again. Expect to get angry. You've been treated unjustly, and anger is natural. Use this anger to strengthen your resolve to change. (I'll show you how to use anger to your benefit in chapter 12.)

STEP FIVE: CHANGE THE WAY YOU SEE YOUR PARTNER

In chapter 1, I described the "romantic blinders" Laura had worn early in her relationship with Bob. But later in therapy with me, she recalled the warning signs:

> There was a voice inside me that was saying: "Watch out. This guy's got a terrible temper and he lied to you about being divorced." Also, I knew he hadn't held a job for more than six months at a time, and that registered. But I didn't let any of *that* matter. I was so in love with him it just didn't seem to make any difference.

Laura had seen a lot about Bob in the beginning of their romance. The same is true for most of us. Usually we know the person we get involved with more than we let ourselves admit, but we choose to ignore the danger signs when they conflict with the romantic picture. However, no matter how hard we push down those unpleasant realities about our partner, there is a small voice within us that tries to get our attention.

At this point in her therapy, Laura needed to turn up the volume on that little voice so that she could evaluate Bob's behavior from a new perspective. I gave Laura the following exercise to help reinforce the part of her that always knew what was going on. It's important that you, too, participate in this exercise.

First, picture your partner behaving irrationally, then ask yourself the following questions:

- Would any reasonable person get so upset over such minor incidents?
- Is constant criticism, picking, and blame-shifting part of a loving relationship?
- Is he just looking for an excuse to attack me?
- Is he blaming me for all those things he doesn't want to take responsibility for himself?
- Does anyone have the right to treat another human being the way he's treating me?

This exercise will validate your inner perceptions of what is going on now; or if you were once in a relationship with a misogynist but no longer are, it will help you to pay closer attention to the same behavioral clues with other men in the future.

If this is the first time that you have experienced full awareness of how unloving and unacceptable your partner's behavior is, you will likely feel quite uncomfortable.

As with all our other work together, I urge you not to allow your discomfort to discourage you or throw you off the track. These perceptions of your relationship are the truth. And, as some smart person once said, the truth hurts. But without the truth you remain a prisoner of distortions and self-doubt.

Go over this list of questions frequently. These recognitions will further motivate you to change your situation. Please remember that it's all right to be angry, to be upset, to cry, and even to feel sorry for yourself right now.

At the same time, however, remind yourself how much courage it has taken just for you to get to this point! Think about the bad relationships you've seen in which people accepted poor treatment without question and without hope of change. *You* are stronger; *you* are trying to change. You are looking at a painful truth, and it's going to hurt. But persevere. Use this list of questions every time you begin to doubt your perceptions and inner voices of reason, every time you find yourself wondering if your partner really isn't right after all, and every time you find yourself making excuses to justify his behavior or taking the blame for his behavior. These questions will get you centered again. Write them down on a piece of paper and carry it around with you. Refer to it whenever your resolve to continue gets shaky or whenever there's a scene between the two of you. Make these questions part of your normal process whenever you think about him. What you are doing is *validating* for yourself what you have always known is true.

SLOW DOWN AND CHECK HOW YOU ARE TREATING YOURSELF

For many women one of the dangers in accepting the truth about their situations is that they may turn their new awareness against themselves. For this reason, I take time out from the work we've been doing to check on how my clients are treating themselves.

Typically, I hear statements like these:

- How could I have been so stupid?
- How could I have let this happen to me?
- I'm furious with myself for being so blind.
- I'm a smart person, so how could I have been so wrong?
- I may be angry at him but I'm even angrier at myself for putting up with it.

It is vitally important that you don't add self-inflicted punishment to the punishment you are already experiencing in your relationship. Instead of putting yourself down for not having seen the truth before, acknowledge yourself for the courage and determination you've shown in looking honestly at yourself and your partner and in making the important and frightening commitment to change your relationship.

The following exercises are designed to help you break your patterns of self-reproach. I developed these interventions specifically to help my clients change how they think about themselves and how they treat themselves when they are hurting.

Thought Stopping

Negative thoughts about yourself will only make you feel more miserable, just at the time when you need all your coping skills to resolve your crisis. To deal with these negative thoughts, try this exercise in thought stopping.

First: Be alert to what you are thinking, particularly in regard to blaming yourself. Watch out for any thoughts such as: "How could I have been so stupid?" or "How could I have put up with this for so long without seeing it?" Also, look out for self-denigrating statements such as: "I hate myself"; "I'm angry at myself"; "I'm sick of being so inept"; "I'm dumb."

Second: In order to stop these self-accusatory thoughts, have a conversation with them. Speak directly to your thoughts as if they were people. I suggest the following dialogue: "Okay, so you're back again. *Stop! Go away!* You can't come in. I have enough trouble without your interference. I don't want you. I don't need you. You serve no useful place in my life, so get out of my head."

Third: Now you need to replace your self-accusatory thoughts and the bad feeling that go with them with good thoughts and good feelings. In order to do this, conjure up a true sense-memory of some wonderful time in your life. Nancy used a vacation memory for this exercise:

> The first time I went to Hawaii, the moment I stepped off the plane someone put a lei around my neck, so that all I could smell was this incredible perfume from the flowers. The air felt gentle and warm against my skin and I thought to myself, "This is paradise."

Find a special moment in your own life to savor and hold on to. Remember how all your senses responded and how good you felt. The more details you can recall, the richer and more satisfying the memory will be. With a little practice, you will be able to put yourself back into the memory and the good feelings at will.

When bad thoughts about yourself arise, *notice them* for what they are, *tell them* to go away, and then use your special memory to *replace them*.

This exercise provides a very good start toward being nicer to yourself. Nancy found that it helped her to interrupt her self-accusatory thoughts. As a result, she felt less emotional pain and less tension. She reported:

> I also got a taste of being in control over how I felt, and that was new for me. I can actually alter those black moods when I get into my Hawaii memories. I have also gotten to see how often I was torturing myself just for having problems!

You may need to practice this thought-stopping exercise many times before you become comfortable with it. It is difficult to break the old habit of beating yourself up when you're feeling bad. However, once this thought-stopping exercise begins to work for you, you will get immediate relief from much of your self-inflicted pain.

Nurturing Yourself When You Are Hurting

Like many of my clients, you've probably spent a great deal of your life taking care of other people. Most women are very skilled at nurturing others. If someone you care about is feeling hurt, alone, and miserable, you know exactly what to do to make him or her feel better. I now want you to use those same skills to comfort yourself. This is a very important part of your preparation for change. You have to learn how to nurture yourself so that you will feel stronger and more capable of tackling your problems.

To begin this phase of our work I ask my clients to make up a list of ten things they would do to comfort someone who was in pain. Here is a sample list:

- Hug them.
- Stroke them.
- Listen to them.
- Assure them that things will get better.
- Fix their favorite meal or snack.
- Take them for a walk in a lovely place.
- Take them out to a show.
- Suggest they take a soothing hot bath.
- Suggest they go for a swim or get involved in some other sport.
- Buy them something that would please them.

Make up a list of your own, with the special things you do to comfort and nurture others.

Things to Do for You

You deserve the same kind of loving attentions that you've been giving to others. Begin now to ask for it. Whether you think you need it or not, ask your children and your friends to hug you; physical contact is extremely important, especially when you are in emotional pain. Begin to devote a certain amount of time each day to doing things that feel good to you. It is essential to your well-being and your mental health that you start taking as good care of yourself as you would of someone else.

Perhaps this seems silly to you; you may view it as pampering or babying yourself, or you may see it as unimportant. However, I assure you that taking care of yourself now is *vitally* important.

The following simple exercises will help you learn how to care for yourself and reduce your stress level. Don't skip ahead, and don't deny yourself this aspect of our work together.

People have a tendency not to take the time to do the things they enjoy, even the simplest and most easily available activities. For this reason, I ask my clients to make a *contract* with themselves. On this contract they list ten simple activities that they agree to do each week. I suggest that each day they do *at least one* of these activities.

Take the little bit of time required to work out a contract list for yourself. Change the activities every few weeks. Try not to approach these activities as if they were medicine. Instead, think of them as old friends you've missed and will enjoy getting to know again.

Nancy's original contract contained negative activities, such as "I will not stay home all day." I had her change these to positive, fun activities she could look forward to. Here is her revised contract:

1. I will take a long bubble bath.
2. I will take a walk on the beach at sunset.
3. I will set aside time to listen to my favorite music.
4. I will hug my friends when we meet and say goodbye.
5. I will go out to lunch with my best friend.
6. I will get a manicure.
7. I will get a massage.
8. I will put on makeup every day.
9. I will start swimming again.
10. I will buy myself some little present every week.

In Nancy's case it was especially important that she do things for herself that involved physical stimulation. Her relationship with Jeff was such that if she wanted physical affection from him, he read it as an invitation to have sex. Sexual relations between them had often been painful and unpleasant for her, so she had stopped seeking any physical affection from him. At this point it was vitally important for Nancy to get some physical pleasure for herself, so I suggested that she swim, take bubble baths, and get massages as often as possible, since she enjoyed these activities.

Jackie, on the other hand, still had a satisfying sexual and affectionate relationship with Mark. On her contract she wrote, "Get Mark to cuddle with me more."

It is very important for you to establish a daily routine where you take time to think about your needs and the things you can do that will give you pleasure. However, thinking about them is not enough. You must *do* them. I urge you to view the contract you make up for yourself as meaningful and binding. If you want to feel better, both mentally and physically, it is essential that you nurture yourself just as you nurture others. Your self-caring activities are the first step toward breaking the painful old pattern of not looking after *you*.

11 | *Healing the Past*

Children have no power. To survive, they must learn early the responses that will enable them to cope with the treatment they encounter in their families. The problem for many of my clients is that they continue to feel in adulthood the same powerlessness they felt as children, even though their current life situations are very different.

As we saw in chapter 7, Jackie's emotional reactions to Mark's mistreatment of her were strikingly similar to those she had as a child when her father was abusive to her. The fear and helplessness she experienced with Mark were directly related to the past. Before her old reactions could be replaced with more effective adult responses, Jackie had to trace them back to their origins. Only by learning how her current behavior was based on old fears that no longer applied could she begin to change her reactions.

This journey back to the past may seem like a detour. Many of my clients get impatient with reexamining their childhood experiences; they are eager to get on with solving their current conflicts with their partners. However, I believe that any new behavior that a woman learns to help her deal more effectively with her partner will become permanent only if she first exorcises those old ghosts from the past that undermine her adult strength.

A Word of Warning

The work we've done together so far has been on a fairly cognitive level—primarily involving your intellect, reason, and thoughts. But even that work may have stirred up some very strong feelings for you. The work I am going to introduce to you now is even more emotionally loaded, for it deals with incidents from childhood. Remembering these incidents can be very upsetting and painful, even for the strongest of us.

I am going to open the door to my office and let you watch some of this work, so that you will see how old events can directly affect current feelings and behaviors. It would be irresponsible of me to suggest that using this book on your own is sufficient to get you through this kind of difficult work. When a woman is in counseling, either individual or group, there is a built-in support system available to her, so that intense emotional responses can be handled. *I urge you not to do this work without such a support system in place.* A therapist, a therapy group, or any other resource such as a women's center, which provides a safe place for you to deal with strong feelings, can be extremely valuable.

While friends can sometimes be quite helpful, a friend cannot provide sufficient support for you when you are trying to handle painful childhood memories. Even the best-intentioned friend will feel inadequate and helpless in the face of the pain and discomfort that may surface when you dig up old experiences.

In addition, if you were a victim of physical and/or sexual abuse in your childhood, I urge you to seek professional help so that you can lay these old demons to rest before attempting new behaviors. There are now self-help groups for victims of child abuse all over the country. There are also a growing number of therapists who specialize in this type of work. Therapy in this area can be extremely effective. It has been my experience that the damage caused by sexual and/or physical abuse is both accessible and specific, and for that reason problems in this area yield to help fairly quickly.

The more traumatic a woman's childhood was, the more damaged her self-esteem as an adult will be. But, no matter how great the damage, tremendous healing can and does take place once these old experiences are confronted and worked through.

It Didn't Start with Your Partner

Nicki told me that when Ed was angry at her she felt small, put down, inadequate, and humiliated. When I asked Nicki to try to recall who else in her life had made her feel that way, she remembered the following incident, which occurred when she was nine years old:

> It was very important to my father that I learn to play the piano, even though I wasn't all that interested in it myself. Nonetheless, I tried very hard to be good at it to please him. But playing in front of people terrified me, and every time I had to perform I blew it. My father wasn't the sort of man who ever raised his voice. He'd get quiet and cold instead. At the recital I was so nervous that I forgot a whole section of the piece I had to play. Afterwards, on the way home, he told me he didn't know how he was ever going to be able to look any of those people in the face again. He said I'd disgraced him in front of everyone and that I was a terrible disappointment to him. He said that it was a lot worse than the fact that I simply seemed to have no talent. I was careless and thoughtless as well and I was too lazy to practice. I was crushed. I'd wanted so much to please him and I'd failed utterly. I held back my tears but I was so humiliated I just felt like dying.

Nicki was very surprised to see that in her marriage she was re-creating her childhood and losing her adult self. To help her get more in touch with her childhood I asked her to bring me a picture of herself as a little girl. When we looked at the photo together, she began remembering many similar incidents in which her father had humiliated her.

To help her to appreciate how young and vulnerable she was when all this happened, I asked her to go down to the local grammar school. She was to watch the children playing and pick out a little girl who reminded her of herself. Then she was to imagine that little girl being berated and put down the way she had been as a child. Nicki needed to recognize that she was that small and defenseless when those painful incidents had happened to her, and that it was this little girl, still living within her, who became so frightened when Ed became abusive.

WHY LOOKING BACK IS ESSENTIAL

It's a mistake to think that if we don't remember or don't acknowledge painful experiences they will just disappear. In fact, great damage is done to us by those phantoms and pieces of memories that swim around in the unconscious, the part of us that never forgets. Unpleasant experiences gain power over us by being denied or hidden, but they can be made to relinquish that power when they are brought out in the open.

Dealing with Feelings from the Past

Working on childhood experiences can stir up a powerful combination of anger over old hurts and grief for the little girl who had to endure them. Acknowledging and dealing with these feelings is a prerequisite to diminishing their control over adult life.

Handling Old Anger

When Nicki began recalling incidents from her childhood she realized that she had a great deal of anger about how she'd been treated. She saw that she'd always had this anger but had never felt able to express it. As we've seen, anger that isn't expressed doesn't just evaporate; it goes underground, where it gets disguised as various symptoms.

The more old anger is pushed out of conscious awareness, the more frightening it becomes. Anger is an uncomfortable emotion for most of us, and repressing it makes it even more uncomfortable.

Nicki found herself remembering many times when she had tried to please her demanding father and had instead met with his disapproval, rejection, and contempt. I urged her not to be frightened by the strong anger these memories provoked and instead to let herself reexperience it. I knew she would find it much less frightening than she imagined.

To help Nicki focus and direct this old anger so that it wasn't overwhelming, I asked her to imagine that she was talking to her father. Using an empty chair to represent him, she was to say all the things she'd always felt but had never been able to tell him. She was to begin with "how dare you" and then finish the sentence. Here is what she said:

> How dare you treat me like that! How dare you humiliate
> me the way you did! Who the hell did you think you were? I
> always looked up to you. I worshipped you. Couldn't you
> tell how much you were hurting me? Nothing I ever did was
> good enough for you. You made me feel like a total failure,
> you bastard. I would have done anything for you, just to get
> you to love me a little.

Nicki was trembling when she finished this exercise. She saw that she'd gotten really angry at her father for the first time in her life and yet nothing terrible had happened. She *could* allow herself to express her anger!

For some of my clients, verbal expression of anger isn't sufficient to release it; they need to act it out physically. I encourage these clients to get a lot of physical exercise during this phase of our work. Playing tennis, racquetball, or other aggressive sports can help the body to release anger and tension.

Nicki, too, needed a physical release from her anger. Although she was an active policewoman and an accomplished athlete, she still carried a lot of tension in her body and frequently suffered from tension headaches and muscle spasms in her neck and shoulders.

My office provided the controlled environment where we could do some of this work together. I asked Nicki once again to picture her father in the empty chair, and then to ventilate her anger physically by beating on the empty chair with a padded foam bat, called a bataka, which I keep in my office. After considerable resistance, thinking she would look foolish doing this, she finally agreed to try the exercise. Raising the bataka over her head with both hands, she brought it down on the chair with a loud *thwack*. She repeated this motion until it became a rhythmic movement. I told her to put words to her rage. As she beat the chair, years of pain came welling up, and she said over and over, "How could you treat me like that? How could you put me down all the time? How could you? *How could you?*" After about thirty seconds Nicki burst into tears and dropped the bataka. I put my arms around her and held her until she'd stopped crying.

After a few moments, when she had calmed down, I noticed that her body was more relaxed. Nicki told me that although it had been frightening to reexperience that rage, she felt much better.

The more Nicki and I worked together, siphoning off her old anger in manageable doses, the more comfortable she became with it. It was a tremendous breakthrough for her to see that she could get very angry, tolerate the feelings, and then pull herself back together again and feel all right.

Because reexperiencing anger is so upsetting, I monitor this work very closely. I don't push my clients further than they are able to tolerate at any given time, and I am careful not to let them leave my office raw and flooded with emotions. Before Nicki left that day I had her relax, close her eyes, and remember a wonderful experience in her life. (This is the exercise I described on p. 183, Thought Stopping.) I asked Nicki to recapture all the physical and sensual memories and not to leave that place in her mind until she felt calm. I always close off highly emotional work with such relaxation techniques.

Although working with angry feelings is dramatic and powerful, I do it not because it is theatrical but because it *works*. Expressing repressed anger in a safe and controlled environment is one of the best antidotes to feeling like a helpless child.

REVISING OLD OPINIONS

We all believe our parents' opinions of us. The story of Nicki's piano recital is a good example—she took her father's critical evaluation of her as the truth. When he called her lazy, careless, thoughtless, talentless, and a disgrace, she believed him. From her little-girl perspective, these were not the words of an angry, critical man. They were fact.

Children don't see that abusive or overly critical treatment is something that is being done *to* them. Instead, they see it as something they have caused by their own failings. When these children reach adulthood, they continue to believe that they got the treatment they deserved. They believe they were being justly punished for their faults.

For Nicki to get free of the negative messages she had received about herself as a child, she needed to bring them out in the open and take a look at them. Having already identified many of the incidents that colored her feelings about herself, she needed now to look at the negative opinions she had internalized about herself as a result of those messages.

When I asked Nicki to make a list of all the bad things her father had told her about herself over the years, she came up with the following:

My Father's Negative Opinions of Me
- I am inconsiderate.
- I am selfish.
- I am thoughtless.

- I am talentless.
- I am inadequate.
- I am an embarrassment to my family.
- I am disappointing.
- I am ungrateful.
- I am a bad person.
- I am a failure.
- I am shiftless.
- I am lazy and will never amount to anything.

I knew that Nicki, as an adult, pushed herself very hard both in her work and in sports. When I asked her to list what she said to herself when she occasionally fell short of her superwoman ideals, she showed me this:

What I Tell Myself When I Fail
- I didn't try hard enough.
- I don't really care about getting ahead.
- I can't even fool myself with that performance.
- If I weren't so lazy, maybe I would have gotten somewhere.
- I'm just incapable of doing anything right.

Nicki immediately saw that she was as harsh a critic of herself as her father had been. She had taken up where he had left off. I asked her to go back to the list of her father's opinions and to write across it in a large, firm hand, *It wasn't true then and it isn't true now!*

At this point Nicki told me that her father had told her some positive things about herself as well. He'd frequently complimented her intelligence, her athletic ability, and her good looks. However, because criticism and negativity colored so much of her relationship with him, and because negative input tends to have more impact than positive input, it was difficult for her to believe his occasional compliments. Ultimately, they only confused her.

Most people had during childhood at least one consistently kind, supportive person who valued them and said positive things about them. For Nicki that person was her mother. For others, that person might be a grandparent or other relative, or it might be a friend of the family or a schoolteacher. Nicki needed to remind herself of how her mother saw her. I asked her to make up a list of her mother's positive opinions of her.

> *My Mother's Positive Opinions of Me*
> • I am smart.
> • I am sweet.
> • I am charming.
> • I am generous.
> • I am talented.
> • I am a hard worker.
> • I am good-natured.
> • I am full of energy.
> • I am lovable.
> • I'm a joy to have around.

After Nicki had made up this list, I said to her, "Isn't it interesting how few of those good labels have been incorporated into your opinion of yourself as an adult?" To help Nicki internalize these neglected positive opinions of herself, I had her write at the bottom of this list, *This is true and always has been.*

I then asked her to perform a ceremony to help rid herself of the negative opinions she had accepted as truth so long ago. She was to do the following:

> *1.* Take the list of negative opinions home with her.
> *2.* Tear the list into as many pieces as she could.
> *3.* Burn the shreds, bury them, or flush them down the toilet.

Nicki told me that she had felt somewhat foolish doing this ceremony but that it had definitely helped to diminish the power of her negative opinions. She had not only destroyed the bad labels for herself but had begun to reclaim some of her good feelings about herself.

Learning to Reparent the Little Child

Nicki now realized that there was a part of her that had been truly hurt when she was little. The child she still carried around inside her had been criticized and picked on so much by her father that she had grown up desperately seeking male approval. Without this approval Nicki felt inadequate and frightened. She needed to heal and reparent the little child so that she could begin to get some of that approval from within herself. To accomplish this, she needed to say to herself, both out loud and through letters, what she's always yearned to hear from her father.

I asked Nicki to write a letter to the hurt little girl inside her. She was not to express any of her negative feelings about herself in this letter; rather, she was to focus on things she as an adult would say to a child who was hurt and upset. Nicki was to tell the child all those loving and tender things she herself had wanted to hear when she was little. This is the letter she wrote:

Hi, Sweetie,

I am really sorry that you got put down so much. You didn't deserve it. You were really a good little girl and I know how much you wanted to do everything right so that everybody, especially Daddy, would love you. But it just didn't work out that way, did it? I think Daddy did love you but he just didn't know how to show it. He bought you lots of things, but I bet you would have traded them all for a big smile and a pat on the back once in a while.

I want you to know that I love you and I'm going to take care of you. I'm going to make sure that nobody else hurts you like that again. You can count on me. I'll never leave you. You are a very special little girl. I want you to know that. You're funny and cute and I know how hard you try to be good and to do things well, and you don't ever have to play that rotten old piano again if you don't want to!

Love from Big Nicki

Many people have a difficult time letting go of their contempt and hatred for the hurt little child they used to be. I've even heard clients insist that they were horrible and ugly as children. Writing the letter to the hurt child within helped Nicki to lift the burden of guilt and self-blame she'd accepted from her critical father. She saw now that as a child she had been an innocent scapegoat of her father's frustrations, and this insight freed her from much of her harsh self-criticism. This process of placing the responsibility where it belongs helps not only to free the innocent child but to help the adult self to be less vulnerable and needy.

As an adult, Nicki had to learn that no amount of approval from the outside would be meaningful to her unless she was secure in her feelings of self-worth. Therefore, the more she could heal the hurt she had experienced as a child, the less would be her frantic need for other people to make her feel good about herself.

Nicki became skillful at identifying those times in her adult life when the voice of her critical father returned to berate and criticize her. She saw how essential it was to push out that harsh voice and replace it with the loving voice she was learning to use toward herself. As a result of the work we did together, Nicki's demeanor began to change noticeably. She was more at ease with herself, her expression softened a great deal, and her body was less rigid. She was making genuine progress in being kinder to and less critical of herself.

Ending the Power of Old Messages

To reinforce the changes Nicki was experiencing I suggested one more exercise to end her father's control over her.

I asked Nicki to imagine herself at a graveside. In the grave was the power her father's negative messages and opinions had over her. I handed her some dried flowers that I keep in my office for this purpose and had her repeat these words:

I hereby lay to rest all of the mean and hurtful things my father said to me when I was little.

I hereby lay to rest the power his criticism had over me.

I hereby lay to rest my hunger for his approval and his praise.

I also bury in this grave my fantasy that my father will one day be the father I always wanted.

Rest in peace.

As with any burial ceremony, there was grief and mourning. Letting go of her fantasy that somehow she would find the magic key and get her father to be the loving parent she'd needed as a child made Nicki very sad.

As an adult, Nicki needed to recognize that her father was limited in what he could give her. He had certain ingrained character traits that had caused him to be hard on her. Accepting the reality that she wasn't going to change him, that nothing she could do would turn him into the warm and loving father she'd yearned for, was very painful for her. She had to accept that if she were going to get her father's love and approval she would have gotten it long ago.

Nicki found sadness and resignation in accepting all this, but there was also a great deal of freedom. All the energy she had spent in the fruitless search for her father's love could now be used in the pursuit of activities that were positive and meaningful to her.

Fears of Being Angry at a Parent

Nicki asked me the same question most of my clients ask when they have contacted their anger at a parent: "Will this work we're doing damage my current relationship with my parent?" Nicki voiced it this way:

Now that I've reexperienced my anger at my father and realized that he isn't going to change, maybe it'll ruin those times when we see each other. After all, he was really a good parent. He never hit me. He tried to give me whatever he could. He sent me to college. He worked hard for all of us. I feel very disloyal for getting so angry at him.

I told her that she could hold on to the parts of her relationship with her father that were good, while letting go of the control he had over her feelings about herself. Now that she was being honest about her feelings toward him, she could expect that the relationship would become one of adult to adult, instead of withholding parent to needy child.

Repressed anger is the single most stressful, toxic, and ultimately destructive element in human behavior. Now that Nicki had let go of her old anger and seen that it was not the frightening monster she'd always believed it to be, she was ready to deal with her anger at her husband, Ed.

Because people are afraid of their anger they don't learn how to channel it, manage it, or express it. In the next few chapters I will show you how I teach my clients to use their anger, both old and current, as a great motivator and energizer. Once a woman can really get angry at her partner's treatment of her, it becomes impossible for her to stay stuck in submissive behavior.

12 | Taking Charge of Your Anger

Paula started her therapy in one of my incest-victims groups. In childhood she had been both physically and sexually abused by her father. Her repressed rage over those terrible crimes had permeated her life. When she married her psychologist husband Gerry she had an understandably low self-image and was already set in the victim role. Once I'd helped her to come to grips with her traumatic childhood, she had to deal with the sad admission that she was also being mistreated by her husband. She was then faced with the task of handling her anger toward him.

Getting in Touch with Anger at Your Partner

The first thing I had Paula do was to write Gerry a letter. She would not send or give him this letter; its purpose was to help her to focus

her thoughts and feelings about Gerry and their marriage. I asked
her to structure the letter along the following guidelines:

- This is what you did to me.
- This is how I felt about it.
- This is how it affected my life.

I told Paula not to worry about feeling sorry for herself but simply
to let it all pour out without holding back. This would be her moment of truth.

Here is the letter she wrote:

Dear Gerry

When we met in college you were so understanding and
so kind. You were the first person who really listened to me
and I was so in love with you that I was ready to do anything
for you. You said you'd protect me and take care of me and I
wanted to believe that. I was still living with my crazy family
then and I couldn't wait to get out of there. I was thrilled
when you asked me to marry you. You were going to be my
safe harbor.

But the moment we got married everything started to
change. You started finding fault with me, with my work, with
everything I did. Instead of being kind and loving you were
picking on me all the time. You made me feel terrible about myself. I trusted you and loved you but you got nastier and
meaner. You used anything you could to beat me down. I never
knew what I did to make you change toward me so much. I
blamed myself and kept trying and trying to win back your
love, but nothing I've done has been good enough or right. It's
been torture. Now I know you were only trying to completely
control me, but you were so ruthless! You started saying I was
"damaged merchandise" because of my father and what he'd
done to me. That was so rotten and heartless of you! I was
eight years old when he started in on me. You know I couldn't
stop him. How dare you use that against me! You more than

anyone else knew how guilty and ashamed I felt about it; and yet you didn't care. You were the first man I'd really trusted but you weren't really worthy of my trust. Do you have any idea how much that hurt me, still hurts me? I'm not sure I can ever forgive you for your cruelty in using that against me.

I allowed you to control my life. You told me what to read, what TV shows to watch, and where we could go on vacations. I haven't made one decision since I've been with you except to give up my work because you never stopped criticizing and ridiculing me. I've been just like a robot! I've done as you wanted, but now I'm asking myself why I gave up my rights as a human being.

Now I think I must have been crazy. I've been with you for over eighteen years and I have no confidence or self-esteem left. I allowed you to control me because I loved you. But now that I'm thinking about the things you've done, I've begun to think I have the wrong idea about what love is.

It's not just me you are mean to. You bully the children all the time too. I'm always having to make up to them for the cruel things you say to them.

I don't know when you started cheating on me but I can't remember a time when you weren't comparing me to other women and letting me know how inadequate and unattractive I was. Then it turned out some of these women were your patients. I should have guessed that by the kind of intimate things you'd tell me about them. What kills me is that when you got caught for having sex with them, you not only blamed them for betraying you but somehow you made it all my fault! I hadn't given you enough love and support! It sounds so crazy to me now, but I bought it. I sat there in that courtroom with you and listened to hours of testimony on what you'd done. I was going to be the "good wife" and stand by you in your hour of need. Have you any idea how humiliating it was for me to do that? To have everyone look at me like I was some sort of fool and then to have you accuse me, as if I were the criminal.

You can't take responsibility for anything, can you? Everything is always somebody else's fault. When Holly was born brain-damaged you even blamed that on me! You've never been a father to her. You act like she's not even your child. I've been all alone with my problems in dealing with her. All the times I wanted you to help me cope, you turned away and acted like I'd brought a leper into the house.

You never ask my opinion on any issue. You discount me as a human being. You're just a self-centered little boy! You have to have it all your way or you throw a temper tantrum. Just who the hell do you think you are, behaving that way? How dare you humiliate me and take me for granted and ignore my feelings like you have? I can't believe I let this happen. I must have some crazy ideas about love and duty, but I'll tell you this: You are not going to control me anymore. I am not going to allow you to treat me the way you have all these years. Not anymore. I swear it.

Paula

Paula was angry and hurt, and when she read her letter aloud to her therapy group, she broke down and cried a few times and had to stop reading until she'd regained her composure. It was an extremely emotional experience for everyone, including me.

Here was a woman who had been passive, depressed, and a victim much of her life. Yet, in her letter to her husband there was a commitment to change her behavior. She'd come a long way in her work, and it was exciting to see her starting to express herself as an adult rather than as a frightened child.

Do's and Don'ts of Dealing with Anger at Your Partner

Paula's letter to Gerry stirred up a great deal of rage. But her anger at him was different from her anger at her father. Her father wasn't active in her life anymore, so of course he was no longer abusing her. Gerry, on the other hand, was extremely active in her life: he was mistreating her on a daily basis. Her anger at him had just surfaced, and naturally she wanted to do something about it—and, like many of my clients, she wanted to do it *immediately*.

DON'T MAKE LIFE DECISIONS

I always caution my clients not to make major life decisions in the heat of the moment. Their judgment is colored by the flood of emotions that are being stirred up. Unless a woman is in physical danger in her relationship, this is not the time to impulsively run to a lawyer or to pack up and leave home.

DON'T TELL HIM OFF

Paula was ready to tell Gerry off or at least to show him her letter. I advised her not to do so. Although I certainly understood her desire to do this, I knew it would not work, for the following reasons:

- He was a master at winning with her.
- He was a master at changing the subject, rewriting history, and sidetracking.
- He would deny whatever she said.
- He would not "hear" her.
- He would blame her for everything, as he always did.
- He would make her back down.
- He would intimidate her.

Like any misogynist, Gerry would experience confrontations, challenges, or complaints about his behavior as assaults on him. Gerry didn't know how to listen to Paula or how to view his role. All he knew how to do was counterattack. For Paula to unleash a torrent of rage at him now would not be any more productive than turning her rage in on herself had been in the past. Further, she would run the risk of irreparably damaging the relationship. If ultimately she decided to leave him, she needed to make that decision from a position of strength, not when she was in an emotional crisis.

Her dilemma now was what to do with all the rage she'd contacted. She was going to be living with Gerry while she was still furious at him. I could help her to siphon off some of that anger, but there was no way to make it all disappear. Instead, Paula would have to learn how to *tolerate* her anger, in the service of becoming an effective adult—a difficult task, but one well worth trying.

Do Find Outlets for Your Anger

Paula's group-therapy sessions provided a safe environment in which to siphon off some of her rage. Use of the bataka, role-playing, and letter-writing also helped to diminish much of her anger in a manageable way.

I also encouraged Paula to get as much physical activity as she could, even if it meant that she would be very tired for a while. I recognized that with four children she couldn't get out very often, so I suggested things she could do at home to help alleviate her distress.

Paula was an artist and could express a great deal of her anger through her work. The pictures she painted during this time aren't likely to hang in any museum, but doing them helped her a great deal. She made a hideous portrait of Gerry, which she worked on whenever she felt angry at him. She also got a lot of satisfaction out of working with clay.

In addition, Paula bought a bicycle and while the children were at school she pedaled furiously through her neighborhood. This helped her to feel less trapped and also made her feel better physically, and she was amazed to see how much energy she had. She had never before realized that her anger could be a source of energy. (In fact, many top athletes and performers use this trick of transforming anger into physical power.)

Anger is a biological response to frustration or insult, and when it is physicalized much of it can be diminished. Any type of exercise—even housecleaning or washing the car—can help.

Stop Feeding Your Partner's Bad Behavior

When Paula's anger became manageable, she had to face the unpleasant truth that almost all her efforts to get Gerry to treat her decently had failed. In fact, her characteristic ways of handling his attacks had actually been feeding and reinforcing them. Every time she defended herself, pleaded with him, or became hysterical, she was being *reactive* rather than *active*; she was doing exactly what he wanted her to do. Her submission and placating gave him clear signals that she was overwhelmed and helpless, which ultimately left him in control.

Many women believe that by yelling back at their partners they are actually standing up for themselves. Of course, this type of behavior is usually ineffective. *If a woman is not actively stating what she will or will not accept, she leaves her partner in charge.* She will appear just as out of control when she's yelling and screaming as when she's pleading or crying. The misogynist has won if he has gotten his partner overwrought, no matter how she displays it.

Following is a list of behaviors that will not work for you. See how many of them are part of your style of reacting to mistreatment by your partner.

- Apologizing
- Pleading
- Crying
- Arguing
- Defending yourself
- Trying to get him to see it your way
- Yelling
- Threatening

Beyond these responses is a whole treasure chest of effective behaviors that many women have simply never learned to use. Before I teach my clients these new behaviors, however, I first have them decide what it is that must change in their relationships.

The Misogynist Has Defined the Relationship Until Now

Gerry had defined how Paula should think, feel, and behave. This gave him a monopoly on what was "right" in their marriage. Her feelings and needs were given no consideration. If any changes were to occur in the relationship, Paula's input had to be respected. To begin this phase of our work, I suggested that Paula start to get into her vocabulary the following phrases:

- This is what I think.
- This is what I believe.
- This is what I will do.
- This is what I will not do.
- This is what I want.

She was to *decrease* her use of these phrases:

- I'm sorry.
- Is this okay?
- Do you agree with me?
- Do you like it?
- If you're going to get upset I'll do what you want.

People who feel good about themselves are able to say, "I can tell you my opinion and let you like it or not like it." In a good relationship there can be two opinions. As we've seen, in the misogynistic relationship only the misogynist's opinions are permitted, and he decides how his partner may express herself.

For Paula to get in touch with what she wanted from her marriage, *as opposed to what Gerry would permit her to have*, she had to define *for herself* her needs, her wants, and her limits.

Defining What You Want

When I asked Paula to make up a list of the things she wanted from Gerry, she came up with the following:

Things I Want
- I want respect.
- I want to be allowed to express myself.
- I want to be heard.
- I want to be taken seriously.
- I want kindness.
- I want understanding.
- I want the right to have my own beliefs and opinions.

These are some of the things you might want from your partner as well. In addition, you may want changes in the power balance in your relationship. If so, your list might include items like:

- I want to be an equal partner in matters concerning money.
- I want my sexual needs to be as important as his.
- I want an equal voice in making decisions that affect both of us.
- I want respect for the work that I do (whether in or out of the house).
- I want us to participate in activities that are important to me, not just the ones he selects.

Don't be afraid to be extremely specific when you make up your list of *wants*. The better you define your wants and needs, the closer you will be to becoming an effective adult. Go into detail about your sexual needs; outline the specific financial arrangements you would like. The more you know about what you want, the better are your chances of getting it.

In addition to your desires relating to better treatment and the balance of power in your relationship, you may have some important *personal* goals. Consider this list:

Things I Want for Myself
- I want to go back to school.
- I want to spend more time with friends and/or family.
- I want to get a job.
- I want to improve my career opportunities.
- I want more help with the housework.
- I want more help with the children.

Make up a list of your particular personal desires. Again, be very specific. Vague statements such as "I want to be happy" or "I want to feel better" do not give you focus or tangible guidelines to begin changing your relationship.

Paula had some very specific complaints about Gerry's treatment of her. I encouraged her to make a list of the behaviors that she would no longer permit. After you read through Paula's list, make up a list of the things that you want to stop permitting in your relationship.

Things I Won't Permit Anymore
- I won't permit him to yell at me.
- I won't permit him to insult me.
- I won't permit him to constantly criticize me.
- I won't permit him to discount me.
- I won't permit him to control me and tell me what to do.
- I won't permit him to humiliate me.

When you make up lists such as these, you establish parameters for yourself and your relationship. Without guidelines it's difficult to learn how to set limits on your partner's bad behavior. You need to know what you can tolerate, will tolerate, and will not tolerate, as well as what it is you want for yourself and for the relationship.

Reclaiming Your Adult Rights

One of the major sources of anger for many of my clients is the sad recognition that their basic human rights have been trampled in what was supposed to have been a loving relationship. To remind these women of their rights, I have written a *Personal Bill of Rights*. Read over these rights. Make them part of your work.

Your Personal Bill of Rights
1. You have the right to be treated with respect.
2. You have the right not to take responsibility for anyone else's problems or bad behavior.
3. You have the right to get angry.
4. You have the right to say *no*.
5. You have the right to make mistakes.
6. You have the right to have your own feelings, opinions, and convictions.
7. You have the right to change your mind or to decide on a different course of action.
8. You have the right to negotiate for change.
9. You have the right to ask for emotional support or help.
10. You have the right to protest unfair treatment or criticism.

There is nothing in this Bill of Rights that is abusive or that attacks anyone. Don't be concerned if these rights sound self-serving to you or if they seem to be in conflict with things you've been taught about what you deserve or can expect in a relationship. These are your basic rights and they must be respected.

13 | Setting Limits With Your Partner

Up until now I have shown you techniques and exercises that I use with my clients to help them change the way they see themselves and their partners and to help them recognize and clarify their feelings. None of those techniques involved dealing with your partner in any direct, confrontational way. Now, however, we will enter the most challenging arena of all: *changing your behavior with him*.

I have been very specific in cautioning you about some of the emotional work I do because it can be too overwhelming or painful for you to attempt on your own. The work in this chapter, however, is *behavioral* rather than *emotional* in nature. It involves some risk-taking, but it is not likely to flood you with rage or grief. These behavioral changes, which are not difficult to learn, can greatly affect the power imbalance that is likely to exist in your relationship. Even if you have been following along up until now without doing the exercises I've suggested, this work can be enormously effective for you.

Rewriting the Script

Women in misogynistic relationships tend to get locked into scripts with their partners in which each plays an assigned role: if he yells, she apologizes; if he criticizes her, she defends herself, etc. To help my clients change the outcome of these little dramas, I first help them to write new scripts.

Paula told me that Gerry became enraged if his dinner wasn't ready when he walked through the front door. When I asked her what she did when this happened, she said, "I tell him I'm sorry and then I try to find some excuse that will calm him down while I scamper around trying to get dinner fixed as fast as I can." Other women give similar responses in this type of situation, using excuses such as:

- I'm sorry, I couldn't get to the market.
- I'm doing the best I can. I'm working hard too.
- I had to work late at the office.

The problem with responses like these is that they are *defensive*. You are immediately placing yourself in a one-down position when you give "good reasons" or explanations for why you didn't do something your partner wanted you to do.

Paula needed to learn some nondefensive responses. I told her to try one of the following the next time Gerry flew off the handle about dinner:

- You're right, dinner isn't ready.
- I don't blame you for being so upset.
- Perhaps I'll do better next time. I'll try.
- Let's eat out instead.

Paula found that this approach had an unexpected payoff: It enabled her to get off her "automatic pilot" responses. She recognized she had some control over the interaction. It also gave Gerry little opportunity to continue his tirade. When she stopped defending herself, she took much of the steam out of his attack.

Paula was beginning to see that Gerry was responsible for his irrational outbursts. If it wasn't a late dinner that he was upset about, it would have been something else. If she allowed herself to get into an argument in which she defended herself, she would lose this important perspective; she would be so preoccupied with protecting her position that she would not see that he was behaving irrationally.

It was a revelation for Paula to discover that the late dinner was not the real issue. It was simply an excuse for Gerry to escalate his psychological warfare against her and to convince her that she didn't care enough about him.

It's very easy to get caught up in an argument. But the very explosiveness and amount of the misogynist's anger is a signal that the anger is inappropriate to the subject at hand. *The anger is about something else.* A reasonable person does not get as upset as Gerry did over a late dinner. Remember, the misogynist has a bottomless pit of rage inside him and it takes very little to set him off. He experiences a late dinner as a direct attack on him, and no amount of pleading or explaining will convince him otherwise.

Nondefensiveness is a good tool here because it is not a form of capitulation. It enables the woman to gain some distance and control without getting swept up in her partner's irrational reactions.

In order to change your relationship, one of you has to start behaving like an adult. It's not likely to be your partner. By using nondefensive responses, you begin to set up a climate that is less explosive. It is essential to establish this climate before you can begin to actually set limits on his behavior.

The Importance of Setting Limits

To take the next step toward rewriting the old script, you must learn how to set limits on your partner's behavior. You will need to clearly define to your partner both what you want and what you will no longer tolerate. Your guidelines for this appear in the lists you made in chapter 12, *Things I Want for Myself* and *Things I Won't Permit Anymore* (see p. 210).

Nicki was terrified at the prospect of challenging Ed. Whenever she had confronted him before, she had been met with a barrage of intimidating tactics that made her back down. Paula's attempts to challenge Gerry had sometimes gotten her a few apologies, but he didn't change his behavior for long, if at all. Therefore, both Nicki and Paula had to give up their old ways of approaching their partners. The same is true for you. You know that the old patterns don't work, but that doesn't mean that nothing you can do will make a difference. Changing *your* behavior *will* make a difference. And even if changing your behavior doesn't change the relationship as much as you'd hoped it would, it will still help you to feel a lot better about yourself.

Like many of my clients, you may experience some stage fright as you prepare to act out the new script. Just think of it as opening night and try to push past your fears. To help with the jitters I always suggest a little rehearsal time. Memorize the phrases below that apply to your situation. Get comfortable with them as part of your assertive vocabulary. Don't try to use them yet, however; just rehearse them to yourself.

New Assertive Statements

- It is not okay for you to talk to me this way.
- It is not okay for you to treat me this way.
- Screaming isn't going to work anymore.
- This is one time you can't intimidate me.
- I know that this has always worked before, but I want you to know that it's not going to work anymore.
- I will not stand here and be screamed at.
- I will discuss this topic with you when you've calmed down.
- I will not accept being put down by you.
- People who care about me don't treat me this way.
- You've controlled me with this behavior in the past but I want you to know that that's over.
- I'm not the same person I used to be.

More Rehearsal Time

When I ask clients to change a behavior, they usually experience a rush of resistance and panic. They fear that awful, catastrophic things will happen if they change. One of the most effective ways I've found to relieve this panic is to give the client ample time to rehearse her new attitudes and dialogue in a safe, risk-free environment. Remember, the more rehearsal you do, the more natural a new behavior will feel when you use it for the first time.

I suggest that your first rehearsal take place alone and in private. Put an empty chair in front of you and picture your partner sitting in it. Imagine that he has begun an attack on you. Pick one of the phrases listed above, such as "I will not stand here and be screamed at," and say it out loud. Repeat it until it comes out sounding strong, believable, and natural.

Now imagine your partner reacting to your new behavior. Allow yourself to experience whatever anxiety comes up. Let both the physical and emotional reactions you usually have to your partner's outbursts rise to the surface. Get used to those reactions; accept the fact that some of them may always be with you, even as you become more active and assertive. The old feelings have been with you a long time and they are very tenacious. However, as you become more successful with new behaviors, these old feelings will get less intense and the discomfort they cause will not last as long. Because you will know what to expect, you will go through the frightening episodes more quickly.

While you are practicing alone with the empty chair, imagine your partner continuing to attack you verbally while you hold your ground, no matter how insulting or humiliating he becomes. Respond only with the phrases from the list, even if you start to sound like a broken record. Remember, you are testing your new strength and resolve.

The following exercise, which may seem quite strange to you, has helped my clients to reinforce their resolve to change and to see that they can't resume their former behavior.

Using the same empty chair, imagine your partner sitting there. Now get down on your knees in front of him and say these words:

> I am a miserable, worthless, disgusting wretch.
> You are powerful, all-knowing, and wonderful.
> I will continue to accept any abuse you heap upon me.
> All your criticisms of me are true.
> You can treat me any way you like and I'll take it.
> I will give up myself in order to get your love.

Most clients feel furious, humiliated, and disgusted with themselves after doing this exercise. One woman told me that she would never have said any of these things to her partner in real life. I agreed with her—no one in her right mind would say such things. However, I asked her, "Hasn't your *behavior* with him been saying these very things all along?"

As a result of doing this exercise, many women realize that although they have not been saying these things aloud, they have been communicating them through their submissive behavior. Remember, it is behavior, not words, that lets other people know what they can get away with in their treatment of you.

Rehearsing with Someone Else

For some of this work, rehearsing with someone else can be more effective than rehearsing alone. Having another person there brings the situation that much closer to reality. This person can be a trusted friend or a relative. It should *not* be one of your children. Make the following agreement with the person:

1. He or she will not judge you.
2. He or she will not give you advice.
3. He or she will support whatever feelings you express.

This person is there to support and encourage you, *not* to tell you what to do or what to feel. I suggest you use a friend rather than a relative for this work, because friends tend to be more objective than family members.

In the following exercise your friend will play the part of your partner. To demonstrate to your friend how your partner behaves with you when you are alone together, pick an unpleasant event from the recent past and act out what happened and what he said to you. For example:

> **YOU** (as your partner): What's the matter with you? I told you to write down that appointment I had. Now I missed it and it's all your fault. You just don't give a damn about me, do you? You just go around with your head up your ass all day. You're selfish. What have you got to do that's so damned important that you can't do a simple thing like this for me?

Use your own dialogue and situation. If your partner is a screamer, scream. If he's a critic, criticize.

While you are acting out what your partner does, notice what *you* are experiencing. You're in his shoes for the first time. If you're really acting like him, you'll see that your behavior is cruel and infantile. Let this experience help to reinforce your commitment to change the situation.

Now that you have demonstrated to your friend how your partner behaves and what he says, your friend will play him, while you play yourself saying some of our new limit-setting statements. For instance:

> **YOUR FRIEND** (as your partner): What's the matter with you? I told you to write down that appointment.
> **YOU** (as yourself): I will not stand here and be yelled at. We will talk when you've calmed down.

Obviously, whatever situation you use, your response should be appropriate to your partner's style of attack.

The simulation of his behavior by another person will intensify your anxiety, because it gets closer to what you will have to deal with when you try this new behavior with your partner. This rehearsal, which is very important, is the bridge to setting limits in the relationship itself.

In addition to learning new things to say, you will learn new things to *think*. You will actually be changing your communication on two levels: *what you say to him, and what you say to yourself.* Think about what goes through your mind in these confrontational scenes between you and your partner. Make a list of what you usually tell yourself when he's attacking you and call it *Old Thoughts.* Nancy wrote down these old thoughts:

Old Thoughts
- He's angry with me.
- I can never win.
- He's going to hurt my feelings.
- I'm helpless.
- Why can't I ever think of anything to say to him?

These statements in Nancy's head had played a big part in keeping her too frightened to challenge her husband, Jeff. Now she had to learn to *interrupt* these old thoughts and replace them with new thoughts. Try these new thoughts for yourself when your partner frightens you:

New Thoughts
- I'm an adult.
- Yelling can't destroy me.
- I can stand how I'm feeling.
- I don't have to make it better or try to fix things.
- He's responsible for his behavior, not me.
- He's behaving like a spoiled brat.
- He's acting like a big baby.
- He's out of control.

What you are doing is using your ability to *think* in order to step back so that you will not get swept up in the intense emotions of the moment. This enables you to break your old patterns of responding. Remember that your old automatic thoughts and reactions will not disappear. Rather, as you change your thinking process, the new thoughts will gradually push out the old ones, and as a result your feelings will change as well. Old thoughts keep us stuck; new thoughts help to free us.

Setting Limits with Him

Until now you have been rehearsing under controlled, predictable conditions. Now it is time to use these new behaviors in the real situation. Your partner is a master of control and intimidation, so your first instinct likely will be to back down in fear. But stay with it. It will be worthwhile.

When Paula reached this point she got cold feet. She told me, "I can't do this. It won't work anyway. I've survived all these years with things the way they are. It's too risky to try to fix it now."

To help her prepare, I had her go back over the *New Assertive Statements* (p. 215) until she was comfortable with them. When the next incident occurred with Gerry she was to use the statements that applied. I reminded her that she was neither attacking him nor leaving herself open to attack. Rather, she was setting limits on what she would and would not accept from him.

At our next session, Paula reported:

> I'd been out with the children and got back in time to start dinner, but Gerry, for some reason, was early that day. He was furious that I wasn't there when he got home. He started carrying on about where I'd been and then went into his old routine of how I spent too much time with the children and neglected him. My first instinct was to tell him where we'd gone and why it was important, but I stopped myself. I told him, "I won't stand here and listen to this." He wasn't making any sense and I wasn't going to defend my-

self. I said, "I won't tolerate your yelling at me." He was so shocked he went white. I was shocked too, that I'd done it. Then he switched into his psychologist routine, which is his other favorite number when all else fails. He said, "Are you premenstrual?" When he saw I wasn't reacting, he went on, "I'm really getting worried about you. Your behavior lately just isn't normal. I suspect it's that therapy you got yourself into. It's making you very cold and calculating." Even though my hands were shaking by then I could see how funny this whole thing was. He was trying to make everything my fault just because I'd stood up to him. I don't know where I got the strength, but I stayed with it. I told him this type of thing wasn't going to work anymore. I was not going to discuss my therapy with him. That did it. He stormed out of the house, slamming the door as hard as he could. He came back after a few hours and sulked all evening. In the past, that would have been my cue to apologize and try to make things nice, but this time I resisted and just let him stew in his own juice.

People like Paula, who have lifelong patterns of being submissive and frightened, often have a tremendous rush of excitement and hope when they take a risk with a new assertive behavior and see that they can survive the experience. When Paula told this story in group, she beamed with pride and a sense of accomplishment. She was amazed that just trying her new, assertive behavior made her feel more powerful and effective in her marriage. Of course, getting accustomed to behaving assertively would take work, but she saw progress immediately. Every time she set limits on Gerry, by letting him know what she would or would not stand for, she got stronger, more sure of herself, and more determined to continue on her new course.

KNOWING WHAT TO EXPECT FROM YOUR PARTNER

When you question or threaten an infantile, insecure person, his response usually will be to escalate his old behavior in an attempt to return the situation to its former state. After all, his behavior has always worked in the past; more of it might work now. Therefore, expect your partner's abuse to increase. To help yourself get through it, remind yourself that you have a great source of power in the relationship: *he is enormously dependent on you.* He will do anything to keep you because he is terrified of being abandoned and alone.

By setting limits and initiating these new self-defining behaviors, you are upsetting the balance of power in your relationship. When you begin to claim some of the power that was owned by him before, expect him to fight you; he's not going to give up his control easily. He may become even more of a bully and a tyrant. He might withdraw, threaten to leave, or try to punish you. Remember that he is a frightened child inside, and that his bullying, controlling behavior is an attempt to cover up his insecurities. It may help you now to remind yourself that only frightened people behave like this. *No one who feels good about himself needs to control another human being.*

Some misogynists respond to their partners' new strengths with a very different kind of manipulation: tears, apologies, and promises to change. When these misogynists act like hurt, scared little boys, they can seem so pathetic that almost any woman would give in to them. However, whether the misogynist uses bullying and threatening or crying and pleading, his goal is the same: to get his partner to give up her attempts to change the relationship and to reestablish the comfortable balance that existed for him before.

All of your partner's reactions are further proof that *you* are the stronger of the two, because you are the one who is willing to take some risks with new behavior, you are more in touch with your feelings than he is, and your survival doesn't depend on dominating and subjugating another human being.

When Gerry became more abusive in response to Paula's new behavior, she sometimes found it difficult to recognize how much power she had in the relationship and how strong she was. If you are experiencing similar difficulty, I suggest you try this shift in your perspective: instead of the old message tape that went, *What's wrong with me that he treats me this way?* use *What's wrong with* him *that he's behaving this way?* This new view will go a long way toward helping you to hold your ground and tolerate your feelings while your partner is becoming increasingly more abusive. Try saying these sentences to yourself when he begins to carry on:

- I don't have to fix it.
- I can stand how I feel.
- He's responsible for his behavior, not me.

In addition, continue to remind yourself:

- Who I am is not dependent on his opinion of me.

Like many of my clients, Paula cared too deeply about the way she appeared to others. It had been essential to her that Gerry saw her as "okay." Once she had struggled free of her intense need for his approval, she realized how destructive and painful it was to allow her sense of self-worth to be dependent on another person's whim.

HOLDING FAST WHILE YOUR PARTNER'S ABUSE IS ESCALATING

Over the next few months, Gerry tried all kinds of strategies to get Paula to give up her new behaviors. He threw tantrums, sulked, became even more critical of her, used his professional expertise to play mind games against her, and began leaving the house for hours at a time without telling her where he was going, making sure each time that he slammed the door loudly behind him. Fortunately, Paula was able to see this behavior for what it was: bravado and bluster designed to get her back in line. She held her ground, and, ultimately, her tactics worked.

There is no way to predict how long it will take for you to see results of your new behavior. There is no way to know how many times you will have to assert yourself and set limits before something starts to shift in your relationship. However, the longer the relationship has been going on, the more firmly entrenched your partner's behavior patterns are likely to be, and therefore the more resistant he's liable to be to change. Also, in a long-term relationship, his dependency is likely to be greater, so his *fear* of change will be greater as well. But don't be discouraged. The important thing is that each time you act in a new way it becomes easier for you, even if your attempts don't produce results immediately. As I explained to Paula, "The relationship didn't get the way it is overnight." She would have to repeat her new, assertive behavior many times before Gerry would take her seriously.

TEACHING YOUR PARTNER HOW TO BEHAVE

Because the misogynist appears to be unaware of how hurtful his abusive behavior is, it becomes his partner's job to show him how to behave. Paula had to make clear to Gerry which of his behaviors made her feel good and which were unacceptable to her.

She would actually be using some simple behavior modification techniques. Part of this involved not reinforcing or rewarding Gerry's negative behavior by responding to it in her old ways. Another important part involved expressing to him her appreciation when he was kind and loving.

I told her that when Gerry was especially nice to her, she should begin her sentences with any of the following phrases:

- I really appreciate it when you . . .
- Thank you for . . .
- I love it when you . . .
- It was nice of you to . . .
- It really makes me feel good when you . . .

Gerry often brought home magazines from his office for Paula to use in her collages, which was thoughtful of him. I told her to be sure to let him know how much she appreciated it. When she did so, Gerry's whole face softened. "He was like a delighted little kid," she said.

Gerry gradually began to treat Paula differently as a result of her behavior changes. Once he saw that she meant business and that the climate between them had altered, he developed a grudging sort of respect for her.

Some misogynists will soften up and become friendlier once they see that they can't push you around anymore. If this happens, more closeness and equality can develop between you.

Getting What You Want for Yourself

Once you have set limits and won some respect from your partner, you will be in a position to approach him about the things you want in the relationship. To begin, refer back to the lists on p. 210; in which you defined your desires and needs. Now narrow down your desires to a few key points so that you won't barrage your partner with too many demands at once.

When I asked Paula to narrow down her desires and focus on what she could realistically expect to put into action at this point, she came up with this list:

- I want an equal voice in money matters, but . . .
- I'm willing to start with my own checking account and my own money.
- I want someone in to help me with the housework and the children.
- I want Gerry to stop being so verbally abusive to the children.
- I want to convert part of the house into a studio for myself so I can paint.

When I asked Paula which item on her list she thought Gerry would most resist, she said, "That's easy. It's the money. He doles out an allowance and then makes me account for every single penny of it." Therefore, we decided to work on the money issue first. If she could handle the most difficult item, she could handle the others.

Paula first had to define very clearly for herself how far she was willing to go if Gerry refused to budge on this major issue. She was clear that she did not want to leave him. With four children, one of them brain-damaged, and no immediate way of supporting herself, she didn't feel ready to make it on her own. But she was willing to get a part-time job. I told her, "That's got to be more than an empty threat if you're going to use it. You have to *mean* it." She replied, "I *do* mean it. Unless I have my own money and can make my own decisions about how to spend it, I'll continue to feel like a child on an allowance."

Although Paula had become a pro at expressing herself assertively, when I asked her what she would say to Gerry about the money issue, she was at a loss. Our conversation continued:

> SUSAN: Well, why not say something like, "It's really important to me that I have my own money in my own checking account. I consider this basic to my self-respect."
>
> PAULA: I can hear his answer to that already: "You don't know how to handle money. I'll decide how the money's going to be handled as long as I'm earning it. Besides, you have nothing to complain about. There's plenty of food on the table."
>
> SUSAN: Then you need to say, "I don't think you heard me, Gerry. I want my own money, and if we can't negotiate something between us, you leave me no choice but to get some kind of job where I get paid for the work I do."

Recognizing that Gerry was volatile and unpredictable, I suggested that Paula rehearse several times by herself how to *tell* him what she wanted, not ask him for it. I also suggested that she speak to him at a time when he was calm.

When Paula did approach Gerry, he responded predictably. But she held her ground, and finally he gave up, yelling "This is total blackmail, but if it means that much to you, all right!" They agreed to meet at the bank a few days later to open a checking account in her name. Gerry then tried to sabotage her again by failing to show up. Paula called me, very upset.

I suggested that she take a look at the want ads in the newspaper and mark off very clearly four or five suitable positions; she was then to leave the paper where Gerry would be sure to see it. Paula objected: "But isn't that a game?" Of course, I agreed, this *was* game-playing, but there seemed little else that Paula could do, because Gerry still wasn't taking her seriously.

The game—and her determination—worked for Paula. Over the course of the next month, Gerry transferred funds into a separate account for her and agreed to maintain it. She was delighted. This seemingly small victory also opened the way for Paula to get other things she wanted, including better treatment for the children.

I am certainly not implying that Paula now has a terrific marriage. Gerry is still infantile and very demanding, they still have a troubled sexual relationship, and he is unwilling to seek counseling. However, Paula has managed, with much hard work and determination, to make dramatic changes in her behavior and the way she feels. She is less depressed these days. She has a studio over the garage, where she paints; she has even sold a few of her pictures. She gets out with her friends more often, and she has help with the housework a few times a week.

Most important, Paula has recognized that Gerry, *not she*, is responsible for his bad behavior. She no longer internalizes his negative comments about her. Some of his remarks still hurt her deeply, but she recognizes them as the expressions of an insecure and frightened man trying to grind her down in order to make himself feel safe. As she said to me in our last session: "I'll probably always have to be his 'good mommy,' but that's a price I'm willing to pay."

In setting limits on your partner's behavior, remember, *your goal is not to change him but to change how he treats you!* You cannot overhaul a man's basic personality by setting limits. However, you can teach him how to treat you better by clearly defining what you will and won't accept. As a result, there will be less emotional chaos in your relationship. It is a slow process, and it takes courage, but it works.

A Word of Warning

When you do anything that will escalate the misogynist's abusive behavior, there is always the danger that he will cross over the line from psychological battering to physical battering. A man who has never struck a woman in his life might impulsively resort to violence when he feels vulnerable. This is a desperate attempt to reestablish control. He is liable to see his partner's newfound strength as "pulling away," which can be very frightening to him. Since his old methods aren't working, he may resort to more violent ones.

Nowhere is it more important to set limits on a man's behavior than when he becomes violent. I have shown you how to set limits verbally; but words are useless in dealing with physical force. If your partner does lose control and becomes violent, *you must get away from him.* You cannot reason with a violent man. Because you are in danger, you must remove yourself from his presence, and if there are children remove them also. Remember that you teach him how to behave by what you do. *If you stay when he is physically violent, you are teaching him that you will accept more violence.* Therefore, go to a relative or a friend, or go to a battered-women's shelter, even if you haven't been battered but just pushed around. Just be sure to *get away from him!*

If physical violence has been part of your relationship, do not attempt any new behavior until you have gotten help with this very dangerous problem. I recommend two books on the subject: *Battered Wives*, by Del Martin, and *Getting Free: A Handbook for Women in Abusive Relationships*, by Ginny NiCarthy. (You will find full information about these and other books in the bibliography.)

If you have had to leave the house for your own safety, the first thing you'll want to know is, "When can I go back?" My professional advice is that this is not the time for you to try to handle things on your own. Your partner may never hit you again, but there is no way to be sure. You will be living with the threat of violence hanging over you unless you insist on getting counseling for both of you. This is a problem that no woman can be expected to handle without professional intervention. If you must go back to get clothes or money, *do not go back alone*. Take a friend or relative with you. The stronger you are during this critical period, the less likely your partner will be to behave violently with you again. That is why it is vital that you be very firm in what you do. If it is *your* home or apartment that you have left, and your partner refuses to leave so that you can return, don't be afraid to call the police for assistance in getting him out.

Remember, it is a sign of courage and strength to seek help when you need it.

14 | Getting Professional Help

If you've done the work I've suggested, your relationship likely has calmed down and become more equitable. However, the situation may still be a long way from where you'd like it to be. Even though you've taken risks and initiated new behaviors, there may be many situations that you simply cannot handle with your partner. As a result, you might find yourself slipping back into your old, destructive behaviors. If this is happening to you, it is time to consider getting professional help.

Many people still cling to the idea that to need such help is a sign of weakness; they believe that we can both diagnose and cure our own emotional problems. Of course, this is simply not true. To seek help when you need it is a sign of courage, strength, and intelligence. If you've tried on your own but can't reach a level of satisfaction in your relationship, therapy may be the answer.

The Relationship Is the Patient

When Nicki discovered Ed's affair, she wanted to leave him, but she decided to stay when he pleaded with her for another chance. After a brief second honeymoon, the marriage soon reverted to its former state, and Ed resumed his affair. His possessiveness, domination, and infidelity caused Nicki excruciating emotional pain. When she tried to tell him how she felt, he quickly turned it back on her, saying that it was her problem, not his. When he said, "If you choose to be miserable, go right ahead. There's nothing I can do about it," Nicki began to believe she was the one who was "sick." Ed further convinced her that if she could learn to control her behavior and her emotions, everything would be fine in their marriage. It was at this point that Nicki started therapy with me.

Nicki and I worked together until she was calmer and felt better about herself. However, her marriage was in serious trouble. If it was to survive, I told her, it was essential that Ed, too, come in for treatment. Since both were responsible for the breakdown of their marriage, both had to work to put it back together again. The *relationship* needed to be the client.

Predictably, Ed was very resistant to the idea of entering therapy. He agreed to see me only after Nicki had threatened to leave him if he did not do so.

Ed turned out to be an exceptional man. After his initial resistance, he worked hard in our sessions and was willing to face his private demons, both past and present. At our last session together Ed made this remarkable statement:

> I really believed that there was nothing wrong with me. It was all her and her problem. Even my affair was her fault because I thought she was frigid. It was really a jolt to come in here and see that I was the one who was being cold and cruel, especially to her. I didn't see it before. I think one of the worst things I went through was seeing that I'd turned her off sexually.

It's been hard to own up to my part of the problems, but now we're both really enjoying each other in every way. I'm not worried about her running around, I'm not sitting in my patrol car imagining her having fun with someone else. We have a real marriage now, instead of a power struggle, and it feels great.

I was thrilled to hear this. The old persecutor-victim cycle had been broken, and the relationship had that genuinely loving quality that is so heartening to see.

Unfortunately, Nicki and Ed were the exception, not the rule. I and many of my colleagues, both male and female, have seen very few misogynists in therapy.

Generally, misogynists view therapy as a threat to their control and dominance at home. The feelings that motivate change—guilt, remorse, anxiety, and sadness—are not a significant part of the misogynist's emotional range. Therefore, these men are not good candidates for the kind of introspection that psychotherapy demands. In addition, because the misogynist is unwilling to accept responsibility for his part in the trouble and is not hurting enough to be motivated to seek help, when he does find his way into therapy it is usually with the idea that therapy is going to "fix" his partner.

My experience with Mark and Jackie is typical in this regard. Mark came into therapy at Jackie's insistence and presented himself to me as a man madly in love with his wife. He didn't like listening to her in our sessions and seemed totally bewildered by her unhappiness with him. He saw our time together as a kind of social gathering; he told long stories about his childhood and his business problems. He was very funny and charming, but I could see that it was going to be extremely difficult to get him to connect with his inner feelings. The only problem they had, as far as Mark was concerned, was that Jackie's constant harping about his business failures was eroding his self-confidence. He insisted that everything would be fine between them if I could somehow get Jackie to be as loving and supportive as she had been when they first got married. The last session I had with them together went something like this:

SUSAN: Jackie has told me about episodes of tremendous emotional violence on your part. You scream, you scare her, you make her cry, and you insult her. Is that how you treat someone you say you love?

MARK: Well, you know, little Jackie is very dramatic. She tends to exaggerate things. I have a temper. Guilty as charged. But insulting? I've never said anything to that woman except that she was the love of my life, the most beautiful, the most sexy, the most exciting woman I've ever met. Now tell me what's insulting about that.

SUSAN: Are you saying that you have no role in the distress and unhappiness that you are both experiencing at this time?

MARK: You bet I do. I've made some very bad business decisions.

SUSAN: I don't want to hear about business. What about your role in this relationship?

MARK: All I've done is try to give her one hundred and ten percent of myself. I'm not out drinking and carousing with the guys. I never hit her. Nobody's been more devoted than I've been to that woman. But somewhere along the line she got the idea that she had to hold the reins. She's got the crazy notion that she's going to handle all the money and put me on an allowance.

JACKIE: I said that I was going to put my salary into a separate account so I could make sure the bills got paid.

MARK: I haven't been on an allowance since I was knee high and I'm not going to be now. No goddamned woman is going to tell me what to do, little honey.

SUSAN: Money is another sidetrack, Mark. We're talking about abusive behavior.

MARK: Listen, I love her and I want to stay with her. Does that make me a bad guy?

SUSAN: If your behavior is as she describes it, then yes, sometimes you are a bad guy.

MARK: Well, little honey, maybe what you need to look at is the fact that you don't like men very much. Who do *you* go home to at night?

SUSAN: We're not talking about me now. We're talking about you. You're here because your marriage is falling apart—the marriage you claim to value and want with a woman you claim to value and want. But at no point in this entire hour have you recognized that you have at least fifty percent of the responsibility in the problems between you.

At this point Mark stood up and said, "It's obvious that if I'm going to be in therapy it's going to have to be with somebody who understands more about business." With that, he left.

Had I been less direct and confrontive with Mark, he would have been quite content to go on telling his funny stories, giving me a lot of history, and generally being the life of the therapeutic party. Like many misogynists, whenever I turned the spotlight on him, he threw up a smokescreen of words, charm, and jokes. When those didn't work, he tried attacking me. The work that needed to be done was never even discussed.

Unless a man is willing to acknowledge that he is at least as responsible as his partner for the difficulties in his relationship, therapy will not be beneficial to him.

There is, however, a group of men that I call pseudomisogynists who can be very receptive to therapy. These are men who in childhood were doted on extensively by their mothers, and who grew up believing that all relationships with women would be like the relationship they had with their mother—that is, geared to their own needs and gratifications. If the pseudo-misogynist hooks up with a woman who cannot express herself or articulate her needs and who believes that any assertion on her part will lead to abandonment, he may wind up behaving like a misogynist. However, he is not a true misogynist; his unpleasant behavior comes from how he was taught to behave to get what he wanted, rather than from a hatred and fear of women. For this type of couple, counseling can be very effective. He may well be the sort of man who, when confronted with how his behavior upsets his partner, is likely to say, "I never knew you felt that way. I'm really sorry. I'll try to pay more attention to your feelings."

The Misogynist's Resistance to Therapy

Unfortunately, most misogynists, when asked to come into counseling with their partners, respond, "You're the one with the problems. Not me." This standard evasion conveniently throws the entire burden of responsibility onto the woman. Some of the other typical responses misogynists use to avoid counseling include:

- I know how to solve my own problems. I don't need a shrink to tell me how to live my life.
- This is how I am. I can't change. If you want to change, go right ahead.
- I know a lot of people who have been in therapy, and it doesn't do any good.
- We can't afford it.
- The shrinks are crazier than the patients.
- I don't have the time.
- You married me this way. Take it or leave it.

I wish I could offer more hope on this subject, but the unfortunate truth is that it is the rare misogynist who is willing to accept treatment. Sometimes a misogynist will agree to try therapy if his partner threatens to leave him, but in many cases such threats do not work. If your partner's defenses are so set in concrete that he refuses help, there's a good chance that he'd rather risk losing you than risk opening up.

Don't give up hope, however. Many churches and synagogues offer couples a variety of counseling resources and communication workshops. If your partner refuses to try therapy, perhaps he will agree to go to a marriage-encounter weekend sponsored by one of these organizations. These workshops and encounter weekends are short-term and limited, but they can provide you and your partner with a new perspective on your relationship.

Such was the case with my clients Carol and Ben. After twenty-six years of marriage, Carol could no longer tolerate Ben's possessiveness. When he refused to consider marriage counseling, she suggested that they try a marriage-encounter weekend. Ben was willing to do this to pacify her. During that intense weekend, in which they were forced to express themselves to each other, Ben saw for the first time how unhappy his wife was. He realized that his choice then boiled down to losing her or agreeing to seek professional help. I worked with them for a little over a year, and when it was time for them to leave therapy Carol wrote Ben this beautiful letter:

> My Dearest Ben,
>
> When we got married, you were my knight in shining armor.
>
> Those first five years we did a lot of struggling together. We had the two girls and your business got on its feet. That's when you started to get so domineering. You were growing in your career and talking about it all day and night and I was stuck at home with the babies. We'd gotten on two different wavelengths and couldn't seem to get off them. It was a merry-go-round . . . good times, bad times, tenderness and abuse. I knew you needed me but I felt left out of our life together.
>
> You made fun of my desire to get an education. When you finally let me go to school, you persecuted me all the time over it. You tried to sabotage my work over and over again. It's taken me over ten years to get my college degree but I've

finally gotten it. On one hand, you helped by paying, but on the other it was some kind of joke. You even ridiculed me in front of the children about it. I had such love-hate for you, I was ready to leave you, even though I still cared so much about you.

Then we went to that encounter weekend and everything started to change. Once you agreed to come see Susan with me it made all the difference. I really feel good about myself now and about our marriage. We've both grown so much lately. We understand each other more each day. That trust I felt in the early years of our marriage is coming back now. I feel more alive about us than ever before. My love for you has been growing and growing to the point where I feel safer and more committed to us each day. I know we're going to make it work.

I love you tons,
Carol

To see a long-term marriage such as Carol and Ben's open up and change is a very exciting experience. The encounter weekend they shared together sparked the beginning of a new life for their relationship.

Help for You

Even if all your efforts to get your partner into counseling with you fail, you can still get help for yourself. A good therapist can provide tremendous support as well as relief from emotional pain.

If you are in a misogynistic relationship, chances are you have lost much of your self-confidence and sense of self-worth. You have had to accept your partner's definition of you as "not okay" and have come to doubt your own perceptions, so that you no longer know what is real and what is not. In therapy you can express your feelings and get validation for your perceptions, which will help you to take back those pieces of yourself that you renounced for the relationship.

Therapy can also give you a chance to get some distance from the center of the storm. It will help you to sort things out so that you can make new choices and decisions based not on fear but on what is in your best interest. There are many more options open to you than you are able to see on your own.

CHOOSING A THERAPIST

If you've decided to try psychotherapy, your first question is likely to be, "How do I choose the right therapist?" This is not an easy task. There are many therapists and many types of therapy, and it can be very confusing. Basically, you need to find someone with whom you feel comfortable. Even in your first session with a therapist you should feel heard, safe, accepted, and not judged. If you continue to be ill at ease with a new therapist after several sessions, *trust those feelings*. Don't assume that there's something wrong with *you* or that it's your resistance to change. Therapy is based on a combination of the therapist's skills and the personal connection between the therapist and the client. It is an intimate and sometimes difficult process. It follows, then, that the relationship with your therapist is as important to your growth as are his or her knowledge and techniques. Do not waste your time, energy, and money with a therapist who is not truly sensitive to your feelings and needs.

My personal belief is that therapy should be active, directive, and time-limited. The therapist should provide you with a great deal of feedback. Too many therapists sit back passively and contribute little to their clients other than an occasional "uh-huh" or "how do you feel about that?" A therapist who actively guides you toward constructive behavioral change will save you a lot of time and money. *Don't be afraid to shop around*. You are the customer and are perfectly within your rights to ask questions and to get straight answers. Most important, *don't be afraid to trust your instincts*.

To help you in your selection process, here are some things to *watch out* for:

- The therapist sits behind a desk so that there is a large barrier between the two of you.
- You are promised a cure in two or three hours for a large sum of money.
- The male therapist who spends a great deal of time commenting on your attractiveness and/or telling you the details of his sex life.
- The therapist is basically passive and nonresponsive, sitting back and nodding without further comments.
- The therapist tells you that it will take many years to help you.

I don't believe that the gender of a therapist is significant. What is significant is the therapist's attitudes about men and women. Many psychotherapists, and particularly psychiatrists and psychoanalysts, are still trained in the traditional Freudian model, which defines women as deficient, hysterical, and masochistic. The Freudian therapist, whether male or female, often sees his job with the female patient as helping her to adjust more adequately to her "proper" role. Health, in this context, means that the woman has learned to become submissive, nurturing, and supportive of her male partner, regardless of how he behaves. If she has ambitions of her own, she is labeled competitive, castrating, and masculine. Surprisingly, this archaic model still permeates an enormous amount of therapeutic practice.

Some male therapists show a strong bias in favor of men when working with couples or with a woman client. These therapists believe that if there is trouble in a relationship, it must be primarily the woman's fault. I've heard male therapists say, "The relationship couldn't be as bad as she's reporting. Maybe she likes bad treatment so she's provoking him."

Unfortunately, misogynists are alive and well in all professions, and psychotherapy has more than its share. Because the profession cloaks the therapist in the mantle of power and authority and tends to duplicate the parent-child relationship, the male therapist who has never worked through his own personal issues about women may act out his private scenarios with his female patients. This situation is particularly dangerous for a woman whose confidence has already been eroded in a misogynistic relationship. If she hooks up with a male therapist who holds the same negative attitudes about women as her partner does, all the negative things she hears about herself at home are reinforced in the therapist's office. It is vitally important, therefore, that you *pay close attention to how your therapist makes you feel*. If your therapist makes you feel exactly the way your partner does, you are with the wrong person! If you hear any of the following remarks from your therapist, it is time to reevaluate your choice:

- Your husband is only trying to keep some order in the family.
- If you stopped being so self-centered and just gave him more support, you wouldn't upset him so much.
- You are behaving like a bad girl.
- You provoke his anger.
- Maybe you enjoy suffering.
- That's no big deal. Everybody loses his temper.
- If you want him to be nicer, why don't you try to be more of a woman?
- Did you ever think that maybe you are too demanding?
- What man wants a woman who is in competition with him?

Also watch out for these labels:

- Castrating
- Ball-breaker
- Hysterical
- Overbearing
- Controlling

Jackie told me that she had first gone into therapy when Mark's business dealings took them to the brink of bankruptcy. She reported the following experience with her male psychiatrist:

> He'd tell me that I was too hysterical and controlling and that no man wanted a woman like that. He told me not to question my husband's business sense or he'd leave me. Meanwhile, Mark was losing all of our money. We'd lost the house because of his deals, and I was getting frantic. I'd call this doctor and he'd say, "Look, we know the basic pathology is in you. You overreact, you overcontrol. Now be a good girl and leave him alone. Let him make the decisions." And I'd say, "But he's losing everything. It's all going down the toilet." And he'd repeat, "The pathology is in you," and then he just stopped returning my phone calls.

I do not mean to imply by any means that I believe all male therapists are misogynists or that they all behave badly with their female clients. On the contrary, many of my male colleagues are sensitive, caring, and understanding about the problems women have in relationships. I'll always remember a group I co-directed with a young male psychiatrist. One woman was very confused about the problems in her ten-year-long marriage. She related a series of incidents in which her husband had been extremely cruel and psychologically abusive toward her—and then asked what she had done wrong. My colleague responded:

> You are being emotionally brutalized very insidiously and on a daily basis. It's not speculative. It's not a matter of opinion, and it is not a matter of sexual politics. You live it every day. You are really okay except that you haven't learned how to protect yourself.

Because this woman had internalized so many of her husband's negative opinions, being validated by another man was tremendously important to her. I could see the enormous relief and gratitude on her face. She clearly felt that someone had truly heard her—perhaps for the first time in many years.

Therapy with someone who values and respects you is a wonderful gift you can give yourself. Just be sure to be as careful in your selection of a counselor as you would be in picking a doctor for your children. The wrong therapist can do you more harm than good.

15 | Knowing When to Leave

Jackie put into practice all the techniques and strategies I have suggested: she set limits, she worked on her emotional growth, and she even got Mark to come into therapy with her. Unfortunately, her efforts did nothing to improve her marriage. In fact, the situation grew worse. Mark sensed that he was losing his control over her and the children, so he escalated his punitive behavior toward them. As his verbal attacks became more vicious, his periods of calm and charm grew fewer and farther between.

Still Jackie clung to the hope that something would happen to make Mark change. At times her old love for him came flooding back, and after ten years of marriage, she had a tremendous emotional investment in the relationship. But more and more she was faced with the realization that only when she and her children totally surrendered to Mark's irrational demands and control could peace be maintained.

The Breaking Point

For a misogynistic relationship to get to the place where a woman wants to leave, there has to be a breaking point. This moment isn't necessarily the time when the relationship actually breaks up. Rather, it is that point at which the woman sees her partner in a different light, if only for a short time. This moment may occur many times before the actual separation. The incident that causes this moment to occur can be a major event, but usually it is just the final act in a series of similar acts.

Each woman has a different tolerance and therefore a different breaking point. There is no way to predict when that moment will occur that finally pushes a troubled relationship over the edge. For Jackie, it took a nasty episode involving her teen-aged son to change how she saw Mark.

My son had committed some federal offense like forgetting to make his bed. Mark was a fanatic about the house, so it never took much to set him off. He seemed to be going out of his way to get after Greg over any infraction of his crazy rules. This time he told Greg he had to run around the block holding a broom over his head. Greg is fourteen now and he's starting to stand up for himself more. He told Mark he just wasn't going to do it. Mark got furious and started to curse him out. He said, "You pimply-faced little prick. When I tell you to jump, the only answer I want to hear out of you is *how high*." At that moment I looked at Mark and he became really ugly to me. I saw how irrational and cruel he was, and I just knew I didn't want to be with this man. I certainly didn't want my children subjected to this kind of abuse anymore. Something really snapped inside of me. I knew it was the beginning of the end.

Jackie had overlooked, apologized for, or taken the blame for Mark's irrational treatment of herself and her children for many years. At her breaking point she saw clearly that no matter how important Mark still was to her, if she and her children stayed with him she would be making the choice for all of them to have a very unhappy life.

Jackie's recognition that the relationship must end came relatively soon after her breaking point had occurred. Much of her love for Mark had been severed, and she knew there was no turning back. For other women, however, the decision to end a misogynistic relationship may take much longer. These women are torn between their outrage over how badly they've been treated, how they see their partners, and their overwhelming need to hold on to the relationship, no matter how it is hurting them.

The decision to end an intimate relationship can never be made lightly or easily. There is always regret and self-recrimination. Even after they acknowledge that their relationship is destructive for them, many women still believe that deciding to leave is wrong and a sign of failure on their part. In truth, what *is* wrong is to accept cruelty, abuse, and unhappiness. It is a far greater failure to stay in a destructive relationship than to find the courage to end it. If you've done everything possible to try to change your relationship and nothing has yielded or shifted, then staying, when you know how miserable it makes you, is wrong. There is nothing sacred about a bad marriage.

Deciding to Leave

I understand fully the enormous turmoil and pain involved in making a decision of this magnitude. What I've seen, and what I know from my personal experience, is that the period during which this decision is made can be a terrible time for you. I want to assure you that your painful and ambivalent feelings are normal and appropriate, and that, no matter how intense these emotions become, you can endure them. I often ask clients to think of this uncomfortable period as similar to the time after a major surgery: the wound feels awful for a while but it does heal. A relationship that you know is destructive for you can be much more painful in the long run than the temporary pain of leaving, for a destructive relationship is like an open wound—it just continues to fester without ever healing.

Fears of Leaving an Addictive Relationship

The more vicious and controlling the misogynist's behavior has been, the more intensely connected to him the woman is liable to feel. The more she has given up her self-confidence and belief in her abilities, the harder it will be for her to face being on her own. She may even be convinced that she cannot survive without him. Jackie was barraged by fears of leaving Mark once she realized that there was no way to save the marriage. Her worst fear was that she would end up alone in a tiny, windowless apartment with a hotplate. Although this fantasy had no basis in Jackie's reality, it was so frightening to her that it prevented her from making the final decision to leave.

Such panic about never-ending loneliness is the fear I hear women express more often than any other. It is not a panic about having friends and other people in their lives but specifically about whether they will find another partner. Many women fear that if they leave their misogynistic relationships, their romantic and sexual lives will be over.

A woman who feels this terror is liable to think that the only solution is to find another man to fill up her emptiness and provide a buffer against loneliness. Although all the old sayings about not jumping from the frying pan into the fire and that this is no time to think about another man may be true, they don't address the terror many women experience once they've decided to get out of a misogynistic relationship.

I have seen this same terror in my hospital work with drug addicts. If you ask an addict who has decided to stop using drugs what he plans to replace his drug highs with, he becomes frightened. He has only a limited repertoire of things that make him feel good. However, after he has been drug-free for six months, he will have many options available to him that he didn't even know existed before.

If you are addicted to a misogynistic partner, you have no more ability to see your life after leaving him than has the addict who decides to give up drugs. Your solution to your panic about loneliness is liable to be another man. But, just as the answer for the addict is not another drug, the answer for you is not another partner. The answer is first to become "clean." Six months after the misogynistic relationship has ended, you will feel like an entirely different person. Not only will you feel different, but you will see your life in a new perspective. Only when the addictive relationship is over do your options become clear. I tell women to think of this period of panic as "withdrawal symptoms" and that the fear of being without a mate is like the fear of not having another drug to make them feel good. This painful time is an emotional metamorphosis. Once it is completed and the "drug" is out of your system, you will be stronger and will see many more options for yourself than you can envision now.

MANAGING YOUR FEARS OF LEAVING

Jackie's depressing vision of her future without Mark came from her little-girl state. Her desperate fear of being forever alone and miserable stemmed from her old feelings of being vulnerable, helpless, and unlovable. In reality, she had a good job, would probably be able to keep her house, and had the ability to make friends easily. Nonetheless, her desperate fears persisted.

Desperate fears paint catastrophic pictures that define the future and the world in bleak and ominous terms. Desperate fears are usually expressed in absolutes such as *never, always*, and *I can't*. Here are some of the desperate fears I hear frequently from women contemplating the termination of their misogynistic relationships:

Desperate Fears
- I'll never find anybody else to love me.
- I can't make it without a man.

- I will be alone forever, and being alone is the most terrifying thing in the world.
- I will never make another friend.
- I can't possibly handle the children by myself.
- I'll never be able to find a job.
- I'll never be able to support myself and/or the children.
- Everyone will see me as a failure for ending the relationship.
- I'm too old to attract another man.
- He'll destroy me if I try to leave. I can never win with him.

Some women panic more over the prospect of no love or sex in their lives, while others are more frightened about money, jobs, and basic survival. Women frequently overwhelm themselves by not being able to separate their practical problems from their desperate fears of catastrophe. Obviously, there are real, practical problems inherent in ending a relationship. These practical fears come from realistic uncertainties regarding finances, the job market, the difficulties in raising children on your own, changes in your social life, and concerns about what your partner might do if you leave. However, practical fears, as opposed to desperate fears, tend to be expressed in terms like *It will be tough to . . .* and *It will be difficult to . . .*

Whatever your concerns are, you must decrease your desperate fears before you can begin to manage and make plans for the real problems with which you will be faced.

CONVERTING DESPERATE FEARS INTO SOLVABLE PROBLEMS

To help you convert your panic into plans for the future, return to the exercise in chapter 9 in which you learned how to separate your *thoughts* from your *feelings* (see p. 163). There, you saw that *feelings* come from *thoughts*, and that once you learn to alter the thoughts that produce the bad feelings, you automatically alter the feelings as well. This same technique can be used to change a desperate fear into a solvable problem. When you change the thought "He's going to destroy me if I try to leave, and I can never win with him," to "I know he'll be a tough adversary but I'll get the best people I can on my team and I'll fight for what is rightfully mine," disaster turns into a manageable problem.

Below I've paired many commonly held *desperate thoughts* with the corresponding *manageable thoughts* stated as solvable problems.

DESPERATE THOUGHT	MANAGEABLE THOUGHT
1. I'll be alone forever and being alone is the most terrifying thing in the world for me.	I know I will have some very lonely times but I will find ways to bring people into my life. I will re-contact old friends and make new ones.
2. I'll never meet another man.	I don't know what life has in store for me, but nobody does. It may take time, but chances are that I will meet somebody when I'm feeling more confident about myself. First, I'll enjoy my freedom.
3. I'll never love anybody the way I love him.	I may not feel those rollercoaster highs and lows again, but they caused me as much pain as pleasure. Maybe next time I can have a more stable and loving if less explosive relationship.
4. People will see me as a failure if I end the relationship.	Some people may see me as a failure, but I'm doing what's in my best interests. I can survive without anybody else's approval.
5. I'll never be able to support myself and/or the children.	Money's probably going to be tight and we might have to lower our standard of living but we'll make it.

6. I'll never be able to find a job.	I may not get the greatest job in the world right away, but I know I can find something because I'm willing to work hard.
7. I'll have a breakdown if I have to work and raise kids at the same time.	It's not going to be easy with all the responsibilities I'm going to have, but a lot of other women have done it, and I'll give it my best effort.
8. He'll take the kids away from me.	He may try to get custody but his chances are slim. I'm a good mother and I'm going to fight for them.
9. I can't make it in the world without him. I can't even balance a checkbook.	I've been helpless about a lot of things up to now and there is much I have to learn about practical problems, but I'm looking forward to handling the practical aspects of life. Once I do, I won't have to put up with someone standing over me, doling out every penny and keeping me on an allowance.
10. I'll lose all my friends because the friends we have now won't be interested in seeing me once he and I are not a couple anymore.	My social life will probably change and I may lose some of the friends we have now, but I'm looking forward to making new ones who will meet me as an individual rather than as an extension of him.

Notice that the *manageable thoughts* not only restate the *desperate thoughts* in such a way as to make them less terrifying, but that the restatements create some solutions and new perceptions. Make up a similar list of your fears in your particular situation, then reshape them in your own words until your *desperate thoughts* become *manageable problems* to which you can find solutions.

Each time a wave of panic starts to wash over you, go back to this list. Look over your fears and your solutions to the problems. As time goes by and you find out how strong and competent you really are, the fearful thoughts will become more remote. Doing this exercise won't reduce all your fears, but converting them into solvable problems can certainly decrease some of your dread of the unknown.

Dealing with Guilt About Leaving

The fear that a woman experiences in deciding to leave her partner is often accompanied by a tremendous sense of guilt about breaking up the relationship.

GUILT OVER ABANDONING HIM

Rosalind felt so guilty about leaving Jim that it was difficult for her to make a move. During the time they lived together Rosalind's once-thriving antiques business went bankrupt, but Jim still wasn't willing or able to keep any kind of steady job. He drank heavily and was very cruel to Rosalind, picking on her about her attractiveness as a woman and how dissatisfied he was with their shattered financial situation. After four years there was virtually no sexual or physical contact between them. When Rosalind tried to discuss Jim's irresponsible behavior, he would provoke a fight, then would leave her for a few days. These separations were agony for Rosalind.

There were at least a dozen times when Rosalind was certain that Jim had left her for good. She would go through the torture of dealing with the breakup, only to have him return and start the whole cycle again. Rosalind's breaking point came over a minor incident about money. She explained:

He was just waiting for me to make a scene about the money so he could pull another one of his grand exits. I knew what he was after and I wouldn't give in to him. He had some cash that I'd taken out of the shop which was supposed to go for groceries, but when I came in I saw that he had on a new pair of running shoes. I said, "Where'd you get the running shoes?" and he said, "They were on sale. They were only fifty dollars." I said, "Where did you get fifty dollars to spend on shoes?" And that's all he needed. He flew off the handle. He said I'd raised my voice and lost control and he was sick of that. He said if he couldn't do what he wanted, he was going to leave. I was so sick of him by then that I just said, "Good. Pack up and get out." But the moment the door closed behind him I knew if he came back I'd take him in again. I know he hasn't got any place to go. I can't abandon him when I know how much trouble he has getting jobs. I'm not going to be just another woman in his life who didn't stick by him just because times got rough. I'd feel too guilty to do that.

Rosalind's guilt over her imagined abandonment of Jim was so great that she continued to allow him to drag her down. She had rescued him so often and for so long that she had come to believe that she owed it to him to take care of him.

Rosalind's relationship with Jim sounded like the relationship between a mother and an irresponsible child. She had been confusing *being needed* with *being loved*. It was important for her to recognize that rescuing Jim never had worked and never would. Unstable, irresponsible people do not get rescued; they continue to fail over and over again, and often they wind up hating their rescuers for making them feel even weaker.

Jim believed that he remained in charge of the situation with Rosalind only if he could leave her whenever he wanted to. Each time he provoked a fight and a separation, he was giving himself the illusion of power and adequacy in the relationship, when in truth he was living like a dependent child.

As Rosalind began to accept the fact that Jim was not going to change, she needed to decide whether her guilt over leaving him was more intolerable than the pain of letting him continue to drag her down emotionally and financially. To help her see how much of her commitment to remain with Jim came from guilt and not love, I asked her to make up a list of reasons for staying in the relationship.

Why I Want to Stay
- He needs me.
- I love him.
- I can't bear to hurt him.
- I can't mess up another relationship.
- I've gone this far with him. I can't leave him now.
- I don't want to be alone again.
- This is still better than nothing.
- No one this good-looking is ever going to be interested in me again at my age.
- When it's good between us it's terrific.
- He can't make it without me.

Rosalind began to see that few of her reasons for wanting to stay with Jim had anything to do with the quality of their relationship.

While she was struggling over the decision to leave him, I suggested that she fortify her resolve with a list that looked at the negative side of the ledger.

Why I Want to Leave
- He makes me feel terrible about myself.
- Nothing I do is ever good enough for him.
- I can't seem to give enough to please him.
- He won't make love to me anymore.
- He's financially irresponsible.
- He's ruined my business and my credit rating.
- He won't get help or take responsibility for any of his problems.
- He insults and humiliates me in front of other people.

- He picks on me about my body and how old I am.
- I'm starting to hate him.

Rosalind was finally able to see that much of her guilt stemmed from her misplaced sense of responsibility to take care of Jim and manage his life for him. I pointed out that the longer she continued to feed Jim's need to be taken care of, the longer she delayed the time when he had to take care of himself.

Rosalind's two lists helped her to see that her love for Jim had been severely damaged by his poor behavior. The only time she felt good in the relationship was when she rescued him and thereby felt needed by him.

We all weigh our decisions mentally, but making up lists like Rosalind's can set out the pros and cons very clearly for you. Rosalind saw that there was little fulfillment for her in staying with Jim. She knew it would be difficult to refuse to take Jim back when he inevitably returned, but she found the strength to do so once she realized that there wasn't much of a relationship left between them.

GUILT ABOUT BEING TAKEN CARE OF BY HIM

When Jeff didn't respond to any of Nancy's efforts to change herself and their relationship, she began to think seriously of leaving him. Her guilt over this decision took a different form from Rosalind's. Jeff was a responsible, competent attorney who made an excellent living and was well respected in his profession. Nancy's guilt about breaking up with him stemmed from the fact that throughout their four-year marriage Jeff had carried the entire financial load. She told me:

> I know I should leave because I'm so miserable with him. I look in the mirror and I can't believe what's happened to me physically in four years. But I still feel like I haven't got the right to just walk out because he's done so much for me. We have this beautiful house. We take all these incredible va-

cations, and socially we're very much in demand. Then when I start thinking about how many times he's mortified me in front of people and how stingy and selfish he is, and how sexually sadistic, I get angry all over again. But I know he loves me and wants me. I start thinking maybe I haven't tried hard enough to make things work out.

Nancy's reaction was typical of those I hear from women who have been "taken care of." To many women, being taken care of means that they owe a peculiar debt of loyalty to their partners.

I explained to Nancy that being loyal didn't mean having to accept mistreatment or lack of respect for her feelings. I also pointed out that she had been a partner in the marriage and had worked very hard to make Jeff happy and to provide him with the kind of home and social life he wanted. Once she saw that her guilt over leaving him was unrealistic, making the decision to leave him became easier for her.

Guilt About the Children

For women with children, there are additional burdens of guilt. These are some of the things I hear from mothers who are contemplating separation or divorce:

- How can I do this to my children? They need their father.
- I can't deprive him of his children.
- The children will be damaged by a divorce. Everyone knows how hard divorce is on kids.
- My parents are divorced and I vowed I would never do that to my children.
- I don't have the right to break up this family just because I'm unhappy.

These concerns are understandable, but many of them are based on false concepts. There is no evidence that children need two parents in order to grow up into healthy adults. But there is a great deal of evidence that children raised in an environment of tension, conflict, and abuse either reenact these behaviors in adulthood or become withdrawn and depressed and take on the role of the victim. Divorces are difficult for everyone, but children can and do survive, provided they have the guidance and continued presence of one loving adult. Children benefit far more from your strength and your ability to make decisions based on reality than they do from staying in a home where they see you tyrannized and are often tyrannized themselves.

GUILT FROM FAMILY AND FRIENDS

Although the decision to divorce or end a relationship is a personal one, friends and/or family members may contribute to a woman's guilt about her decision by trying to make her change her mind and stay in the relationship.

In deciding whether to leave, you will need all your courage to withstand the onslaught of well-meaning advice givers. It may help you to remember that family members often have strong philosophical or personal reasons for discouraging you. These reasons may have little to do with what's best for you and your children. Family members may see your decision to break up the marriage as a reflection on them. You may hear things like, "There's never been a divorce in this family before"; "Your father and I stuck it out. Why can't you?" or, "It can't be as bad as you say. After all, he isn't beating you."

I give my clients specific tools for dealing with this kind of input. Nondefensive, self-protective responses can help to shield a woman from the guilt created by other people's disapproval. Here are some phrases you might use to assert yourself when family or friends become judgmental and critical:

- I'm sorry you feel that way, but this is my decision to make on my own.

- I know there's never been a divorce in the family but I can't let that influence me.
- I know you stuck it out but I don't choose to do that.
- I need your support and understanding, not your advice.
- Thanks for your concern, but I don't choose to discuss it.
- This subject is off limits.
- I am not doing this to hurt you. I am doing it for me.
- Stop blaming yourself and stop blaming me.

The reactions from family and friends can run the gamut from support to total disapproval and everything in between. However, the stronger they see you becoming and the more assertive you can be about your position, the less you will be manipulated by guilt and by their reactions to you.

There are all sorts of reasons for the reactions of family members. Primary among them is likely to be their concern that you will become financially and/or emotionally dependent on them. When their pressure gets to you, remind yourself that *they have not been living your life or feeling your feelings.*

Well-intentioned friends may also muddy the water for you at a time when total support would help. Couple-friends may fear losing the two of you as a social unit. They may also be concerned that your neediness will be draining on them. Again, remember that although they may be well intentioned, they are not in your shoes.

Appropriate guilt serves to restrain most of us from committing harmful antisocial acts. Certainly this kind of guilt is necessary for society to continue. But the guilt that many women feel when leaving a misogynistic partnership has little relationship to the "crimes" they may have committed. Most of this guilt comes from a misplaced sense of responsibility for other people's behavior, an intense need for the approval of others, and a willingness to put oneself last. In this context, guilt becomes a psychological ball and chain. The only purpose it serves is to seriously diminish a woman's ability to leave a destructive relationship and to take care of herself.

Preparing for Your Partner's Reactions

As we have seen, the misogynist needs to be in control at all costs, yet underneath the facade of power he is very dependent. When the object of his dependency threatens to pull away from him, all his old terrors get stirred up. For this reason, your attempts to leave him are liable to be met with considerable resistance. Because he is threatened, he may exhibit behavior you have never seen before. Again, the more prepared you are for your partner's reactions, the better you will be able to handle the guilty feelings and the fears that his reactions are liable to cause.

He May Become Pathetic

The breaking point for Nancy came when she and Jeff took a long-awaited vacation in Europe. In the first session after they'd come home she reported:

> You know how much I had been looking forward to this, but it turned into a disaster. He humiliated me, screamed at me in public places, left me without money constantly, and blamed me for everything that went wrong, including delayed flights and lost baggage. He was a monster. Once he stormed out of a restaurant leaving me there without a cent to pay for the meal. I had to sit there like a bad kid and wait for him to come back and pay the bill so I could leave. The trip just intensified everything that's wrong in the marriage. He just treated me like excess luggage everywhere we went. By the time we were heading home I'd made up my mind to leave him. On the plane back I told him I wanted a divorce. I was so furious with him that after I said that I refused to speak to him. I just let him sit there and stew, all the way back to LA. As soon as we got in the house he started pleading and apologizing to me. He said he didn't know why he behaved that way. But I said it was no good. I wasn't going to

stand for any more humiliating scenes with him and I wasn't
going to be treated the way he treated me anymore and that
was that. Then he just broke down. He started crying and
sobbing like a little boy. I couldn't believe it. He cried and
cried and told me he loved me and he couldn't live without
me. He said he'd do anything in the world for me if I just
wouldn't leave. He was so pathetic that I just caved in. Now I
don't know what to think.

It isn't unusual for a man like Jeff not to take his wife seriously
until she threatens to leave him. Sometimes this can be a real moment of truth for a relationship. In any case, Nancy decided to give
Jeff the benefit of the doubt.

My concern was that Jeff, who had not responded positively to
any of Nancy's increasing self-confidence and assertiveness, knew
only one way to behave in the marriage. Before he could treat her
differently, he would have to learn new responses and behaviors.
Still, Nancy hoped that his last-minute promises would be followed
by substantial changes in his behavior toward her.

The marriage was calm and more loving for a few weeks after
their return, but Jeff didn't follow through on his promise to go into
counseling. Instead, he convinced Nancy that he didn't need outside help because "look how wonderful it can be between us without it." Once Jeff began to feel safe again and was no longer
threatened with losing her, he resumed his former behavior. Nancy
was bitterly disappointed. It was at this point that her decision to
leave became final in her mind.

Even the most abusive misogynist can become pathetic when he
feels threatened with abandonment. He may cry, beg, and even
break down. He may apologize and promise to do better. He may
remind you of all the wonderful times you've shared together and
how much he still loves and needs you. All of these reactions on his
part can flood you with a renewal of compassion and tenderness
toward him.

The vital question that you must ask yourself before you change
your mind about leaving the relationship is: Have any of his apolo-

gies and promises ever been followed by a *sustained* behavioral change?

He May Become Self-Destructive

Some misogynists become self-destructive when they feel threatened with abandonment. This is particularly true of those who have a history of alcoholism, drug abuse, or episodes of depression. A woman may come genuinely to fear that if she leaves her partner he will not be able to survive. He may sponsor this idea and try to convince her that she must stay in order to protect him from himself.

One client of mine, whose husband had a history of substance abuse, decided to leave her marriage after eight years of mistreatment. The night she told her husband that she wanted a divorce, he got very drunk and had a serious auto accident. She saw that he was trying to hold on to her by becoming so helpless and pathetic that she would stay and take care of him. When he realized that she wasn't going to stay, he started threatening suicide. At this point I advised her to involve as many of his family members and friends as she could to serve as a support system for him during the divorce. Having his family behind him made him feel less isolated and desperate, and eventually the crisis passed.

There is no way to predict whether your partner will follow through on threats to hurt or kill himself. Obviously, people do sometimes commit these acts. But staying with your partner is no guarantee that you can save him from himself. And if you stay for these reasons, it virtually guarantees that your partner will use this form of emotional blackmail whenever he feels threatened with abandonment.

There are many mental health and therapy resources available to help a man who is self-destructive or has patterns of instability. If he chooses not to use any of these and instead focuses on you entirely for his emotional security, you need to clarify for yourself the realistic limits of your responsibility to him. If he intensifies his self-destructive behavior and you've done everything possible to help him find other sources of support and help, it is time to recognize that to be self-destructive is ultimately his choice.

HE MAY BECOME THREATENING

If your partner sees your decision to leave him as a betrayal, as many misogynists do, he may become vindictive and to try to "get you."

Whatever arenas your partner controls the most firmly in your relationship are likely to be the arenas where he will become the most vindictive.

If he's always kept tight control of the money, he may threaten to withdraw all financial support. The more financially dependent you are on him, the more weight his threats may seem to carry. He may threaten to take all the credit cards, close the bank accounts, and convince you that he has the power to ruin you.

If your partner knows that you are vulnerable about the children, he may use custody as a threat against you. He may tell you that if you're the one who wants to go, then get out. He and the children are not going anywhere.

If you fear that your partner may implement his threats against you, it is essential that you get competent legal counsel. Learning exactly what your legal rights are in regard to money, property, and custody is your greatest defense against his threats.

Do not play the victim and leave important decisions to your partner because you feel guilty about leaving him. Chances are that many of his threats are empty. Remember, he's a bully, and often when you stand up to a bully he will back down. You will be much less frightened of him if you know your legal rights.

A WORD OF WARNING

If your partner threatens physical violence against you or your children, I urge that you err on the side of caution and find a safe place to stay until the legal aspects of your separation are settled. Separation is the ultimate stress test for a misogynist. I can't state this strongly enough: a man who has never been violent before may get violent at this point.

Planning Ahead

When you decide to leave a relationship, you are faced with a number of uncertainties about the future. The more you know about where you are going and how you are going to get there, the less frightening this time will be.

Any life decision is made easier if you *plan first.* Plans bring a sense of order and structure to what otherwise may seem like chaos and provide you with a road map for the future.

Each woman, depending on her situation, her age, and her experience, will have her own particular type of plan. Nancy had not worked outside the home in over four years when she decided to leave Jeff. In those years she had become frightened of the job market and doubtful about her abilities to perform in it, and her appearance had changed so drastically that returning to the fashion industry seemed unrealistic to her. She knew also that Jeff would fight her bitterly over money and property. Because he was an attorney, he would be a particularly formidable opponent.

The first thing Nancy needed to do was to consult an attorney to learn what she could expect when she actually filed for divorce. But she was afraid even to do this, because Jeff checked over everything she spent and might find out she'd seen an attorney. At my suggestion, Nancy found a divorce lawyer who did not charge for the initial consultation.

Because Jeff had been very secretive about money, Nancy had no idea what their assets really were. Therefore, her next step was to formulate a plan with her attorney that would protect whatever financial interests she could while enabling her to earn her own living so that she would not be totally dependent on the eventual divorce settlement.

Nancy was ambivalent about a career. Her skills and previous experience equipped her to do many things, but she needed a specific goal to work toward. I suggested she make up a *goal list* of jobs that interested her, including the training, skills, and plusses and minuses of each job. Here is the list she brought in one week later:

JOB	PLUSSES	MINUSES	TRAINING REQUIRED
Fashion coordinator	Good money Nice clothes Travel I'm experienced Recognition	It's a ratrace I'm too overweight The money isn't worth all the anxiety and competition	None
Veterinarian	I love animals I'm good in science Respected position Good money	Schooling is expensive Schools are hard to get into Training too long	Four years
Secretary	I have office skills and experience Benefits good	I hate office work It's boring Not good money	None
Travel agent	Travel Meeting people New places I speak three languages I know what people need from an agent	School costs $700	Ten-week course

If you are thinking about changing careers or starting a career for the first time, this kind of goal list can help you see your strengths and weaknesses, your likes and dislikes, and what training you might need. Nancy found that the job of travel agent had the greatest number of plusses. Her only problems were that it would take time to train and there would be an initial financial outlay. She had a small savings account left from when she had worked before, which she decided to use for this purpose.

As soon as Nancy made her decision, she became afraid that Jeff wouldn't "let" her take the travel-agent course. I pointed out that while he might offer some resistance, once he saw how determined she was he would likely settle down, especially since she was willing to pay for it herself. To Nancy's surprise, however, Jeff barely noticed that she'd started something new in her life.

Nancy's other major concern was that she wasn't being honest with Jeff about her long-range plans. She began to see the two of us as co-conspirators plotting behind Jeff's back.

> NANCY: Aren't I really lying to him about what I'm doing going to school?
> SUSAN: What would happen if you didn't withhold that information?
> NANCY: He would start up all his legal machinery against me. He'd probably cut off all the money; or he might even kick me out of the house.
> SUSAN: Isn't that a heavy price to pay for being honest?

Obviously, total honesty is desirable when dealing with someone who is operating from a position of goodwill and concern, but Nancy was dealing with a man who could turn vengeful and mean. Jeff was certainly far more concerned with losing control over her than with what she wanted or how she was feeling.

Withholding information from someone who is volatile, unpredictable, and punitive is a survival strategy. Misogynists do not act reasonably or fairly with their partners. Therefore, it is extremely important that you do whatever you must to protect yourself. You may have to withhold information. There is nothing noble about being honest if you know from the outset that you will be mistreated if you are.

Your plans may involve housing, dealing with the children, or learning how to combat loneliness and isolation. Drawing up a list of your goals and plans for attaining them can help to diminish your fear of the unknown.

The time frames for plans can vary greatly depending on the circumstances a woman faces. One client of mine decided that she would divorce her husband after her youngest child was graduated from high school. She decided to wait out the two years because she knew how disruptive the divorce would be for her entire family, especially her youngest daughter. Other women, like Jackie and Rosalind, can leave their relationships whenever they want to. In such cases, plans for the future focus primarily on ways to combat loneliness.

Many women find that making plans for the future provides a surge of hope, even though it may take time to carry out those plans and there may be a few false starts before they begin to move ahead. I always remind my clients that false starts are not a sign of failure, nor do they indicate that there is something wrong with the plan. Rather, they are a manifestation of the anxiety and fear that are an inevitable part of any major life change. Sticking with your goal, in spite of any uneasy beginnings, will add to your strength.

What to Expect After Leaving

Intimate relationships do not end simply. The legal ending, which often seems the most difficult, can actually be easier than the emotional ending, because the legal ending is final, at least in the eyes of the law. The emotional ending, however, can be much more painful and can actually take longer. Your heart may keep you hooked in long after your mind or the courts have told you it's over.

ENDING IT EMOTIONALLY

Despite the fact that she knows how badly she's been treated, a woman's emotional connections to her misogynistic partner may pull her toward him after she has ended the relationship. As I discussed earlier, misogynistic relationships can be addictive. The more toxic the relationship was, the harder it may be to end it emotionally. As with a drug addiction, the stronger the addicting drug, the more intense the highs and lows, and the harder it is to break the addiction.

Wanting Him Back

Laura left Bob and filed for divorce after a humiliating event at a New Year's Eve party. But her feelings remained painfully confused long after the breakup.

> He'd been nasty to me all evening and I kept trying to make it up to him by taking his arm and being affectionate, giving him all my attention, but nothing I did was right. If I took his arm, I did it the wrong way. If I walked into the party, I did that wrong. He was just being an asshole about everything. Then, when I was having a discussion with a couple about the women's movement, he came over and started listening and suddenly he just threw his drink in my face. I was totally stunned. He'd done some rotten things before, but that was it! I just got up, got my things, and left. He followed me out screaming like a madman, yelling at me all the way down to the parking lot. When he saw I wasn't listening to him he grabbed me by the sleeve and ripped the sleeve right out of my dress, yelling, "You're my wife and when I talk to you you listen to me and you don't walk away." I said, "Forget it. You are not going to humiliate me again. I don't have to take this kind of crap anymore." Then he pulled off his wedding ring and threw it on the ground. I couldn't believe he'd done that. But that was the end for me. I knew I couldn't live with that man anymore. I didn't go home that night, and I filed for divorce right afterward, but what's happened since is that we just can't seem to stay away from each other. I don't know why, but I can't seem to really let him go out of my life.

Even after her divorce, Laura continued to see Bob, to sleep with him, and to be obsessed with him. She was beginning to feel that she was doomed to be hooked to him for the rest of her life.

I told Laura that she was like any other addict: she couldn't have just a little bit of what she was addicted to. She would have to go "cold turkey" and not see Bob at all for a time.

I told her what I tell all my clients who are trying to break up addictive relationships: they need to make a contract with themselves stating that they will have absolutely no social or sexual contact with their ex-partners for at least ninety days. If there are children involved or legal issues in dispute, obviously there will be some things to deal with your partner about. However, arranging visits with the children or appointments with the lawyers doesn't mean going out to dinner or going to bed with him.

Laura agreed to the contract terms. One week after she'd cut off contact with Bob she told me:

> I feel so bad all the time. I got a cold right away, and I find myself crying in the car all the way to work and all the way home. I feel like I'm never going to feel good and I'm never going to stop crying.

As with any addiction, there were withdrawal symptoms, but, as usually happens, once she got past the first few weeks, Laura noticed that she was thinking of Bob less, feeling lighter and freer, and that while she still yearned to be with him from time to time the pain was decreasing steadily.

I suggest that any woman who has broken up with a misogynistic partner make this same contract with herself. Think of it as your *emotional divorce decree*. Until you do this, you will remain very married, no matter what your legal divorce decree may say.

After Jackie broke up with Mark, she was surprised to find that much of her anger and outrage against him began to disappear and she wanted him back again. She thought about the wonderful, romantic times they'd had together and how terrific he could be. You may find yourself at this point thinking along these lines:

- It couldn't have been as bad as I remember.
- We really did have some fun together.
- He sounds so miserable when I talk to him. I can't do this to him.
- Maybe leaving is what will get him to see the light. Now we can get back together again and it will be different.
- I've got a lot of years invested in this relationship. I just can't let it go completely.
- If I miss him this much, maybe it was a mistake to leave him.

It is typical at this stage to start minimizing the outrages in order to justify your desire to reconnect with your partner. Jackie needed all her strength to combat this tendency. She developed a clever technique to prevent herself from weakening:

> I'd find myself obsessing about how good it felt when he held me, how he smelled, the strength of his arms, and I'd think, "Oh, God. I must have that feeling again." So at those times I'd *force* myself to go into the den and take out a box of checks that I'd saved. They were checks he'd written in the course of our marriage and they were all for his crazy business schemes, none of which ever came to fruition. I'd start looking at those checks for five thousand dollars, ten thousand, twenty thousand . . . all the money he'd gotten my family to loan him, all the money that I'd earned working at two jobs so that we'd be able to survive while he couldn't spend it fast enough. The hunger I felt to have him close to me just evaporated as I looked at those checks. It worked every time.

You can use a similar method to combat wanting your partner back at this time. Refer back to the list you made up on pp. 166–167, *How Your Partner Has Been Behaving*. Focus on one or two specific scenes that you had with your partner that were particularly terrible for you. Re-create the whole scenario in your mind. See his face, hear his voice, and remember as many of his words as you can. Most important, remember *how you were feeling at that moment*. Then ask yourself if you want to feel that way again.

Ambivalence after separation is very common. However, it is particularly treacherous with the misogynist, because when he's trying to pull you back in, his Jekyll and Hyde behavior enables him to be exactly the man you want him to be. He is a master at the art of seduction. He knows your vulnerabilities and how to exploit them for his own purposes. But, should you yield to his temptations and go back, he will resume his old behavior. Remember, he made no real effort to change when you were together. You may have a short period of calm or even of good times, but soon his controlling and demeaning behavior will begin again. And it may be even worse this time, because he has the added justification of getting back at you for having abandoned him.

The emotional divorce is the most difficult time a woman will go through after breaking up a misogynistic relationship. Ending a relationship is much like experiencing a death in the family. It is the death of your hopes, of your way of life, and of your sense of yourself as part of a couple. As with any death, it has to be mourned. If you don't go through this mourning, it will return later to haunt you. Recognize that grieving is essential to healing. Yell, cry, scream, pound your pillow, and, most important, marshal all the support, comfort, and friendship you can find. Remember, it is strength to reach out for help from others when you need it, and weakness to give in to the old inner voices that berate you for going through a bad time.

STARTING TO FEEL BETTER

Something new and wonderful also happens at this time. Suddenly, you find yourself *not needing to justify, explain, or apologize to anyone*. You can now make your own decisions without the panic or fear of what your partner might do. Rosalind was delighted that she no longer had to "walk on eggs," and although she felt shaky some of the time, she also had the exhilarating feeling of knowing that no one else was running her life for her. She told me:

> The tension was so thick when Jim was around that it could have been cut with a knife. Now I come home at night and it's safe and comfortable. It's my place again instead of his. And even though I get depressed some of the time, it's still so much better than how it used to be when I felt inadequate and lousy about myself with him.

Rosalind's loneliness and depression were gradually being replaced by a growing inner strength and determination about her work and her new life. I suggested that she say aloud to herself whenever she thought about going back to Jim or about what lay ahead for her in the future, "*I won't let anybody mistreat me ever again.*"

Helping the Children Through

Separation is a confusing time for children, but when a misogynistic family breaks up and the father is gone, the positive effects on the children can usually be seen immediately. Many women have reported to me that after the divorce their children began to do better in school and were happier and less anxious. As Jackie said:

> We're all doing better now that Mark is gone. We have a peaceful home now. My son is doing better in school and my daughter likes coming home again. She used to invent reasons for not being in the house because it was so tense and miserable around us. Now both of them bring their friends home, which Mark never let them do, or if they did he'd crit-

icize and pick on their friends. It feels like we're a real family now.

I advise that during this period of readjustment you explain to your children exactly *why* you got out of the relationship. In very clear terms, let them know that what they saw and experienced was true. Daddy was an angry, controlling person; he was unpredictable and often scary. Obviously, the older the children, the more information they can deal with, but even very young children need to be told that abusive behavior is not acceptable.

I realize that in most cases the children, especially young ones, will continue to have a relationship with their father or stepfather. Giving your children this kind of information may hurt that relationship, but it is far more important that you put what is best for your children ahead of what may be best for your former partner.

Your honesty with your children validates what they have known all along on some level. When you tell them that their perceptions are right, you release them from the self-blame they may have taken on for the problems of the family. By putting the responsibility for the bad behavior where it belongs—on the adults in the family—you are freeing them from future patterns of self-hatred.

One of the most important parts of this validating process is to acknowledge to your children that they were not adequately protected against their father's rage. Jackie agreed that she needed to do this with her children but she felt terribly ashamed of her failure in this area. I told her to let the children know that she hadn't defended them because she hadn't known how to defend herself, and to let them express their feelings to her. Later she told me:

> It was a very tearful scene. It was all I could do to get the words out. I told them I was sorry that I had allowed them to be frightened and put down the way they'd been. I told them that there was nothing they had done to deserve the kind of treatment they'd taken from Mark. I tried to assure them that I had learned a lot since then and would never let it happen

again. My kids were just so wonderful it made me cry. They said, "Mom, we forgive you. When are you going to forgive yourself?"

In my work as a therapist I have seen many people yearn for this kind of validation from their parents. It is an enormous gift to your children for you to be truthful and open about these painful experiences. A dialogue like the one Jackie had with her children can go further than you can imagine toward rebuilding their damaged self-esteem and trust in you as a loving parent. More than anything else, it will solidify your relationship with your children in the most positive way.

16 | *Finding Yourself Again*

Every woman who has been in a long-term misogynistic relationship has had to barter away parts of herself in order to keep the peace. You may have had to give up or let falter a promising career, academic pursuits, or other activities and interests of which your partner didn't approve. Perhaps you have also had to let go of people who were important in your life because your partner felt jealous of or threatened by them. How exciting it will be for you to realize that there is nothing to prevent you from taking all of these valuable things back into your life again!

Taking Back What You Lost

What you may have forfeited will most likely fall into four basic categories, which I have listed below. Please make up your own list of the things you have given up in the service of keeping peace in your relationship.

GOALS & ASPIRATIONS	BELIEFS & OPINIONS	PEOPLE	ACTIVITIES & INTERESTS
Career advancement	Religious beliefs and/or political beliefs that conflicted with his	Seeing old friends	Athletics (such as tennis, skiing, joining a gym)
Getting a degree		Spending more time with family	
Getting a job	Opinions about people, the world, and events	Spending more time with the children	Joining a special interest club (such as bridge, debating, cycling, or a glee club)
Taking a training program	Values and ethics	Having people visit more often	
Taking workshops		Making new friends	Attending musical, theatrical, or film events
			Going camping, hiking, or other outdoors activities
			Taking classes just for fun (such as cooking, language, art and dance)

Once Rosalind had ended her destructive relationship with Jim, she began to rebuild not only her failing business and her confidence in herself, but other neglected pursuits as well. She told me:

> I've got so much more energy and funds available to me now that he's out of my life. I had never realized what a drain he'd been in so many ways. I'm not only rebuilding my shop but I've been able to get back into my china painting, which I couldn't afford to do when Jim was around. Remember I

told you that I'd set aside part of my shop for his furniture-refinishing business? Well, I'm using that space for a new kiln and a drying closet. I can sit in the shop and do my painting and I'm just loving it. I'm getting pretty good at it, so I've decided to put out a little catalog just for china work. It's a nice adjunct to the advertising art I've always specialized in. I have cleared out one side of the shop window just for my china pieces. They're starting to sell, and I'm so thrilled with myself over it, I'm about to burst.

It was moving to see the pride that Rosalind took in her accomplishments, and I was extremely touched when she presented me with one of her exquisitely painted china vases as a token of her appreciation for the hard work we'd done together.

A toxic relationship takes up an enormous amount of energy. There is nothing more exhausting than tension and conflict and nothing more exhilarating and energizing than a commitment to be kind to yourself and to let yourself be you. Many women experience this kind of regeneration once they begin to bring back into their lives the things they once cared about.

Part of the dramatic improvement in Carol and Ben's marriage came about because Carol held fast in her determination to take the classes she wanted and to get her degree. Ben found, to his amazement, that the woman she became was far more fascinating and exciting than the woman he'd tried to make her into. In our last session he told me:

> Before, all I wanted was somebody who wasn't going to leave me. The worst thing I could think of was that if she could stand on her own two feet she could also go. But now that I feel better about myself I'm not so afraid anymore. She's finished school and has a job, and to tell you the truth, I'm damned proud of her. She's not this dependent little girl anymore. She's more like a real person. She stands up for herself, and you know what? I like it! She's more fun. She's alive and she's interesting. I tell you, I'm more in love with her than I've ever been.

It was wonderful to see this twenty-seven-year marriage evolve into a relationship that was a source of such happiness and rediscovery.

Jackie had not renounced educational or vocational goals, but she had let go of many of her friends and the little pleasures that meant so much to her. One of the first things she took back for herself when Mark left the house was the pleasure of going to the movies with her friends.

> I hadn't been to the movies for years because Mark didn't like them. It was okay to sit around and watch TV incessantly, but if we actually went out to a film he'd be so obnoxious that it just wasn't worth it to me. He'd announce in a loud voice, as soon as we got into the theater, "This better be good." And if it wasn't, it was my fault for dragging him there. He made me so tense it was hard for me to ever enjoy a picture with him. But now I have a bunch of people I can go to the movies with, including a new man I've been dating who's a real film buff. It's just been so much fun to go to the movies and not worry about whether someone is going to embarrass me or put me on the spot if the picture's no good.

It's important not to discount or devalue the interests and activities that please you. If they are important to you, they are part of what makes you who you are. Being able to go to the movies comfortably may not sound like much of an accomplishment, but for Jackie it represented a hard-won shift in her ability to do as she pleased without worrying about anyone else's approval.

THE BENEFITS OF BUILDING UP OTHER AREAS OF YOUR LIFE

Many women look to intimate relationships for almost all of their emotional gratification. The trap for a woman in a misogynistic relationship is that not only does this narrow her world, but it can set her up to accept any kind of treatment because she has so little to support her in her own life. When Nancy had married Jeff she had let go not only of her career but of many of her friends. Once she had regained much of her self-confidence in therapy, she began re-connecting with many of these people. Her friends had missed her, and Nancy had forgotten how much fun it was to go out with them. She also found that once she had completed her travel-agent course and begun working, she was far less vulnerable to Jeff's hostile behavior. Diversifying her life gave her a new perspective on her-self and on her marriage, and she stopped overloading the partner-ship with too many emotional demands, needs, and expectations. By the time she left therapy, Nancy was still ambivalent about staying with Jeff. But she knew that she was solid enough with her-self not to be afraid of making the decision to leave if she had to, be-cause she was no longer looking to the marriage to fill up her entire life.

Many women are genuinely surprised at the confidence and ex-citement that results from expanding their horizons and becoming more independent. One radio caller told me recently:

> I have a wonderful success story to share with you and your listeners. I'm fifty-eight years old and I was married to an emotionally abusive man for over forty years. I don't know how I did it but I finally got up the guts to get out. I want to tell you I was really terrified at first. I'd never worked and I didn't think anyone would hire me, but I found a job in an automotive-supply store running the desk and taking orders. I get to meet lots of people every day. I'm going out and going square dancing and I'm just having a ball.

It is essential for every woman to see that the more she has going on in her own life, separate and apart from her partner, the better she will feel about herself and the less panic she will have about any major life changes.

Certainly none of this is meant to diminish or devalue the plea-sures of being in a relationship. We all have a basic human desire to be close to other people and to be coupled. But being part of a cou-ple should not mean having to limit your world or lose yourself.

How Your Children Can Benefit from Your New Strength

One of the great benefits of taking back yourself is that it gives you the chance to reverse much of the negative role modeling and messages that your children may have internalized. Women often express to me deep concerns about keeping their sons from becoming misogynists and their daughters from being victims after they have spent many years in a misogynistic household. What I tell these mothers is that no matter how old the children are, once the misogynistic cycle has been broken and there has been a dramatic change in the mother's behavior, much of what the children have learned about how men and women behave can be altered.

A woman's courage to rebuild her life and to bring back into it those things that define her as an individual sets up a powerful new role model for children of both genders. Sons will begin to see women as valuable and worthy of respect, while daughters will learn that they too are valuable and entitled to good treatment. Children are remarkably resilient and flexible. Seeing Mother happy and confident in herself enhances any child's sense of well-being. Therefore, the greatest teacher in the world for your children is your new, confident behavior.

Keeping Yourself from Doing It Again

By the time Rosalind terminated therapy she was doing very well, feeling good about herself, her business, and her new accomplishments. I hadn't seen her for about six months when I got a panicky phone call from her one afternoon. She came into the office the next day extremely agitated, and our discussion went like this:

ROSALIND: I'm doing it all over again. I met a new man named Les. He's gorgeous and exciting, but the same things are starting to happen, just like with Jim. Why do I need to do this to myself? What's wrong with me?

SUSAN: Tell me what happened.

ROSALIND: Les and I were hiking. I'm really into doing that with him, but a few days ago we were climbing a really steep slope and I just couldn't keep up with him. I was struggling and pushing myself but I couldn't. I asked him to slow down and he refused. Then he got mad and started yelling back at me that I was a lazy bitch and what was the point of hiking if I wasn't going to exert myself. I felt like I was hanging him up so I finally quit and just went back down the trail and waited for him at the car. He came back two hours later and he was furious. He said I'd ruined his hike and that he should have known better than to take an old woman like me on a hike. I started doing what I always do, apologizing and blaming myself, even though I was really hurt. And then I caught myself and I remember thinking, "Why am I apologizing to him? He's the one who's behaving like an idiot, not me." That's when I realized I'd done it again. I'd picked another one. I've been so upset with myself that I had to see you.

SUSAN: First of all, I think you are telling me a glorious success story. What you will see, when you stop beating yourself up, is that you quickly identified your feelings and your responses and you knew when you were being mistreated.

Rosalind had actually taken pretty good care of herself. She'd stopped herself when she found herself apologizing, she'd seen that it was Les and not she who was behaving badly, and, most important, when she'd found that Les was making her feel bad about herself, she'd paid attention. There was nothing in her story to indicate that she was doomed to a life of picking men who would mistreat her.

Old behavior doesn't disappear overnight. Changes always involve two steps forward and one step back. The fact that Rosalind had slipped back into apologizing didn't mean that she had lost all the gains she'd made in therapy.

She also didn't need to berate herself for picking another psychologically abusive man. *Any woman can be attracted to a misogynist.* Being attracted to a misogynist is not the problem. Staying and accepting abuse for long periods of time is! I assured Rosalind that she was doing very well. It was obvious from what had happened on the hike that she was no longer willing to tolerate mistreatment, no matter how charismatic, exciting, or handsome a man was.

The other exciting news about Rosalind's story was that she had begun to trust herself, and trusting yourself, even when you make mistakes, is the real foundation of emotional security.

Many women who have been in misogynistic relationships ask me, "How can I ever trust another man again?" I tell them it is not important to worry about trusting who *he* is; the important trust comes from the knowledge and security that you can manage whatever life throws at you.

Despite Rosalind's bad experience with Jim, she hadn't locked herself off by becoming guarded and suspicious. But many women do make this mistake. They believe that they'll be safe if they close off their emotional world and avoid relationships altogether. But real safety comes from the freedom to make choices, to trust your feelings, and to know that you will be able to take care of yourself should things not work out. Suspiciousness and the refusal to connect with another man may give you the illusion of safety, but in reality it just keeps you emotionally frozen.

NOT EVERY MAN IS A MISOGYNIST

As important as it is to be able to identify mistreatment, it is equally important not to start labeling *misogynist* any man with whom you are unhappy. Rosalind had presented clear evidence that Les had been both insulting and abusive to her. However, some women, in their fervor to avoid getting into another misogynistic relationship, make the mistake of seeing all men as misogynists.

The fact that you may feel bad in a relationship with a man

doesn't automatically mean he's being abusive to you. Some men are withholding, some are noncommunicative, some are not affectionate, and some are not ready for a relationship and may reject you. Some men are extremely moody, some lose their tempers easily, some like to argue, and some may disagree loudly with anything you have to say; but none of these behaviors, in and of itself, defines a man as a misogynist. Remember, a misogynist is a man who needs to control women. He does this in an aggressive way, by using intimidation and criticism, by demeaning her, by breaking down her confidence in herself, and by keeping her off balance with unpredictable switches from charm to rage.

You mustn't let your new awareness of misogynistic behavior and its effects prejudice you against all men. It is no more realistic to see every man as a misogynist than it is to overlook mistreatment when it is leveled at you.

FINDING LOVE AGAIN

There are many wonderful, caring, sensitive men who do like women and who value their company and their uniqueness. These men are not threatened by a woman's intelligence, ambition, or competence, because they are secure and solid in their own sense of adequacy. They don't have to grind women down in order to feel good about themselves.

Laura found just such a man two years after she stopped seeing Bob. I received this wonderful letter from her along with a wedding invitation.

> Dear Susan,
>   Remember how worried I was that (a) I would never fall in love again; (b) I'd never get over what's-his-name; and (c) the days of romance were over for good? Well, I'm writing to tell you that you were right and I was wrong. I met a really terrific guy. He doesn't yell, he isn't demanding or insanely possessive, and I love him completely. I think I used to overlook men like him because I thought they weren't flashy or

exciting enough, but guess what? I don't miss for a second all those crazy scenes I had with Bob. I used to think all that fighting was love and passion. But Randy is tender and soft-spoken and twice as exciting as Bob ever was. He's just a joy to be with.

I so much want you to come to our wedding so you can be part of this really special day for us.

Love and many, many thanks,
Laura

Many women who have been in misogynistic relationships worry that a kind, respectful man will not be exciting or romantic, but Laura found she could have a loving relationship with a man without the chaos she'd always believed was part of romance. The excitement in a misogynistic relationship comes as much from anxiety, tension, and the unpredictability of the man's behavior, as from love and passion.

Finding Your Balance as a Woman

Many people today are confused about what to expect and how to behave in a relationship. Old, rigid stereotyped roles are often rejected by couples, but they are unsure about what to replace them with. Women agonize over how to respond to their new-found freedom without becoming tough or hard. Men are concerned with how to be caring and sensitive without losing their masculinity. Both men and women are likely to have careers and ambitions of their own—often by choice, and often by economic necessity, as well.

I believe our goal as contemporary women is to hold on to those qualities that make us unique—our intuition, our comfort with feelings and strong emotions, and our ability to nurture—while letting go of those self-denying behaviors that have not served us well. Being a woman no longer means having to be passive, submissive, and self-denigrating. Nor does it mean becoming an "honorary man" by imitating traditional male behavior. There is no contradiction between being a loving, giving woman and taking care of yourself and acting in your own best interests. The most wonderful gift that you can give yourself and any man you become involved with is your sense of self-worth and, with it, your expectation of love and good treatment.

Bibliography

Titles especially recommended for further reading are annotated.

Arcana, Judith. *Our Mother's Daughters*. Berkeley, CA: Shameless Hussy Press, 1979.

Bell, Donald. *Being a Man: The Paradox of Masculinity*. Brattleboro, VT: The Stephen Greene Press, 1982.

Blacker, K.H., M.D. "Frightened Men: A Wish for Intimacy and a Fear of Closeness." *The International Journal of Psychoanalytic Psychotherapy* 6 (1977).

Blanck, Gertrude, and Ruben Blanck. *Ego Psychology: Theory and Practice*. New York: Columbia University Press, 1974.

Botwin, Carol, with Jerome L. Fine, Ph.D. *The Love Crisis: Hit-and-Run Lovers, Jugglers, Sexual Stingies, Unreliables, Kinkies and Other Typical Men Today*. New York: Bantam Books, 1979. Botwin is always fun to read, and she offers some good insights into several recognizable types of men; all of whom make unsatisfactory partners. Of particular relevance is the section titled "The Bastards."

———. *Love Lives: Why Women Behave the Way They Do in Relationships.* New York: Bantam Books, 1983. Easy, readable overview of the different roles and behaviors women adopt in relationships with men. Be sure to read the sections on "The Nurse" and "The Elusive or Abusive Man Specialist."

Bowen, Murray, M.D. *Family Therapy in Clinical Practice.* New York: Jason Aronson, 1978.

Branden, Nathaniel, *The Psychology of Romantic Love.* Los Angeles: J.P. Tarcher, 1980.

———. *The Psychology of Self-Esteem.* Bantam Books, 1971.

Brownmiller, Susan. *Against Our Will: Men, Women, and Rape.* New York: Bantam Books, 1976.

Caplan, Paula, *The Myth of Women's Masochism.* New York: E.P. Dutton, 1985. A book that finally recognizes that women do not need, enjoy, or seek out suffering but rather have learned dependent and submissive behaviors that set them up for mistreatment in their quest for love and approval. The book effectively shatters many long-held beliefs that women are inherently masochistic.

Chesler, Phyllis. *Women and Madness.* New York: Avon Books, 1973.

Cleckley, Hervey. *The Mask of Sanity.* St. Louis: C.V. Mosby, 1975.

Cowan, Connell, and Melvyn Kinder. *Smart Women, Foolish Choices: Finding the Right Men and Avoiding the Wrong Ones.* New York: Crown, 1985. A readable attempt to answer the paradox of why competent women so often pick men who make them miserable. Particularly relevant are the sections on addictive love and a chapter called, "How Exciting Men Can Make Women Miserable."

Dowling, Colette. *The Cinderella Complex: Women's Hidden Fear of Independence.* New York: Summit Books, 1981. A classic. One of the most important and controversial books ever written for women and a must for women in a misogynistic relationship. Dowling clearly details how women have been trained to be dependent and to fear that independence will lose them love.

Dubbert, Joe. *A Man's Place: Masculinity in Transition.* Englewood Cliffs, NJ: Prentice-Hall, 1979.

Dworkin, Andrea. *Women Hating: A Radical Look at Sexuality.* New York: E.P. Dutton, 1976.

Forward, Susan, and Craig Buck. *Betrayal of Innocence: Incest and Its Devastation.* New York: Penguin Books, 1979. The first contemporary book for the general public on the subject of incest. Important to understanding women in misogynistic relationships, since so many have been victims of incest and other forms of child abuse.

Friday, Nancy. *Men in Love, Male Sexual Fantasies: The Triumph of Love Over Rage.* New York: Dell Publishing, 1981.

Friedan, Betty. *The Feminine Mystique.* New York: Dell Publishing, 1963.

Goldberg, Herb. *The Hazards of Being Male: Surviving the Myth of Masculine Privilege.* Signet Books/NAL, 1977.

Gordon, Barbara. *I'm Dancing as Fast as I Can.* New York: Harper & Row, 1979. Gordon's excellent book painfully details both her relationship with a misogynistic lover, who abused her physically and psychologically, and her encounters with cruel and callous professionals whom she turned to for help.

Hacker, Frederick, M.D. *Crusaders, Criminals, Crazies: Terror and Terrorism in Our Time.* New York: W.W. Norton, 1976.

Halpern, Howard. *How to Break Your Addiction to a Person.* New York: Bantam Books, 1983. One of the books I recommend regularly on my radio program. Halpern does an excellent job of exploring the components of addictive relationships and how early attachment hunger makes us vulnerable to becoming love junkies.

Harrington, Alan. *Psychopaths.* New York: Simon and Schuster, 1972.

Hilberman, Elaine, M.D. "The Wife-Beater's Wife Reconsidered." *American Journal of Psychiatry* 137:11 (November 1980)

Horney, Karen, M.D. *Feminine Psychology*. New York: W.W. Norton, 1967, 1973.

——. *Neurosis and Human Growth: The Struggle Toward Self-Realization*. New York: W.W. Norton, 1942, 1970.

——. *New Ways in Psychoanalysis*. New York: W.W. Norton, 1939, 1964.

——. *Self-Analysis*. New York: W.W. Norton, 1942, 1968.

Kernberg, Otto, M.D. *Borderline Conditions and Pathological Narcissim*. New York: Jason Aronson, 1985.

——. *Object Relations Theory and Its Application*. New York: Jason Aronson, 1981.

Kiley, Dan. *The Peter Pan Syndrome: Men Who Have Never Grown Up*. New York: Dodd, Mead, 1983. A bit cutesy, but nevertheless a good description of another type of male character disorder. Peter Pans frequently exhibit some misogynistic traits, and Kiley shines a clear light on their behavior and its effect on their partners.

King, Florence. *He: An Irreverent Look at the American Male*. New York: Stein and Day, 1978.

Klein, Carole. *Mothers and Sons*. New York: Houghton, Mifflin, 1984.

Komarovsky, Mirra. *Dilemmas of Masculinity: A Study of College Youth*. New York: W.W. Norton, 1976.

Korda, Michael. *Male Chauvinism: How It Works*. New York: Ballantine Books, 1973. A good exploration of the attitudes that have demeaned women in the workplace, in relationships, and in society in general.

Lederer, W. *The Fear of Women*. New York: Grune and Stratten, 1968.

Lerner, Harriet Goldhor. *The Dance of Anger: A Woman's Guide to Changing the Patterns of Intimate Relationships*. New York: Harper & Row, 1985. A book that offers women valuable guidelines for understanding and handling this most frightening and difficult emotion.

Lowen, Alexander, M.D. Narcissism: *Denial of the True Self*. New York: Macmillan, 1983.

Martin, Del. *Battered Wives*. San Francisco: Volcano Press, 1981. Still one of the definitive works on the subject of physical abuse and the two actors in the drama of violent relationships.

Masterson, James. *New Perspectives in Psychology of the Borderline Adult*. New York: Brunner/Mazel, 1978.

Mellen, Joan. *Big Bad Wolves: Masculinity in the American Film*. New York: Pantheon Books, 1977. A book that describes the important role that films have had in shaping our perceptions of masculinity and "real men." The mistreatment of women has often been portrayed in films as both acceptable and a proof of manliness.

Miller, Jean Baker, M.D. *Toward a New Psychology of Women*. Beacon Press, 1977.

Moulton, Ruth. "The Fear of Female Power: A Cause of Sexual Dysfunction." *The Journal of the American Academy of Psychoanalysis* 5 (1977).

Naifeh, Steven, and Gregory White Smith. *Why Can't Men Open Up?: Overcoming Men's Fear of Intimacy*. New York: Clarkson M. Potter, 1984. It's no news that a number of men are closed, guarded, and have a difficult time with feelings and expressing themselves. This book deals with the conscious and unconscious fears underlying these difficulties and what women can do to facilitate change in their partners.

NiCarthy, Ginny. *Getting Free: A Handbook for Women in Abusive Relationships*. Seattle: The Seal Press, 1982. Primarily addressed to women who have been physically battered by their partners, this detailed and compassionate guide to building a new life is also highly recommended to victims of emotional abuse. It contains many self-assessment activities that can help women clarify their experience and goals.

Norwood, Robin. *Women Who Love Too Much: When You Keep Wishing and Hoping He'll Change*. Tarcher/St. Martin's Press, 1985. Another book I recommend quite regularly on the air. Written by a therapist who understands women's needs and feelings. The book takes an in-depth look at how women willingly give up big chunks of themselves in order to be in a relationship.

Olsen, Paul. *Sons and Mothers: Why Men Behave as They Do.* New York: Fawcett Books, 1982.

Paul, Jordan, and Margaret Paul. *Do I Have to Give Up Me to Be Loved by You?* Minneapolis, MN. CompCare Publications, 1983. The Pauls are specialists in clarifying and changing communication styles between couples. The book offers good examples of nondefensive communication, which are valuable for women in misogynistic relationships.

Peele, Stanton, with Archie Brodsky. *Love and Addiction.* New York: Signet/NAL, 1976.

Russell, Diana E. H. *Rape in Marriage.* New York: Macmillan, 1982.

Russianoff, Penelope. *Why Do I Think I Am Nothing Without a Man?* New York: Bantam Books, 1983. Highly recommended. An important book for every woman, especially for women who are involved with misogynists. Russianoff speaks sensitively to the universal female dilemmas of low self-esteem and the feelings of desolation and fragmentation many women experience unless they are connected to a man. She shows how these patterns are learned and can be unlearned.

Sager, C.J., and B. Hunt. *Intimate Partners: Hidden Patterns in Love Relationships.* New York: McGraw-Hill, 1978.

Sanford, Linda Tschirhart, and Mary Ellen Donovan. *Women and Self-Esteem.* New York: Penguin Books, 1985. Written by two feminist authors, this book is an excellent and comprehensive look at how society and family interact to damage female self-worth and emotional well-being. There are valuable suggestions on how to repair this damage and stop feeling like a second-class citizen.

Trafford, Abigail. *Crazy Time: Surviving Divorce.* New York: Bantam Books, 1984. The title says it all. A readable and compassionate book that provides guidance and support through one of life's most difficult and painful experiences.

Weissberg, Michael, M.D. *Dangerous Secrets: Maladaptive Responses to Stress.* New York: W.W. Norton, 1983. A good overview of family violence and abuse and the terrible damage that these behaviors create. The book deals insightfully with such issues as wife-beating, alcoholism, and the physical and sexual abuse of children. Painful and realistic.

ABOUT THE AUTHORS

SUSAN FORWARD, PH.D., is an internationally renowned therapist, lecturer, and author of the number-one *New York Times* bestsellers *Toxic Parents* and *Men Who Hate Women and the Women Who Love Them*, as well as *Obsessive Love; Betrayal of Innocence: Incest and Its Devastation; Money Demons; Emotional Blackmail; When Your Lover Is a Liar;* and *Toxic In-Laws.* In addition to her private practice, for five years she hosted a daily ABC Talk-radio program. She has also served widely as a group therapist, instructor, and consultant in many Southern California medical and psychiatric facilities, and she formed the first private sexual abuse treatment center in California. She lives in Los Angeles and has two grown children.

Susan Forward maintains offices in Sherman Oaks, California. For further information call (818) 986-1161.

JOAN TORRES is an award-winning freelance writer with extensive movie and television credits.